D1613782

JOURNAL FOR THE STUDY OF THE OLD TESTAMENT
SUPPLEMENT SERIES
119

Editors
David J. A. Clines
Philip R. Davies

JSOT Press
Sheffield

TELLING QUEEN MICHAL'S STORY

An Experiment in
Comparative Interpretation

edited by
David J.A. Clines
Tamara C. Eskenazi

Journal for the Study of the Old Testament
Supplement Series 119

For
Heather McKay
and
David Eskenazi
affectionate critics, admired companions

Published by JSOT Press
JSOT Press is an imprint of
Sheffield Academic Press Ltd
The University of Sheffield
343 Fulwood Road
Sheffield S10 3BP
England

Printed on acid-free paper in Great Britain
by
Billing & Sons Ltd
Worcester

British Library Cataloguing in Publication Data

Clines, David J.A.
    Telling Queen Michal's story : an experiment in
    comparative interpretation.—(JSOT supplement,
    ISSN 0309-0787:v.119).
    1. Title II. Eskenazi, Tamara C.
    III. Series
    222.4

    ISBN 1-85075-301-6

CONTENTS

PREFACE

This book is something of an experiment. Its purpose is to provide readers with the raw materials for developing their own reading of the Michal story. It does not offer a unified portrait of this biblical character, which readers would then be free to adopt or reject; rather, it invites readers to form their own assessment interactively with the disparate readings of the Michal story collected here. We hope it is a more reader-involving book than most works of biblical criticism.

At the same time, this book presents some guidance in how one might go about the business of coping with divergent interpretations. The Michal figure is complex and tantalizing, and in consequence has given rise to a variety of interpretations. Rather than cite only those writers about Michal whom we agree with or else feel inclined to refute, we have presented in their own words the diverse readings of several writers. The introductory chapter, 'Michal Observed', however, offers some thoughts on evaluating these readings; nevertheless, even this overview proceeds rather inductively, moving outward from particular points of interpretation, like 'Why does Michal love David?', to general observations about what may count as interpretation and what had better be termed speculation.

The programme of 'comparative interpretation' goes further, however, than recognizing that there have been divergent interpretations; further, too, than suggesting how we should proceed when confronted with such variety. There is also implicit in the programme a belief that *all* interpretations are relevant to the task of interpretation, precritical, popular, moralistic and imaginative readings as well as scholarly, learned and sober. A sober interpretation is not necessarily a good one, nor is a sermonic one necessarily a bad one. All kinds of interpretation are grist for our mill, for all the interpretations are interpretations generated by this story, interpretations therefore for which this story is more or less responsible.

Although we do make use of Michal for our literary and critical purposes, we aim at going beyond mere 'use'. As Saul's daughter and David's wife, Michal has already been used, and abused, enough.

Instead, we seek to restore her to her rightful place in the tradition
and in memory. By calling her Queen Michal (deliberately if
somewhat anachronistically, since wives of Hebrew kings are not
usually called 'queens' in the Hebrew Bible), we recall that she is both
a king's daughter and a king's wife and the first in ancient Israel to
hold this position. Perhaps the effect of the multiple readings brought
together in this volume will be to enable her enigmatic yet engaging
presence in the biblical text to emerge more powerfully and more
distinctly.

How to use this book? First, we should point out what kinds of material it contains.

Encyclopaedia Entries
W. Ewing and J.E.H. Thomson, 'Michal', in *The Temple Dictionary
of the Bible*, ed. W. Ewing and J.E.H. Thomson.
D. Harvey, 'Michal', in *Interpreter's Dictionary of the Bible*, ed.
George A. Buttrick.
G.P. Hugenberger, 'Michal', in *International Standard Bible Encyclo-
pedia*, ed. G.W. Bromiley.
N.J.D. White, 'Michal', in *Encyclopaedia Biblica*.

Surveys of Interpretations
Tamara C. Eskenazi, 'Michal in Hebrew Sources'.
Louis Ginzberg, *The Legends of the Jews. IV. Bible Times and Char-
acters from Joshua to Esther*, pp. 116-17, 273-75.
Abbey Poze Kapelovitz, 'Michal: A Vessel for the Desires of Others'.

Literary Studies
Robert Alter, *The Art of Biblical Narrative*, pp. 114-25.
Adele Berlin, 'Characterization in Biblical Narrative: David's Wives',
Journal for the Study of the Old Testament 23, pp. 69-85.
David J.A. Clines, 'X, X *ben* Y: Personal Names in Hebrew Narrative
Style', *Vetus Testamentum* 22, pp. 266-87 (266-67, 269-72).
J. Cheryl Exum, 'Murder They Wrote: Ideology and the Manipulation
of Female Presence in Biblical Narrative', in A. Bach (ed.), *The Plea-
sure of her Text. Feminist Readings of Biblical and Historical Texts*,
pp. 45-68.

Biblical Commentary
Walter Brueggemann, *I and II Samuel*, pp. 251-53.

Studies of Bible Characters
Edith Deen, *All the Women of the Bible*, pp. 96-100.
Abraham Kuyper, *Women of the Old Testament*, pp. 109-12.
H. Lockyer, *All the Kings and Queens of the Bible*, pp. 224-25.
H. Lockyer, *The Women of the Bible*, pp. 109-11.
Norah Lofts, *Women in the Old Testament: Twenty Psychological Portraits*, pp. 107-21.
Maurice Samuel, *Certain People of the Book*, pp. 191-206.
Adin Steinsaltz, *Biblical Images: Men and Women of the Book*, pp. 141-51.

Christian Sermons
W.G. Blaikie, *The First Book of Samuel*, pp. 307-309, and *The Second Book of Samuel*, pp. 95-96.
Alexander Whyte, *Bible Characters: Gideon to Absalom*, pp. 171-81.

Historical Study
Zafrira Ben-Barak, 'The Legal Background to the Restoration of Michal to David', in *Studies in the Historical Books* (ed. J.A. Emerton; Supplements to Vetus Testamentum, 30), pp. 15-29.

Previously Unpublished Papers
Richard G. Bowman, 'The Fortune of King David/The Fate of Queen Michal. A Literary Critical Analysis of 2 Samuel 1–8'.
David J.A. Clines, 'The Story of Michal, Wife of David, in its Sequential Unfolding'.
Tamara C. Eskenazi, 'Michal in Hebrew Sources'.
Abbey Poze Kapelovitz, 'Michal: A Vessel for the Desires of Others'.
Peter D. Miscall, 'Michal and her Sisters'.
Robert Polzin, 'A Multivoiced Look at the Michal Narratives'.

Imaginative Writing
Robert Ehle, 'The Grace of God', *Tikkun* 3/4, pp. 56-60 [short story].
Shoshanna Gershenzon, 'Michal bat Shaul' [poem].

A good way to start using these materials would be to re-read the biblical texts about Michal, reproduced at the beginning of this book. After that we suggest you might read one or two of the encyclopaedia articles, for a quick overview of the key moments in the story of Michal. Then one might sample one of the readings of the Michal character that is sensitive to the literary dimensions of the material (e.g. the extract from Alter or from Berlin). After that, the reader is invited to try something as different as possible, e.g. the sermonic piece by Alexander Whyte, the account of Jewish traditions about Michal in Ginzberg, or the short story by Ehle. After that, we suggest, read what you will until you can no longer bear being tantalized by the multiplicity of possible interpretations or enraged by the prejudices of the writers. When you have got a feel for what passes as readings of the Michal story, try the Introduction ('Michal Observed'), where you will be led through the story from beginning to end, with comparative observations on the way the various moments of the plot are handled in the interpretations; here you will be encouraged to develop, out of the specific problems of interpretation highlighted by the biblical text itself and by the diverse readings, some ground-rules or principles for your own reading.

One of the many surprises awaiting us when we began work on this book was the large amount of material written about Michal, hidden at times in unexpected places. Our collection is by no means exhaustive, though we hope that it is representative. Regretfully, we left out several important readings because their format did not lend itself to incorporation in the present work. Among them were the numerous commentaries, and other studies like that of J.P. Fokkelman, *Narrative Art and Poetry in the Books of Samuel* (Assen: van Gorcum, 1981–90). The study of S.J. Teubal, in her *Hagar the Egyptian* (San Francisco: Harper & Row, 1990), appeared too late to be included.

The history of this book will, like history usually, explain very little. But it needs to be told. The Society of Biblical Literature in the United States has a Group that works on Narrative Research on the Hebrew Bible and that meets each year at the Annual Meeting. This Group, chaired by Tamara C. Eskenazi and J. Cheryl Exum, took the Michal story as its theme for its 1988 session in Chicago. The session consisted of papers by A. Berlin, R. Bowman, J.C. Exum and R. Polzin, with responses by P.D. Miscall and D.J.A. Clines. This immensely enjoyable symposium was the initial impetus for the present book, which contains papers on Michal by all the participants; its coming into being is due in large part to the goodwill, collegiality and simple pleasure in the text engendered by the Narrative Research on the Hebrew Bible Group, and a testimony to the indispensability of congenial interpretative communities for scholarly creativity.

EDITORS' NOTE

The reprinted extracts in this volume are reproduced in the exact form of their original publication, with a few minor exceptions: biblical references are normalized to the JSOT Press housestyle, as are inverted commas and the transliteration of Hebrew words (but a simplified system is sometimes retained), and obvious errors are corrected.

The page numbers of the original publication are indicated within square brackets throughout the texts. Cross-references within this volume are to page numbers of the present book, followed by the original page numbers in square brackets where appropriate.

ABBREVIATIONS

AB	Anchor Bible
ANET	J.B. Pritchard (ed.), *Ancient Near Eastern Texts*
Ant.	Josephus, *The Antiquities of the Jews*
AV	Authorized Version (= KJV)
BSOAS	*Bulletin of the School of Oriental and African Studies*
BZAW	Beihefte zur *ZAW*
CBQ	*Catholic Biblical Quarterly*
HUCA	*Hebrew Union College Annual*
IDB	G.A. Buttrick (ed.), *Interpreter's Dictionary of the Bible*
JBL	*Journal of Biblical Literature*
JSOT	*Journal for the Study of the Old Testament*
KJV	King James Version (Authorized Version)
Luc.	Lucianic (Greek) text of the Old Testament
LXX	Septuagint
MT	Masoretic text
NEB	New English Bible
NRSV	New Revised Standard Version
OLP	Orientalia lovaniensia periodica
Pesh.	Peshitta (Syriac) version of the Bible
Ps.-Jerome	Pseudo-Jerome
Qu. Heb.	Jerome, *Quaestiones hebraicae in II Regum et in II Paralipomena*
RSV	Revised Standard Version
RVm	Revised Version, marginal note
USQR	*Union Seminary Quarterly Review*
Targ.	Targum
ZAW	*Zeitschrift für die alttestamentliche Wissenschaft*

THE BIBLICAL STORY
OF MICHAL
IN HEBREW AND ENGLISH

THE BIBLICAL STORY OF MICHAL IN HEBREW

1 Samuel 14.49-51 (1)

(49) וַיִּהְיוּ֙ בְּנֵ֣י שָׁא֔וּל יוֹנָתָ֥ן וְיִשְׁוִ֖י וּמַלְכִּי־שׁ֑וּעַ וְשֵׁם֙ שְׁתֵּ֣י בְנֹתָ֔יו שֵׁ֤ם
הַבְּכִירָה֙ מֵרַ֔ב וְשֵׁ֥ם הַקְּטַנָּ֖ה מִיכַֽל:

(50) וְשֵׁם֙ אֵ֣שֶׁת שָׁא֔וּל אֲחִינֹ֖עַם בַּת־אֲחִימָ֑עַץ וְשֵׁ֤ם שַׂר־צְבָאוֹ֙ אֲבִינֵ֔ר בֶּן־נֵ֖ר
דּ֥וֹד שָׁאֽוּל:

(51) וְקִ֧ישׁ אֲבִֽי־שָׁא֛וּל וְנֵ֥ר אֲבִֽי־אַבְנֵ֖ר בֶּן־אֲבִיאֵֽל:

1 Samuel 18.12-29 (2)

(12) וַיִּרָ֥א שָׁא֖וּל מִלִּפְנֵ֣י דָוִ֑ד כִּי־הָיָ֤ה יְהוָה֙ עִמּ֔וֹ וּמֵעִ֥ם שָׁא֖וּל סָֽר:

(13) וַיְסִרֵ֤הוּ שָׁאוּל֙ מֵֽעִמּ֔וֹ וַיְשִׂמֵ֥הוּ ל֖וֹ שַׂר־אָ֑לֶף וַיֵּצֵ֥א וַיָּבֹ֖א לִפְנֵ֥י הָעָֽם:

(14) וַיְהִ֥י דָוִ֛ד לְכָל־דְּרָכָ֖ו מַשְׂכִּ֑יל וַֽיהוָ֖ה עִמּֽוֹ:

(15) וַיַּ֣רְא שָׁא֔וּל אֲשֶׁר־ה֖וּא מַשְׂכִּ֣יל מְאֹ֑ד וַיָּ֖גָר מִפָּנָֽיו:

(16) וְכָל־יִשְׂרָאֵל֙ וִֽיהוּדָ֔ה אֹהֵ֖ב אֶת־דָּוִ֑ד כִּֽי־ה֛וּא יוֹצֵ֥א וָבָ֖א לִפְנֵיהֶֽם:

(17) וַיֹּ֨אמֶר שָׁא֜וּל אֶל־דָּוִ֗ד הִנֵּה֩ בִתִּ֨י הַגְּדוֹלָ֤ה מֵרַב֙ אֹתָ֤הּ אֶתֶּן־לְךָ֙ לְאִשָּׁ֔ה
אַ֚ךְ הֱיֵה־לִּ֣י לְבֶן־חַ֔יִל וְהִלָּחֵ֖ם מִלְחֲמ֣וֹת יְהוָ֑ה וְשָׁא֣וּל אָמַ֗ר אַל־תְּהִ֤י יָדִי֙
בּ֔וֹ וּתְהִי־ב֖וֹ יַד־פְּלִשְׁתִּֽים:

(18) וַיֹּ֨אמֶר דָּוִ֜ד אֶל־שָׁא֗וּל מִ֤י אָֽנֹכִי֙ וּמִ֣י חַיַּ֔י מִשְׁפַּ֥חַת אָבִ֖י בְּיִשְׂרָאֵ֑ל
כִּֽי־אֶהְיֶ֥ה חָתָ֖ן לַמֶּֽלֶךְ:

(19) וַיְהִ֗י בְּעֵ֥ת תֵּ֛ת אֶת־מֵרַ֥ב בַּת־שָׁא֖וּל לְדָוִ֑ד וְהִ֧יא נִתְּנָ֛ה לְעַדְרִיאֵ֥ל
הַמְּחֹלָתִ֖י לְאִשָּֽׁה:

THE BIBLICAL STORY OF MICHAL IN ENGLISH*

1. *1 Samuel 14.49-51*
(49) Now the sons of Saul were Jonathan, Ishvi, and Malchishua; and
the names of his two daughters were these: the name of the first-born
was Merab, and the name of the younger Michal; (50) and the name of
Saul's wife was Ahinoam the daughter of Ahimaaz. And the name of
the commander of his army was Abner the son of Ner, Saul's uncle;
(51) Kish was the father of Saul, and Ner the father of Abner was the
son of Abiel.

2. *1 Samuel 18.12-29*
(12) Saul was afraid of David, because the LORD was with him but
had departed from Saul. (13) So Saul removed him from his presence,
and made him a commander of a thousand; and he went out and came
in before the people. (14) And David had success in all his under-
takings; for the LORD was with him. (15) And when Saul saw that he
had great success, he stood in awe of him. (16) But all Israel and Judah
loved David; for he went out and came in before them.
(17) Then Saul said to David, 'Here is my elder daughter Merab; I
will give her to you for a wife; only be valiant for me and fight the
LORD'S battles'. For Saul thought, 'Let not my hand be upon him, but
let the hand of the Philistines be upon him'. (18) And David said to
Saul, 'Who am I, and who are my kinsfolk, my father's family in Israel,
that I should be son-in-law to the king?' (19) But at the time when
Merab, Saul's daughter, should have been given to David, she was
given to Adriel the Meholathite for a wife.

---

*   The text is from the Revised Standard Version, copyrighted 1971 and 1952
by the Division of Christian Education of the National Council of the Churches of
Christ in the U.S.A.

(20) וַתֶּאֱהַ֛ב מִיכַ֥ל בַּת־שָׁא֖וּל אֶת־דָּוִ֑ד וַיַּגִּ֣דוּ לְשָׁא֔וּל וַיִּשַׁ֥ר הַדָּבָ֖ר בְּעֵינָֽיו׃

(21) וַיֹּ֣אמֶר שָׁא֗וּל אֶתְּנֶ֤נָּה לּוֹ֙ וּתְהִי־ל֣וֹ לְמוֹקֵ֔שׁ וּתְהִי־ב֖וֹ יַד־פְּלִשְׁתִּ֑ים וַיֹּ֤אמֶר שָׁאוּל֙ אֶל־דָּוִ֔ד בִּשְׁתַּ֛יִם תִּתְחַתֵּ֥ן בִּ֖י הַיּֽוֹם׃

(22) וַיְצַ֨ו שָׁא֜וּל אֶת־עֲבָדָ֗ו דַּבְּר֨וּ אֶל־דָּוִ֤ד בַּלָּט֙ לֵאמֹ֔ר הִנֵּ֨ה חָפֵ֤ץ בְּךָ֙ הַמֶּ֔לֶךְ וְכָל־עֲבָדָ֖יו אֲהֵב֑וּךָ וְעַתָּ֖ה הִתְחַתֵּ֥ן בַּמֶּֽלֶךְ׃

(23) וַיְדַבְּר֞וּ עַבְדֵ֤י שָׁאוּל֙ בְּאָזְנֵ֣י דָוִ֔ד אֶת־הַדְּבָרִ֖ים הָאֵ֑לֶּה וַיֹּ֣אמֶר דָּוִ֗ד הַֽנְקַלָּ֤ה בְעֵֽינֵיכֶם֙ הִתְחַתֵּ֣ן בַּמֶּ֔לֶךְ וְאָנֹכִ֖י אִֽישׁ־רָ֥שׁ וְנִקְלֶֽה׃

(24) וַיַּגִּ֜דוּ עַבְדֵ֥י שָׁא֛וּל ל֖וֹ לֵאמֹ֑ר כַּדְּבָרִ֥ים הָאֵ֖לֶּה דִּבֶּ֥ר דָּוִֽד׃

(25) וַיֹּ֨אמֶר שָׁא֜וּל כֹּֽה־תֹאמְר֣וּ לְדָוִ֗ד אֵֽין־חֵ֤פֶץ לַמֶּ֙לֶךְ֙ בְּמֹ֔הַר כִּ֗י בְּמֵאָה֙ עָרְל֣וֹת פְּלִשְׁתִּ֔ים לְהִנָּקֵ֖ם בְּאֹיְבֵ֣י הַמֶּ֑לֶךְ וְשָׁא֣וּל חָשַׁ֔ב לְהַפִּ֥יל אֶת־דָּוִ֖ד בְּיַד־פְּלִשְׁתִּֽים׃

(26) וַיַּגִּ֨דוּ עֲבָדָ֤יו לְדָוִד֙ אֶת־הַדְּבָרִ֣ים הָאֵ֔לֶּה וַיִּשַׁ֤ר הַדָּבָר֙ בְּעֵינֵ֣י דָוִ֔ד לְהִתְחַתֵּ֖ן בַּמֶּ֑לֶךְ וְלֹ֥א מָלְא֖וּ הַיָּמִֽים׃

(27) וַיָּ֣קָם דָּוִ֗ד וַיֵּ֣לֶךְ ׀ ה֣וּא וַאֲנָשָׁ֞יו וַיַּ֣ךְ בַּפְּלִשְׁתִּ֗ים מָאתַ֣יִם אִ֔ישׁ וַיָּבֵ֤א דָוִד֙ אֶת־עָרְלֹ֣תֵיהֶ֔ם וַיְמַלְא֣וּם לַמֶּ֔לֶךְ לְהִתְחַתֵּ֖ן בַּמֶּ֑לֶךְ וַיִּתֶּן־ל֥וֹ שָׁא֛וּל אֶת־מִיכַ֥ל בִּתּ֖וֹ לְאִשָּֽׁה׃

(28) וַיַּ֣רְא שָׁא֔וּל וַיֵּ֕דַע כִּ֥י יְהוָ֖ה עִם־דָּוִ֑ד וּמִיכַ֥ל בַּת־שָׁא֖וּל אֲהֵבַֽתְהוּ׃

(29) וַיֹּ֣אסֶף שָׁא֗וּל לֵרֹ֛א מִפְּנֵ֥י דָוִ֖ד ע֑וֹד וַיְהִ֥י שָׁא֛וּל אֹיֵ֥ב אֶת־דָּוִ֖ד כָּל־הַיָּמִֽים׃

1 Samuel 19.8-18 (3)

(8) וַתּ֖וֹסֶף הַמִּלְחָמָ֣ה לִֽהְי֑וֹת וַיֵּצֵ֨א דָוִ֜ד וַיִּלָּ֣חֶם בַּפְּלִשְׁתִּ֗ים וַיַּ֤ךְ בָּהֶם֙ מַכָּ֣ה גְדוֹלָ֔ה וַיָּנֻ֖סוּ מִפָּנָֽיו׃

(9) וַתְּהִי֩ ר֨וּחַ יְהוָ֤ה ׀ רָעָה֙ אֶל־שָׁא֔וּל וְה֗וּא בְּבֵית֥וֹ יוֹשֵׁ֖ב וַחֲנִית֣וֹ בְּיָד֑וֹ וְדָוִ֖ד מְנַגֵּ֥ן בְּיָֽד׃

(10) וַיְבַקֵּ֨שׁ שָׁא֜וּל לְהַכּ֧וֹת בַּחֲנִ֛ית בְּדָוִ֖ד וּבַקִּ֑יר וַיִּפְטַ֣ר מִפְּנֵ֣י שָׁא֗וּל וַיַּ֤ךְ אֶת־הַחֲנִית֙ בַּקִּ֔יר וְדָוִ֣ד נָ֔ס וַיִּמָּלֵ֖ט בַּלַּ֥יְלָה הֽוּא׃

(20) Now Saul's daughter Michal loved David; and they told Saul, and the thing pleased him. (21) Saul thought, 'Let me give her to him, that she may be a snare for him, and that the hand of the Philistines may be against him'. Therefore Saul said to David a second time, 'You shall now be my son-in-law'. (22) And Saul commanded his servants, 'Speak to David in private and say, "Behold, the king has delight in you, and all his servants love you; now then become the king's son-in-law"'. (23) And Saul's servants spoke those words in the ears of David. And David said, 'Does it seem to you a little thing to become the king's son-in-law, seeing that I am a poor man and of no repute?' (24) And the servants of Saul told him, 'Thus and so did David speak'. (25) Then Saul said, 'Thus shall you say to David, "The king desires no marriage present except a hundred foreskins of the Philistines, that he may be avenged of the king's enemies"'. Now Saul thought to make David fall by the hand of the Philistines. (26) And when his servants told David these words, it pleased David well to be the king's son-in-law. Before the time had expired, (27) David arose and went, along with his men, and killed two hundred of the Philistines; and David brought their foreskins, which were given in full number to the king, that he might become the king's son-in-law. And Saul gave him his daughter Michal for a wife. (28) But when Saul saw and knew that the LORD was with David, and that all Israel loved him, (29) Saul was still more afraid of David. So Saul was David's enemy continually.

3. *1 Samuel 19.8-18*

(8) And there was war again; and David went out and fought with the Philistines, and made a great slaughter among them, so that they fled before him. (9) Then an evil spirit from the LORD came upon Saul, as he sat in his house with his spear in his hand; and David was playing the lyre. (10) And Saul sought to pin David to the wall with the spear; but he eluded Saul, so that he struck the spear into the wall. And David fled, and escaped.

(11) וַיִּשְׁלַח שָׁאוּל מַלְאָכִים אֶל־בֵּית דָּוִד לְשָׁמְרוֹ וְלַהֲמִיתוֹ בַּבֹּקֶר וַתַּגֵּד לְדָוִד מִיכַל אִשְׁתּוֹ לֵאמֹר אִם־אֵינְךָ מְמַלֵּט אֶת־נַפְשְׁךָ הַלַּיְלָה מָחָר אַתָּה מוּמָת:

(12) וַתֹּרֶד מִיכַל אֶת־דָּוִד בְּעַד הַחַלּוֹן וַיֵּלֶךְ וַיִּבְרַח וַיִּמָּלֵט:

(13) וַתִּקַּח מִיכַל אֶת־הַתְּרָפִים וַתָּשֶׂם אֶל־הַמִּטָּה וְאֵת כְּבִיר הָעִזִּים שָׂמָה מְרַאֲשֹׁתָיו וַתְּכַס בַּבָּגֶד:

(14) וַיִּשְׁלַח שָׁאוּל מַלְאָכִים לָקַחַת אֶת־דָּוִד וַתֹּאמֶר חֹלֶה הוּא:

(15) וַיִּשְׁלַח שָׁאוּל אֶת־הַמַּלְאָכִים לִרְאוֹת אֶת־דָּוִד לֵאמֹר הַעֲלוּ אֹתוֹ בַמִּטָּה אֵלַי לַהֲמִתוֹ:

(16) וַיָּבֹאוּ הַמַּלְאָכִים וְהִנֵּה הַתְּרָפִים אֶל־הַמִּטָּה וּכְבִיר הָעִזִּים מְרַאֲשֹׁתָיו:

(17) וַיֹּאמֶר שָׁאוּל אֶל־מִיכַל לָמָּה כָּכָה רִמִּיתִנִי וַתְּשַׁלְּחִי אֶת־אֹיְבִי וַיִּמָּלֵט וַתֹּאמֶר מִיכַל אֶל־שָׁאוּל הוּא־אָמַר אֵלַי שַׁלְּחִנִי לָמָה אֲמִיתֵךְ:

(18) וְדָוִד בָּרַח וַיִּמָּלֵט וַיָּבֹא אֶל־שְׁמוּאֵל הָרָמָתָה וַיַּגֶּד־לוֹ אֵת כָּל־אֲשֶׁר עָשָׂה־לוֹ שָׁאוּל וַיֵּלֶךְ הוּא וּשְׁמוּאֵל וַיֵּשְׁבוּ בְּנָיוֹת:

1 Samuel 25.43-44 (4)

(43) וְאֶת־אֲחִינֹעַם לָקַח דָּוִד מִיִּזְרְעֶאל וַתִּהְיֶיןָ גַּם־שְׁתֵּיהֶן לוֹ לְנָשִׁים:

(44) וְשָׁאוּל נָתַן אֶת־מִיכַל בִּתּוֹ אֵשֶׁת דָּוִד לְפַלְטִי בֶן־לַיִשׁ אֲשֶׁר מִגַּלִּים:

2 Samuel 3.12-16 (5)

(12) וַיִּשְׁלַח אַבְנֵר מַלְאָכִים ׀ אֶל־דָּוִד תַּחַתוֹ [תַּחְתָּיו] לֵאמֹר לְמִי־אָרֶץ לֵאמֹר כָּרְתָה בְרִיתְךָ אִתִּי וְהִנֵּה יָדִי עִמָּךְ לְהָסֵב אֵלֶיךָ אֶת־כָּל־יִשְׂרָאֵל:

(13) וַיֹּאמֶר טוֹב אֲנִי אֶכְרֹת אִתְּךָ בְּרִית אַךְ דָּבָר אֶחָד אָנֹכִי שֹׁאֵל מֵאִתְּךָ לֵאמֹר לֹא־תִרְאֶה אֶת־פָּנַי כִּי אִם־לִפְנֵי הֱבִיאֲךָ אֵת מִיכַל בַּת־שָׁאוּל בְּבֹאֲךָ לִרְאוֹת אֶת־פָּנָי:

(14) וַיִּשְׁלַח דָּוִד מַלְאָכִים אֶל־אִישׁ־בֹּשֶׁת בֶּן־שָׁאוּל לֵאמֹר תְּנָה אֶת־אִשְׁתִּי אֶת־מִיכַל אֲשֶׁר אֵרַשְׂתִּי לִי בְּמֵאָה עָרְלוֹת פְּלִשְׁתִּים:

(11) That night Saul sent messengers to David's house to watch him, that he might kill him in the morning. But Michal, David's wife, told him, 'If you do not save your life tonight, tomorrow you will be killed'. (12) So Michal let David down through the window; and he fled away and escaped. (13) Michal took an image and laid it on the bed and put a pillow of goats' hair at its head, and covered it with the clothes. (14) And when Saul sent messengers to take David, she said, 'He is sick'. (15) Then Saul sent the messengers to see David, saying, 'Bring him up to me in the bed, that I may kill him'. (16) And when the messengers came in, behold, the image was in the bed, with the pillow of goats' hair at its head. (17) Saul said to Michal, 'Why have you deceived me thus, and let my enemy go, so that he has escaped?' And Michal answered Saul, 'He said to me, "Let me go; why should I kill you?"' (18) Now David fled and escaped, and he came to Samuel at Ramah, and told him all that Saul had done to him. And he and Samuel went and dwelt at Naioth.

4. *1 Samuel 25.43-44*

(43) David also took Ahino-am of Jezreel; and both of them became his wives. (44) Saul had given Michal his daughter, David's wife, to Palti the son of Laish, who was of Gallim.

5. *2 Samuel 3.12-16*

(12) And Abner sent messengers to David at Hebron, saying, 'To whom does the land belong? Make your covenant with me, and behold, my hand shall be with you to bring over all Israel to you.' (13) And he said, 'Good; I will make a covenant with you; but one thing I require of you; that is, you shall not see my face, unless you first bring Michal, Saul's daughter, when you come to see my face'. (14) Then David sent messengers to Ishbosheth Saul's son, saying, 'Give me my wife Michal, whom I betrothed at the price of a hundred foreskins of the Philistines'.

(15) וַיִּשְׁלַח֙ אִ֣ישׁ בֹּ֔שֶׁת וַיִּקָּחֶ֖הָ מֵעִ֣ם אִ֑ישׁ מֵעִ֖ם פַּלְטִיאֵ֥ל בֶּן־לָֽיִשׁ׃

(16) וַיֵּ֨לֶךְ אִתָּ֜הּ אִישָׁ֗הּ הָל֧וֹךְ וּבָכֹ֛ה אַחֲרֶ֖יהָ עַד־בַּֽחֻרִ֑ים וַיֹּ֨אמֶר אֵלָ֤יו
אַבְנֵר֙ לֵ֣ךְ שׁ֔וּב וַיָּשֹֽׁב׃

2 Samuel 6.12-23 (6)

(12) וַיֻּגַּ֗ד לַמֶּ֣לֶךְ דָּוִד֮ לֵאמֹר֒ בֵּרַ֣ךְ יְהוָ֗ה אֶת־בֵּ֨ית עֹבֵ֤ד אֱדֹם֙
וְאֶת־כָּל־אֲשֶׁר־ל֔וֹ בַּעֲב֖וּר אֲר֣וֹן הָאֱלֹהִ֑ים וַיֵּ֣לֶךְ דָּוִ֗ד וַיַּעַל֩ אֶת־אֲר֨וֹן
הָאֱלֹהִ֜ים מִבֵּ֨ית עֹבֵ֥ד אֱדֹ֛ם עִ֥יר דָּוִ֖ד בְּשִׂמְחָֽה׃

(13) וַיְהִ֗י כִּ֧י צָעֲד֛וּ נֹשְׂאֵ֥י אֲרוֹן־יְהוָ֖ה שִׁשָּׁ֣ה צְעָדִ֑ים וַיִּזְבַּ֥ח שׁ֖וֹר וּמְרִֽיא׃

(14) וְדָוִ֛ד מְכַרְכֵּ֥ר בְּכָל־עֹ֖ז לִפְנֵ֣י יְהוָ֑ה וְדָוִ֕ד חָג֖וּר אֵפ֥וֹד בָּֽד׃

(15) וְדָוִד֙ וְכָל־בֵּ֣ית יִשְׂרָאֵ֔ל מַעֲלִ֖ים אֶת־אֲר֣וֹן יְהוָ֑ה בִּתְרוּעָ֖ה וּבְק֥וֹל
שׁוֹפָֽר׃

(16) וְהָיָה֙ אֲר֣וֹן יְהוָ֔ה בָּ֖א עִ֣יר דָּוִ֑ד וּמִיכַ֨ל בַּת־שָׁא֜וּל נִשְׁקְפָ֣ה ׀ בְּעַ֣ד הַחַלּ֗וֹן
וַתֵּ֨רֶא אֶת־הַמֶּ֤לֶךְ דָּוִד֙ מְפַזֵּ֣ז וּמְכַרְכֵּ֣ר לִפְנֵ֣י יְהוָ֔ה וַתִּ֥בֶז ל֖וֹ בְּלִבָּֽהּ׃

(17) וַיָּבִ֜אוּ אֶת־אֲר֣וֹן יְהוָ֗ה וַיַּצִּ֤גוּ אֹתוֹ֙ בִּמְק֣וֹמ֔וֹ בְּת֣וֹךְ הָאֹ֔הֶל אֲשֶׁ֥ר נָֽטָה־ל֖וֹ
דָּוִ֑ד וַיַּ֨עַל דָּוִ֧ד עֹל֛וֹת לִפְנֵ֥י יְהוָ֖ה וּשְׁלָמִֽים׃

(18) וַיְכַ֣ל דָּוִ֔ד מֵהַעֲל֥וֹת הָעוֹלָ֖ה וְהַשְּׁלָמִ֑ים וַיְבָ֣רֶךְ אֶת־הָעָ֔ם בְּשֵׁ֖ם יְהוָ֥ה
צְבָאֽוֹת׃

(19) וַיְחַלֵּ֨ק לְכָל־הָעָ֜ם לְכָל־הֲמ֣וֹן יִשְׂרָאֵ֗ל לְמֵאִ֣ישׁ וְעַד־אִשָּׁ֔ה לְאִ֣ישׁ חַלַּ֣ת
לֶ֗חֶם אַחַת֙ וְאֶשְׁפָּ֣ר אֶחָ֔ד וַאֲשִׁישָׁ֣ה אֶחָ֑ת וַיֵּ֥לֶךְ כָּל־הָעָ֖ם אִ֥ישׁ לְבֵיתֽוֹ׃

(20) וַיָּ֥שָׁב דָּוִ֖ד לְבָרֵ֣ךְ אֶת־בֵּית֑וֹ וַתֵּצֵ֞א מִיכַ֤ל בַּת־שָׁאוּל֙ לִקְרַ֣את דָּוִ֔ד
וַתֹּ֗אמֶר מַה־נִּכְבַּ֨ד הַיּ֜וֹם מֶ֣לֶךְ יִשְׂרָאֵ֗ל אֲשֶׁ֨ר נִגְלָ֤ה הַיּוֹם֙ לְעֵינֵי֙ אַמְה֣וֹת
עֲבָדָ֔יו כְּהִגָּל֥וֹת נִגְל֖וֹת אַחַ֥ד הָרֵקִֽים׃

(21) וַיֹּ֣אמֶר דָּוִד֮ אֶל־מִיכַל֒ לִפְנֵ֣י יְהוָ֗ה אֲשֶׁ֨ר בָּֽחַר־בִּ֤י מֵֽאָבִיךְ֙ וּמִכָּל־בֵּית֔וֹ
לְצַוֺּ֨ת אֹתִ֥י נָגִ֛יד עַל־עַ֥ם יְהוָ֖ה עַל־יִשְׂרָאֵ֑ל וְשִׂחַקְתִּ֖י לִפְנֵ֥י יְהוָֽה׃

(22) וּנְקַלֹּ֤תִי עוֹד֙ מִזֹּ֔את וְהָיִ֥יתִי שָׁפָ֖ל בְּעֵינָ֑י וְעִם־הָֽאֲמָהוֹת֙ אֲשֶׁ֣ר אָמַ֔רְתְּ
עִמָּ֖ם אִכָּבֵֽדָה׃

(23) וּלְמִיכַל֙ בַּת־שָׁא֔וּל לֹֽא־הָ֥יָה לָ֖הּ יָ֑לֶד עַ֖ד י֥וֹם מוֹתָֽהּ׃

(15) And Ish-bosheth sent, and took her from her husband Paltiel the son of Laish. (16) But her husband went with her, weeping after her all the way to Bahurim. Then Abner said to him, 'Go, return'; and he returned.

6. 2 Samuel 6.12-23

(12) And it was told King David, 'The LORD has blessed the household of Obed-edom and all that belongs to him, because of the ark of God'. So David went and brought up the ark of God from the house of Obed-edom to the city of David with rejoicing; (13) and when those who bore the ark of the LORD had gone six paces, he sacrificed an ox and a fatling. (14) And David danced before the LORD with all his might; and David was girded with a linen ephod. (15) So David and all the house of Israel brought up the ark of the LORD with shouting, and with the sound of the horn.

(16) As the ark of the LORD came into the city of David, Michal the daughter of Saul looked out of the window, and saw King David leaping and dancing before the LORD; and she despised him in her heart. (17) And they brought in the ark of the LORD, and set it in its place, inside the tent which David had pitched for it; and David offered burnt offerings and peace offerings before the LORD. (18) And when David had finished offering the burnt offerings and the peace offerings, he blessed the people in the name of the LORD of hosts, (19) and distributed among all the people, the whole multitude of Israel, both men and women, to each a cake of bread, a portion of meat, and a cake of raisins. Then all the people departed, each to his house.

(20) And David returned to bless his household. But Michal the daughter of Saul came out to meet David, and said, 'How the king of Israel honored himself today, uncovering himself today before the eyes of his servants' maids, as one of the vulgar fellows shamelessly uncovers himself!' (21) And David said to Michal, 'It was before the LORD, who chose me above your father, and above all his house, to appoint me as prince over Israel, the people of the LORD—and I will make merry before the LORD. (22) I will make myself yet more contemptible than this, and I will be abased in your eyes; but by the maids of whom you have spoken, by them I shall be held in honor.' (23) And Michal the daughter of Saul had no child to the day of her death.

2 Samuel 21.7-9 (7)

(7) וַיַּחְמֹל הַמֶּלֶךְ עַל־מְפִיבֹשֶׁת בֶּן־יְהוֹנָתָן בֶּן־שָׁאוּל עַל־שְׁבֻעַת יְהוָה
אֲשֶׁר בֵּינֹתָם בֵּין דָּוִד וּבֵין יְהוֹנָתָן בֶּן־שָׁאוּל:

(8) וַיִּקַּח הַמֶּלֶךְ אֶת־שְׁנֵי בְּנֵי רִצְפָּה בַת־אַיָּה אֲשֶׁר יָלְדָה לְשָׁאוּל
אֶת־אַרְמֹנִי וְאֶת־מְפִבֹשֶׁת וְאֶת־חֲמֵשֶׁת בְּנֵי מִיכַל בַּת־שָׁאוּל אֲשֶׁר יָלְדָה
לְעַדְרִיאֵל בֶּן־בַּרְזִלַּי הַמְּחֹלָתִי:

(9) וַיִּתְּנֵם בְּיַד הַגִּבְעֹנִים וַיֹּקִיעֻם בָּהָר לִפְנֵי יְהוָה וַיִּפְּלוּ שְׁבַעְתָּיִם
יָחַד וְהֵם הֻמְתוּ בִּימֵי קָצִיר בָּרִאשֹׁנִים תְּחִלַּת קְצִיר שְׂעֹרִים:

1 Chronicles 15.29 (8)

(29) וַיְהִי אֲרוֹן בְּרִית יְהוָה בָּא עַד־עִיר דָּוִיד וּמִיכַל בַּת־שָׁאוּל נִשְׁקְפָה
בְּעַד הַחַלּוֹן וַתֵּרֶא אֶת־הַמֶּלֶךְ דָּוִיד מְרַקֵּד וּמְשַׂחֵק וַתִּבֶז לוֹ בְּלִבָּהּ:

7. *2 Samuel 21.7-9*

(7) But the king spared Mephibosheth, the son of Saul's son Jonathan, because of the oath of the LORD which was between them, between David and Jonathan the son of Saul. (8) The king took the two sons of Rizpah the daughter of Aiah, whom she bore to Saul, Armoni and Mephibosheth; and the five sons of Merab the daughter of Saul, whom she bore to Adriel the son of Barzillai the Meholathite; (9) and he gave them into the hands of the Gibeonites, and they hanged them on the mountain before the LORD, and the seven of them perished together. They were put to death in the first days of harvest, at the beginning of barley harvest.

8. *1 Chronicles 15.29*

(29) And as the ark of the covenant of the LORD came to the city of David, Michal the daughter of Saul looked out of the window, and saw King David dancing and making merry; and she despised him in her heart.

David J.A. Clines

MICHAL OBSERVED:
AN INTRODUCTION TO READING HER STORY

> The text provides our window on Michal, offering us only a glimpse, the
> kind of view a window gives, limited in range and perspective. We are, as
> it were, outside, watching her, inside, watching David.[1]

What This Book Is

In form, this book is an anthology of interpretations of the story of
Michal, daughter of Saul and wife of David. It includes both
'scholarly' and 'unscholarly' readings of her story, both imaginative
reconstructions of the life of Michal and straightforward explications
of the texts about her, both brief encyclopaedia articles and lengthy
essays, both Jewish and Christian perceptions of her character, both
reprinted studies and new publications. In this Introduction I address
the questions that such a compilation raises for scholars and students
of biblical literature, and to draw attention to the variety of interpretation to which the story leaves itself open.

In intention, this book is by no means a mere anthology of variant
interpretations that may provoke curiosity, puzzlement or derision. It
aims rather to raise the question of what interpretation in general is,
and whether there is in practice any means for judging particular interpretations. It refuses to prejudge the value of an interpretation on
grounds extrinsic to the interpretation itself, such as the scholarly cre-
dentials or otherwise of the interpreter, the audience addressed by the
interpreter, or the date at which the interpretation was written.

The programme of this book is not to study the *history* of interpretation, or to attempt to organize that history into a meaningful

---

1. J. Cheryl Exum, *Arrows of the Almighty. Tragedy and Biblical Narrative*
(Cambridge: Cambridge University Press, forthcoming), ch. 4.

sequence of 'progress' or 'development'. Rather, it is to put in the hands of readers the materials for *comparative interpretation*, that is, for comparing interpretations and developing critical principles for coping with the variety of interpretations that actually exist. Because my interest is in *interpretation*, and specifically in the interpretation of these particular texts, it is success in interpretation that is for me the yardstick of this evaluation. The materials printed in this book may have served, in their own contexts, other functions beside that of interpretation—exhortation, historical reconstruction or imaginative writing, for example—and they may have served those functions very successfully. But such functions are not my concern here; I am inviting the reader to have in one hand the biblical text and in the other the succession of interpretations collected in this volume and to wonder and worry about what it is that has been going on in the name of Michal.

What This Introduction Is

This Introduction has two main intentions. The first is to view synoptically the various interpretations collected in this volume, that is, to compare and contrast their readings of certain key moments in the Michal story. The second is to develop from this comparison of actual interpretations some principles about interpretation in general. Questions of what is valid or legitimate in interpretation are always raising themselves whenever we tangle with actual and particular readings, and I hope that by starting from the side of the actual rather than of the theoretical I may have some useful answers to suggest.

The first task therefore will be to identify what it is I have in mind when I speak of 'the Michal story', and the second will be to move through the story itself, comparing and contrasting the offerings of these authors on certain major elements in the story. In the course of the comparative work, certain principles in interpretation will begin to emerge; and at the conclusion of this Introduction some summary statements about the programme of 'comparative interpretation' will be made.

What the Story of Michal Is

It has to be acknowledged at the outset that the idea of a 'story of

Michal' is something of an artificial construct. For what we find in the text of 1 and 2 Samuel is a few episodes within the story of David, in which Michal figures. There are only four such episodes, to which we may add three further notations that concern Michal. There is, in addition, one further reference to Michal in the Bible, in 1 Chronicles. These then are the passages about Michal (printed in full, in Hebrew and English, on pp. 16-25 above):

Notations	Episodes
(1) *1 Samuel 14.49-51* The ancestry of Michal	
	(2) *1 Samuel 18.12-29* Michal becomes David's wife (3) *1 Samuel 19.8-18* Michal saves David from Saul's anger
(4) *1 Samuel 25.43-44* Michal is given to Palti as a wife	
	(5) *2 Samuel 3.12-16* David demands Michal from Palti (6) *2 Samuel 6.12-23* Michal despises David dancing before the ark
(7) *2 Samuel 21.7-9* Michal's children (8) *1 Chronicles 15.29* Michal despises David	

The biblical Michal is certainly no more than a marginal character in the David story; nevertheless, the material concerning her forms a coherent sequence and creates in readers' minds a distinctive picture of her as a character. Despite the brevity of the episodes in which she appears, she emerges as an interesting, complex, and developing person. Those who write about Michal always seem to believe that they know enough about her as a character to make assessments of her personality and inferences about her motivations which the text does not make explicit. It may be that the text itself, in its very unforthcomingness about her, invites such gap-filling; and it will be a goal of this Introduction to consider ways of determining the value of the numerous inferences drawn by various authors from the texts[1].

---

1. Quotations in this chapter are from works printed in this volume. The first

The Story of Michal, Step by Step

1. *Why does Saul permit David to marry Michal, when he prevented him from marrying his older daughter Merab to whom he was promised?*

The Biblical narrative seems plain enough. It is clear that Saul was 'afraid' of David and his popularity with the people, and that he was 'in awe' of him (18.15). This fear apparently leads Saul to hope for David's death. He promises him to his elder daughter Merab on condition that he carry on Saul's battles against the Philistines. Saul hopes that David will lose his life in some such battle: 'Let not my hand be upon him', he thinks, 'but let the hand of the Philistines be upon him' (18.17).

So Saul would like David to be dead, but not so much as to want to kill him himself. He would like David to be killed by someone else, accidentally as it might seem. We cannot say that Saul really has a definite plan to have David killed, for there is a good chance that David will survive all his engagements with the Philistines, and will earn even greater adulation from the people. We suspect that Saul does not appear to be entirely serious about doing away with David.

The sequence of vv. 17 and 19 indicates that Saul's plan has been ineffectual. For a time arrives 'when Merab should have been given to David', presumably after David has been successful enough against the Philistines to deserve the princess's hand. Nevertheless, Saul does not give her to David, but marries her to Adriel the Meholathite. It is not clear why Merab needs to be given to another man if Saul's principal motivation is the death of David, for even after becoming the king's son-in-law David could presumably still be sent out on missions against Philistines, with all the attendant risks. Readers inevitably ask themselves whether they are being told the real story.[1]

Michal enters the story in a reprise of the Merab incident. For Michal, Saul explicitly requires a dowry—a hundred Philistine fore-

---

page reference is to the page in the present volume, and the second reference, in square brackets, is to the original page number, in the case of works previously published.

1.   Here and elsewhere in this chapter I am speaking about what 'readers' do and fail to do. Inevitably I am extrapolating from my own experience of being a reader, as well as observing what other readers who have committed their readings to paper have made of the text. But I am not suggesting that all readers actually read in the ways I speak of, far less that all readers should.

skins. As with Merab, it is Saul's hope that David will be killed by the Philistines. For the second time, David is successful against Philistines, but this time the king gives him his daughter as a wife. Why does he do so this time, and not the first time? There is a narrative gap here, which readers naturally try to fill.

How are we to explain Saul's behaviour? Is it that Saul is 'wavering between desire to destroy David and reluctance to promote him to be the king's son-in-law'?[1] Has Saul in fact any 'reluctance' to make David his son-in-law? Is the question of succession to the throne at all an issue in this narrative? Or is it a question entirely of Saul's fear of David, and of half-hearted attempts to dispose of David?

Or is it perhaps just a token of Saul's neurosis that he changes his mind? And can we accept 'sheer spite' as a reason for Saul's breaking of his promise?[2]

Or may it be that Saul has some finer feelings, and cannot bring himself, when the crunch comes, to marry his daughter to a man he hopes to send to an early grave? Is it, as Maurice Samuel puts it, that 'Saul shrank from having to pray for his daughter's widowhood'?[3]

Or is the broken engagement not Saul's doing at all? Is it perhaps David himself who becomes at the last moment reluctant to marry the king's daughter?[4] Might there indeed, be some truth in David's protestation—which most readers have taken as false humility: 'Who am I, and who: are my kinsfolk, my father's family in Israel, that I should be son-in-law to the king?' Does he feel some unaccountable sense of unworthiness to marry into the royal family? Or is it perhaps Michal who stands behind the scenes? Can we perhaps suppose that the sentence that immediately follows the news of Merab's marriage elsewhere, 'Now Saul's daughter Michal loved David', signifies that 'Michal worked against the marriage' to Merab?[5] To the same effect, Lofts asks:

> [I]s it safe to overlook the possibility that Michal had a hand in the business? She was in love with David. She was, as the later events in the

1. N.J.D. White, 'Michal', p. 285 [363].
2. N. Lofts, 'Michal', p. 238 [112].
3. M. Samuel, 'Three Wives', p. 272 [194].
4. Cf. Samuel, 'Three Wives', p. 272 [194].
5. Samuel, 'Three Wives', p. 272 [194].

story prove, a crafty and resourceful young woman. She could play, successfully, a very double game. . .[1]

Among this profusion of explanations for Saul's motives, which shall we choose? Unless we are to find all explanations equally plausible and interesting, we shall have to use some standard by which to judge among them. It is not very novel to suggest that the most useful standard is the question: Is there anything in the text that supports this interpretation? Various interpretations may be supported by elements in the text, and so finding some anchor in the text will not of itself determine that an interpretation is 'correct' or 'acceptable'. But it is among interpretations with *some* anchor in the text that we must decide. Those that have no anchor in the text, however interesting or attractive, we cannot allow as *interpretations* of the text. They may even be better ways of telling the underlying story that comes to expression in the text, but they are not better ways of explaining the text. And *that*, I argue, is what interpretation is.

In this case, whatever we think of Saul's motives, and however refined and subtle our analysis of his character, we cannot overlook the explicit signals sent by the narrator, that Saul was 'afraid' of David and for that reason wanted him to be killed. We are entitled to consider for what exact reasons Saul was afraid of David, or how much he wanted him to be killed, and we can look for clues in the narrative to answer our questions. What we cannot do is to fasten upon an entirely different motivation for Saul, as if we knew better than the narrator. Unless we have reason to suspect that the narrator is an unreliable one (for example, if the narrator explicitly told us that Saul was afraid but never gave us any evidence in Saul's words or actions that he was afraid), then we cannot know better than the narrator. The narrator's narrative is all we have; we have no access to Saul or his mind apart from what the narrator tells us, explicitly or implicitly. For we are not in the business of reconstructing the real thoughts of the historical personage Saul, but of understanding the characterization that the narrator has presented to us.

So when it comes to our question here, Why does Saul permit David to marry Michal, having prevented him from marrying Merab, to whom he was promised?, we have to ask which of the proposed solutions has some anchor in the text. Can it be that 'Saul shrank from

---

1. Lofts, 'Michal', p. 238 [112].

having to pray for his daughter's [Merab's] widowhood'?[1] Hardly, because we cannot put our finger on anything in the text that will support that. There is no hint that Saul felt any differently about his two daughters, or that if he was reluctant to make Merab a widow he would not have been equally reluctant to make Michal a widow. Perhaps the real-life Saul 'shrank' from quite a few things which we are not told of in the text; but we can know nothing of the real-life Saul, only of the character Saul in the narrator's text.

No more can we feel comfortable with the idea that Saul is reluctant to make David his son-in-law. For the text clearly says that Saul offers Merab to David *in order that David will go off to fight Philistines and get himself killed.* Saul is not 'reluctant' to have David marry Merab; rather, *he intends that David should not marry Merab.* The idea of marrying Merab is invented by Saul as a way of getting David killed. Nor can we allow that 'sheer spite' is the reason for Saul's not keeping his promise. For he never intended to keep his promise, he never intended that David would survive long enough to marry Merab.

Let us be clear: Saul never changed his mind about David's marriage to Merab, and we read that in the text; it is not some psychological reading of a dead man's mind. The text says that Saul offered Merab to David *and* that Saul intended David to die before the marriage could take place. So it is *the text* that tells us that Saul was not sincere, and that the offer of Merab was only a way of ensuring David's death. And it is *the text* that tells us that the reason why Saul wanted David to be dead was because he 'was afraid' of him.

Can it be, we go on to ask, that it is David himself who has last-minute nerves about marrying Merab, as Maurice Samuel suggests? Is it that David feels some sense of unworthiness at marrying into the royal family? If we are to take any notice of the text, we must reply, perhaps he does have nerves about it, perhaps he feels unworthy. Perhaps his protestation is sincere. *But that is not the reason why the marriage does not go ahead.* The reason lies with Saul, who never intended it in the first place, and then, when it ought to have happened, makes sure it does not, by marrying Merab off to a different man.

Was Saul any more sincere when he offered David Michal? The text is equally plain. Michal is intended by Saul as a 'snare' for David,[2]

---

1.   Cf. Samuel, 'Three Wives', p. 272 [194].
2.   We can hardly agree with Z. Ben-Barak that 'the motive for this marriage is

which can only mean that Saul thinks that by proposing a bride-price of a hundred Philistine foreskins he is sending David to certain death. If David agrees to the bride-price, Michal will prove to be his entrapment. Saul's intention was to make David fall by the hands of the Philistines, so says the text explicitly (v. 25).

Then why does Saul allow David to marry Michal when he did not allow him to marry Merab? We must look even more closely at the text for the answer. Saul's intention is the same in both episodes, and so is David's acceptance of Saul's proposal. What is different? In the first case, David is supposed to 'be valiant' for Saul and 'fight the LORD's battles' (v. 17). In the second case, the king desires a hundred foreskins of the Philistines so that he may be avenged of his enemies (v. 25). We all know what accomplishing the second task will look like, and the narrative itself depicts its fulfilment, with David 'giving' to Saul the two hundred foreskins that he has 'brought' (v. 27). But how would anyone know when the first task had been accomplished? There, David had not been sent into some particular battle and told to win it. He had not been commissioned to decapitate some Philistine hero like Goliath. He had been told to *go on* being valiant for Saul and fighting the LORD's battles. When, pray, will he have done enough fighting and being valiant to be allowed to stop and get married to Merab? Only Saul will decide that, and he is obviously going to decide that David can stop only on the day he meets with a fatal accident. There does seem to have been some day envisaged for the marriage, the 'time of the giving of Merab to David' (v. 19), but when that day arrives, David is presumably still being valiant and Merab has inadvertently been given to Adriel. Things are different in the case of Michal, and Saul has shot himself in the foot if he was hoping for a replay of the Merab affair. No doubt Saul thinks that the bride-price of a hundred Philistine foreskins is an impossible target to meet. Perhaps Saul has not been reckoning with David's men, who no doubt co-operate enthusiastically, excessively even, in getting their leader happily married. In any case, when David arrives at court with his bloody parcel, there can be no denying that the bride-price has been

Michal's love for David' (p. 79 [19]); the motive rather is Saul's plan to be rid of David, and Michal's love for David only happens to be a useful cover-story. Cf. J.C. Exum, 'Murder They Wrote: Ideology and the Manipulation of Female Presence in Biblical Narrative', p. 182 [50]: 'From Saul's perspective, Michal's love for David may be convenient but otherwise largely gratuitous'.

delivered. There cannot even be any quibble about the arithmetic. Saul
cannot deny that David is now entitled to Michal. The story is therefore a story *at Saul's expense*, a story of David's superior luck, a story
that proves that Yahweh is with David—which is exactly what Saul
'sees' and 'knows' as a result of the way things turn out (v. 28). Saul
had never wanted either of his daughters to marry David; because he
is unlucky, he fails to prevent the second marriage even though he
managed to prevent the first.

2. Why does Michal love David?

At first sight, the text seems perfectly plain:

> Saul's daughter Michal loved David (18.20).

Readers of this sentence, however, generally find themselves confronted by two choices. They can

1. take this notation as a datum of the story, and not reflect on it further.
2. take this notation as an invitation to identify the reason why Michal
   loved David.

With the first choice, we may accept that love is not always capable of
explanation, and consider that, if the narrator says nothing explicit
about the reason for Michal's love, the *reason* itself cannot be important for the story, however fundamental the *fact* of the love may be.
With the second choice, we may feel that the story cries out for, or at
least permits, an exploration into the motive for Michal's love; however arbitrary falling in love may be from the outsider's point of
view, people who fall in love commonly claim to have reasons. Does
this narrator mean us to suppose that Michal's love is arbitrary, or
does the narrator believe that enough reasons have already been provided in the story for intelligent readers to draw their own conclusions? Does not the very absence of explanation itself invite readers
not to take the 'fact' at its face value? That at least is the view of
Alter: 'Michal's love is stated entirely without motivated explanation;
this does not mean, of course, that it is inexplicable, only that the
writer wants us to conjecture about it'.

Interpreters of the Michal story divide over this issue. Either they
confine their comments to the *fact* of Michal's love, or they offer
some explanation of it.

Matters are complicated somewhat by the fact itself. For this is the

only time in biblical Hebrew narrative when a woman is said to love a
man.[1] Might it be, then, that a quite unique event demands some explanation which a more everyday kind of event could manage without? In that case, should we perhaps worry whether the distinction
between the two choices as set out above is very secure after all? Or
further, even if we are not to be busy exploring for *reasons* for
Michal's love, does the uniqueness of the narration not perhaps imply
something about Michal that the text does not make explicit? Should
we say, for example, that Michal 'must have been a woman of unusual
strength of mind to declare her love in that age'?[2] Despite these in-
centives for thinking of explanations, it has to be admitted that there
are plenty of interpreters who see no call here to *explain* at all, and
who take the 'fact' as a datum of the story.

Those who do explain try to find something in David's character
that might have been attractive to Michal. Here are some possibilities:

(1) [T]he closeted young girl from the aristocratic family. . . fell in love
with the village hero; and his simplicity—or crudeness—was not disturbing to her but doubtless had a certain charm of its own.[3]

(2) Michal had been deeply impressed by the young man who had killed
the giant Goliath.[4]

(3) She loved David, attracted no doubt by the heroism and chivalry of the
young soldier (18.20).[5]

(4) It is easy to suppose that she and David had often met when her
brother, a great admirer of David, had brought him home. And to a king's
young daughter the brave and strong David became a great hero.[6]

(5) [T]he beautiful young man who could accompany his music with
songs of his own making, who had easy good manners and an air of
confidence and high destiny, proved as attractive to Saul's daughters and
sons as to the king himself.[7]

(6) She saw David slighted by her father, whose fitful affections she

---

1.   So R. Alter, 'Characterization and the Art of Reticence', p. 68 [118]; White,
'Michal', p. 285 [363].

2.   H. Lockyer, 'Michal', p. 227 [224].

3.   A. Steinsaltz, 'The Princess and the Shepherd', p. 281 [147].

4.   A. Kuyper, 'Michal', p. 224 [109].

5.   W. Ewing and J.E.H. Thomson, 'Michal', p. 175 [463].

6.   E. Deen, 'King Saul's Daughter—David's First Wife', p. 141 [97].

7.   Lofts, 'Michal', p. 236 [109].

mistrusted; she saw him needing the protection and guidance of one
whose affections were as steady as they were deep.[1]

Are any of these explanations to be called 'speculative'? None of them
is explicit in the text, but are they in any way implicit? Are they reasonable ways of filling a gap in the text, or do they, lacking any
anchor in the text, fall into the category of the 'speculative'?

Let us suppose that we had begun to read the story with 18.20,
'Now Saul's daughter Michal loved David', having no prior knowledge about the principal characters. In order to understand the sentence at all, we should have had to go back over the preceding pages
to discover who they are, that Saul is a king of Israel, that David is a
young man, an Israelite, and a warrior, and so forth. We would be
filling out the gaps in this sentence by reference to previous sentences.
It is no different when, knowing the identity of the characters, we go
back over the preceding story to discover what it is about David that
lies behind Michal's 'loving' him.

There is nothing that the reader *must* supply in order for the narrative to have logical coherence, it must be admitted. On the other hand,
it is difficult to resist some of the explanations just quoted, for they
seem to do little more than recapitulate facts that the narrative has already presented. It is *true*, according to the text, that David is found
to be attractive by both Saul and his son Jonathan (as Lofts notes),[2]
and to make this comment at the point where the daughter also is said
to 'love' David seems to be wholly appropriate and enlightening. We
might not be so sure, initially, that the other comment by Lofts is so
clearly anchored in the text: 'Michal was far from being alone in her
adoration for him. Half the women in Israel were in love with him
then.'[3] She is thinking of 1 Sam. 18.16, 'All Israel and Judah loved
David'; even if we ought to distinguish between the kind of 'love' the
populace as a whole bear him and Michal's kind of 'love' (perhaps we
should, perhaps we shouldn't), should we not allow that the cross-
referencing of Michal's love to the Israelites' love is useful comment?
Perhaps there is something suspicious in the fact that Lofts wants to
say that '*half* the women in Israel were in love with him' while the
biblical narrator wants to say that '*all* Israel' loved him; perhaps Lofts

1. Samuel, 'Three Wives', pp. 270-71 [192].
2. Lofts, 'Michal', p. 236 [109].
3. Lofts, 'Michal', p. 237 [111].

means something different by 'being in love with'. Nevertheless, to background Michal's love with the love Saul and Jonathan and all Israel feel for David (Saul's love in 16.21, Jonathan's in 18.3) is in general quite acceptable; it is the normal kind of duty a commentator performs.

If such comment is acceptable, let us ask now, Is there anything in the six explanations quoted above that we should resist? Of course, explanations differ in their explanatory power, but there is one simple yardstick for establishing the a priori possibility of an explanation: Is it to do with the *person* Michal, or is to do with the *character* Michal? There may or may not have been an historical person named Michal, daughter of Saul; in either case, we have no access to her. We can only access the character Michal in the pages of 1 and 2 Samuel. We cannot know anything about Michal the person that the pages of Samuel do not tell us directly or indirectly. We cannot know what was going on in her head, we cannot know her motivations; but we can make, on the basis of the text, reasonable guesses and inferences about the character Michal, and about the circumstances that were impacting on her. And we can build on those inferences further inferences about how a typical person in those circumstances and in that culture is likely to have behaved.

In short, we can say, with reasonable probability, that Michal was 'deeply impressed by the young man who had killed the giant Goliath'[1] because the narrative enables our belief that the character Michal knows that David had killed Goliath (David and Michal are both members of Saul's household, 18.2), and that the character Michal is impressed by it (the Israelite women sing victory hymns in praise of David, 18.7, and Michal is an Israelite woman). On the other hand, we cannot say of the character Michal that David's rustic simplicity (or crudeness!) had a certain charm for her[2]—for there is no anchor for that in the text. This observation—or its opposite—may well have been true about the *person* Michal, but we shall never know. We are in no position to tell whether, assuming that David *was* possessed of rustic simplicity, this trait endeared him to Michal or was a perpetual difficulty for her affection for him. We do not know whether Michal saw it as 'simplicity' or 'crudeness' (the parenthesis in Steinsaltz's sentence is revealing). The objection to this explanation of

---

1. Kuyper, 'Michal', p. 224 [109].
2. Steinsaltz, 'The Princess and the Shepherd', p. 281 [147].

Michal's love is not so much that it is untrue as that it is unfalsifiable; it does not connect with anything in the text, so there is no way of arguing against it. Whatever the comment is, therefore, it is not interpretation, for interpretation is interpretation of texts. I myself call it 'speculation', which does not mean that it is not interesting, not intriguing or even not true about the historical person Michal (assuming there *was* such a person), but that it is not an *interpretation of this text* about this character Michal.

Things are a little more complicated in the case of the sixth comment quoted:

> (6) She saw David slighted by her father, whose fitful affections she mistrusted; she saw him needing the protection and guidance of one whose affections were as steady as they were deep.[1]

The first clause, that she saw David slighted, is undoubtedly an interpretation. For the character Michal is in a position to see the way in which Saul is treating David. Whether it is an ultimately convincing interpretation will depend on whether we agree that the text shows David being 'slighted' by Saul, but that is not the issue here. What of the second clause, that she mistrusted Saul's fitful affections? The issue is perhaps not so straightforward, but I think that we can certainly reference the fitful affections of Saul, who both loves David and seeks to kill him, and we can plausibly infer that this Michal is aware of her father's attitudes to David; and we can further assume that any normal character will mistrust such a person as Saul. This textual warrant and these reasonable inferences from the text permit us to assent to the phrase 'whose fitful affections she mistrusted'—at least if we could add a 'probably' to it.

But it is quite different with the second half of the comment. For there is nothing in the text that suggests that the character Michal sees David as needing her protection and guidance; she does indeed offer David her protection when she lets him down through the window to escape Saul (19.12-17), but there is no hint that she has such activities in mind when she begins to love him. The problem with this comment is, then, not that it is 'psychological'—since all the comments made on this text are bound to be psychological in one way or another, nor that the text is not explicit on the subject—since there are many things that can be reasonably and safely inferred from texts that are not explicit,

---

1.   Samuel, 'Three Wives', pp. 270-71 [192].

but rather that there is nothing in the text that could support or deny the comment. The unfalsifiable is not interpretative.

3. Does David love Michal?

The text never says that David 'loves' Michal. But whether he does or not is not a question that arises for the casual reader. The most natural implication is that husbands love their wives, especially newly married wives, and readers generally take it for granted if the text does not alert us to the contrary. We should of course pay due heed to the cultural context of the narrative, in which marriages are usually arranged and are not love matches. Nevertheless, most readers still assume, in reading biblical narratives, that they may rely on husbands loving wives, even if the text does not say so explicitly. Even when we read that David is excited by the thought of marrying into the royal family ('It pleased David well to be the king's son-in-law', 18.26), readers may still not suppose that this means that he does *not* love Michal; it would be a natural instinct to believe that her status as the king's daughter simply makes Michal all the more attractive to him.

In this case there is more to it than a general assumption. For in this narrative we learn that David has been set a task by Saul which he needs to accomplish if he is to marry Michal. He is to pay Saul as a bride-price a hundred Philistine foreskins, presumably to be acquired by killing their owners first. When David fulfils this requirement twice over, it is reasonable to suppose that we are seeing a sign of his enthusiasm for the marriage. As the writers in the *Temple Dictionary of the Bible* put it:

> She loved David,. . . a love reciprocated, if we may judge from the liberal fashion in which the strange dowry was provided (vv. 25ff.).[1]

Such a conclusion is no doubt natural enough, but we nevertheless must ask whether the text encourages us to draw it. Is David's love for Michal a mere narrative gap which we should unhesitatingly fill? Or is the absence of explicit reference, especially when Michal's love for him has become explicit, itself an hint that the love is *not* 'reciprocated'? Alter remarks:

> [W]e were told twice that she loved him while all that could be safely in

---

1. Ewing and Thomson, 'Michal', p. 175 [463].

ferred from his attitude toward her was that the marriage was politically useful.[1]

David's excessive dowry could be a sign of his enthusiasm for the *marriage*, as a marriage into the royal family, rather than as a sign of his enthusiasm for Michal herself. But we cannot tell. Alter has pointed to several such places in the David narrative where we readers are left in the dark, tantalized into speculating and ultimately compelled into forming opinions of David's character without due evidence—or else leaving more in abeyance than we find comfortable to do. Writing more generally of the character David, Alter asks:

> What does David feel, what is he really thinking, when he responds to Saul or Saul's spokesmen? Does he genuinely feel humble as a poor Ephraimite farm boy suddenly taken up by the court? Is he merely following the expected effusive formulas of court language in these gestures of self-effacement before the king? Or. . .is he through his protestations of unworthiness being careful not to appear too eager to marry into the royal family because of what such a desire might suggest about his political ambitions? The narrator leaves these various 'readings' of David hovering. . .[P]recisely by not specifying, the narrator allows each its claim.[2]

Perhaps this question of David's love for Michal is one of those cases where 'by not specifying, the narrator allows each [reading] its claim'. The effect on readers will be that their image of David will retain a certain fluidity; either David's love for Michal or his absence of love for Michal could become a resource for understanding future developments in the story. Each view is an interpretation of the text, for each has some anchor in the text; neither is a speculation. But which view is better it is hard, or even impossible, to tell.

4. *How should we judge Michal's lie to her father?*

Having let David down from the window in order to escape Saul, Michal tells Saul's messengers who come for him that he is sick in bed (19.14). When they return with Saul's order that David be brought to him in the bed, they find that Michal has put a dummy in the bed to deceive the messengers into thinking that David is still in it (19.16). When Saul learns of the deception, Michal justifies her action in letting David escape by saying that he threatened her life if she did not

---

1. Alter, 'Characterization and the Art of Reticence', p. 69 [120].
2. Alter, 'Characterization and the Art of Reticence', p. 119 [of the original publication, not reprinted in this volume].

help him escape (19.17).

We know that Michal's answer to the messengers, 'He is sick' (19.14), is a lie, because we have just learned from the narrator that David is not in bed but out the window. We *assume* that Michal's answer to Saul, 'He said to me, "Let me go; why should I kill you?"' (19.17), is also a lie; but we do not *know* that; for there has been no report of David's speech against which we could check it. Perhaps she is lying to protect herself; or perhaps David had said such words. If he did, perhaps he was serious, perhaps he was giving her a line she could use.

The question before us here is how we are to evaluate this action of Michal's. It is possible, of course, to give an account of the narrative without making any judgments about the characters' behaviour; but readers generally find themselves taking sides with or against characters, and even professedly neutral interpreters, like the authors of encyclopaedia articles, not infrequently tip their hand. When we read, for example, of Michal's 'clever ruse',[1] or that '[t]his lie sharply contrasts Michal with her brother Jonathan, who defended David against Saul even at the risk of his own life',[2] we are encountering *evaluation.*

One way writers convey their evaluation is by headlining the story, that is to say, offering a brief overview of the narrative. One may begin thus:

[W]e come to that episode when Michal risked her own life to save the husband she loved.[3]

[W]hen Saul sent messengers to kill David, Michal contrived his escape.[4]

In the first of these headlines, the writer ensures that we will read the story as *an example of Michal's love for David*; by calling him not 'David' but 'the husband she loved' he casts the story in that light, even though in this episode the text says nothing above love. We ourselves might feel that this headline is quite in keeping with the movement of the Michal story as a whole, that this reading is implicit in the text, but we should be aware that such an opinion is our own interpretative and evaluative judgment.

What of the headline that 'Michal risked her own life to save'

1. White, 'Michal', p. 285 [363].
2. G.P. Hugenberger, 'Michal', p. 205 [348].
3. Lockyer, 'Michal', p. 227 [225].
4. D. Harvey, 'Michal', p. 204 [373].

David? We know that Saul is unpredictable and given to wild frenzies;
we know that he has several times 'tried' to kill David, and we can
guess that Michal will make him furious. But is it equally possible to
substantiate from the text that Michal's own life is at risk? That seems
harder to sustain.

In the second of these headlines, the episode is evaluated as 'Michal
contriv[ing] his escape'. This evaluation compels us to consider the
text more closely, for if we were casual readers we might have found
ourselves referring to this episode as the story of 'David's escape'
rather than of 'Michal's contrivance'. Where does the emphasis lie, we
ask ourselves, having read Harvey's sentence, and is it correct to see
Michal as the principal character? When we read the text again, we
notice that Michal is indeed very active: she warns David to 'save your
life tonight', lets him down through the window, takes the teraphim,
lays them on the bed, covers them with clothes, speaks to Saul's messengers, is addressed by Saul, and replies to Saul. With Michal's
words to Saul the episode concludes.

Of David, on the other hand, nothing is said except that he 'went off
and fled away and escaped'—which is not very strongly participating
in the action.[1] Elsewhere throughout the episode he is not acting, but
acted upon.[2] Messengers are sent by Saul to his house, Saul intends to
kill him in the morning, he is warned by Michal, he is let down from
the window by Michal, messengers are again sent by Saul to take him,
he is spoken of by Michal, messengers are for a third time sent to see
him, Saul questions Michal about his escape, and Michal replies quoting him (or, putting words into his mouth). The headline devised by
Harvey is therefore in this instance amply supported by the text; it becomes an interpretative and evaluative tool for the episode as a whole.

We turn now to the primary evaluative question in this episode,
namely, the question of Michal's lie. The issue is how we are to respond to this event. For readers mostly have an underlying baseline of
morality, which they believe they share with the narrator, in which
husbands love wives and murder and lying are wrong—unless there is

---

1. 'These three verbs for the one in Michal's breathless instructions underline
David's singleminded attention to the crucial business of saving himself', says Alter,
'Characterization and the Art of Reticence' (p. 68 [120]).

2. 'At a critical moment he obeyed her implicitly; there is no other record of his
putting himself into human hands, a passive taker of orders' (Lofts, 'Michal', p. 239
[113]).

something said to the contrary. For most writers, Michal's lie is easily justified; but we need to stress that, because they operate on an unspoken moral baseline, they feel the need to justify it

Michal is usually seen as being faced by a simple choice: she is caught in a conflict of loyalties between her father and her husband, and there is little doubt in most writers' minds that loyalty to the husband must come first. It helps that, in the eyes of these writers, the father Saul is bad, a madman, and rejected by God, and that the husband David is virtuous, brave, and pious. Here are some samples of interpretations based on this set of disjunctions:

[A]s a truehearted wife, she tricked her father and his emissaries.[1]

[F]or love of David, she. . . flung aside conventionalities and braved her father's fury.[2]

[S]he was even prepared to betray her father for David's sake, as when she tricked Saul. . .[3]

This is Michal's hour, and here she is established. Here her romanticism fuses with realism. She was not alone in defying her father's madness against David. . .[4]

[T]he moment had come when she must face reality and choose between her father and her husband. And as she betrayed Saul. . .[5]

Clever woman that Michal was, she evaded her father's question . . . When Michal dared to defy a madman king like her father in order to save her husband, she must have possessed real courage.[6]

Hardly a writer can be found who does not approve of Michal's decision. The most negative note is struck in the following remark:

When Michal is angrily reproached by her father for letting [David] escape, she parries the blow by a falsehood. . . On this somewhat mean conduct of hers a light is incidentally shed by the mention of the image. . .[7]

This author will go on to make unfavourable remarks about Michal on

1. Lockyer, 'The Woman who Tricked her Father', p. 230 [109].
2. White, 'Michal', p. 286 [363].
3. Steinsaltz, 'The Princess and the Shepherd', p. 282 [148].
4. Samuel, 'Three Wives', p. 275 [199].
5. Lofts, 'Michal', p. 239 [114].
6. Deen, 'King Saul's Daughter—David's First Wife', p. 142 [98].
7. W.G. Blaikie, 'Michal in the Books of Samuel', p. 94 [307-308].

the grounds of the presence of the teraphim in her house; for him, Michal can do nothing right since she is a heathen idol-worshipper and plainly 'not one in religion with David'.

At the other extreme, the most positive appreciation of Michal's lie comes from a writer who fastens on the fact that once Michal has spoken it the episode comes to an end, with the implication that Saul is satisfied to accept it:

> She kept her head. David had gone, it was essential for her own well-being to remain on good terms with her father. So she said that David had threatened to kill her unless she aided his escape. And Saul believed her. Anything pointing to David's villainy would be credible to him; besides, he trusted Michal. It is a tribute to this woman's skill in the gentle art of sail-trimming that both David. . .and Saul. . .should equally have had faith in her partisanship.[1]

For this writer Michal emerges, remarkably enough, as creditable both from David's point of view and Saul's. But even when, as with other writers, she is seen as Saul's betrayer, there is rarely a whiff of criticism for her behaviour.

Why is there such unanimity among writers on this issue? We might have expected it to be a point of dissension, since it is a question whether or not to approve of telling lies. No commentator seems even to feel a need to excuse Michal's lie; even if it is a 'betrayal' of Saul, there is no doubt that it is the right thing to do because the only alternative has been cast as a 'betrayal' of David. No one seems to think that Michal's decision to side with her husband against her father is difficult for her. If she needs courage (Deen), it is courage to defy a madman, not courage to be disloyal to her father. And if she flings aside conventionalities (White), like loyalty and obedience to her father, we are to understand, these are mere stale conventionalities that should not put any constraint on a woman of her type.

It remains interesting to consider whether any re-evaluation of the characters of Saul and David could make the present episode more problematic. Suppose that we regard Saul as more a victim of fate than of flaw, and suppose that his rejection by Yahweh seems to be grounded upon a mere technicality over how many days he should have waited for Samuel to arrive for the sacrifice—will we view Michal's action in the same light as if we have determined that Saul is

---

1. Lofts, 'Michal', p. 240 [115].

a thoroughly bad man who no longer deserves anything from anyone? And suppose that we regard David as a selfish prig rather than as a man after God's own heart—will we feel quite so certain that Michal does right not to hesitate to side with David against Saul? Or suppose even that we conclude that David's sole motivation throughout the story so far has been to accomplish the demise of Saul's house—for which purpose, we might suppose, he entered the palace and charmed both Jonathan and Michal (not to mention Saul himself)—might we not be tempted to decide that, in enabling David to escape from Saul, Michal makes the biggest mistake of her life?

5. *Has the presence of the image (teraphim) any significance for the characterization of Michal?*
The reference to the image that Michal puts under the bedclothes in order to deceive Saul's messengers into thinking that David himself is still in the bed has attracted the attention of many writers. Commonly, they find here evidence that Michal, unlike David, is a worshipper of non-Israelite gods. For example,

> We have no record that Michal had David's faith in God's protecting power. She no doubt believed in idols. . . [S]he was not a believer in David's God.[1]

> She kept teraphim in her room—idols; she had neither David's devotion to God, nor the tact to conceal her lack of it.[2]

> As a Jewess, she had, perhaps, prayed to the Covenant God. But we know that she persevered in idolatrous practices.[3]

Others stress that the possession of teraphim does not necessarily imply the worship of foreign gods, but they judge it to be evidence of second-rate religious behaviour. Thus:

> '[T]eraphim'—images which were kept and used by persons who in the main worshipped the one true God. . . The use of them was not a breach of the first commandment, but it was a breach of the second. . . The use of the images implied an unspiritual or superstitious state of mind; or at least a mind more disposed to follow its own fancies as to the way of worshipping God than to have a severe and strict regard to the rule of

---

1. Deen, 'King Saul's Daughter—David's First Wife', p. 142 [98].
2. Samuel, 'Three Wives', p. 275 [199-200].
3. Kuyper, 'Michal', p. 225 [110-11].

God. . . When we read of these images we are not surprised at the defects
of character which we see in Michal.[1]

Whether the keeping of teraphim was idolatrous in the strict sense
or not is really rather a secondary matter, however. The important
question is rather whether it can have anything whatever to do with an
evaluation of the character of the Michal of the biblical story. We
cannot of course complain against such readings that there is nothing
in the text explicitly suggesting that Michal's possession of teraphim is
a bad sign; for reading between the lines and bringing into the fore-
ground cultural conventions assumed by the narrator are everyday
legitimate means of interpretation, as we have already seen. But there
is one facet of the story which almost every writer who comments on
the teraphim in connection with Michal leaves out of account: it is the
fact that the teraphim are to be found in *David's* house! If their presence in the bedroom casts any aspersions on Michal and her character, it must cast exactly the same aspersions on David.

One author at least appears at first to recognize this implication as a
possibility, but hastens to dismiss it as unthinkable:

> It is impossible to suppose that David could have either used, or counte-
> nanced the use of these images. God was too much a spiritual reality to
> him to allow such material media of worship to be even thought of.[2]

This is pure assertion, of course, which flies in the face of the plain
evidence of the text. Given the presence of teraphim as household
objects in the stories of Israel's ancestors (Gen. 31.19-37), it is hard to
believe that any criticism attaches to Michal here—or at least no more
criticism than would attach to David also.

*6. Has David's escape any significance for the Michal story as a
whole?*

Most writers see no symbolic significance in the episode of David's
escape; they are carried along by the narrative thrust. The narrative
itself does not signal how crucial this event is for the relationship of
Michal and David. The first-time reader will naturally think this a
temporary separation between the couple, and will no doubt be surprised as the story unfolds to discover that David never returns to
Michal or for Michal. David and Michal will in fact never meet again

1. Blaikie, 'Michal in the Books of Samuel', pp. 94-95 [308].
2. Blaikie, 'Michal in the Books of Samuel', p. 95 [308].

until after she has been married to another man, and, much later, has been taken from him by David after he has become king in Jerusalem. At the very least, the seven years that David will rule in Hebron (1 Kgs 2.11) will have elapsed. A second-time reader might not unnaturally therefore be looking again at the narrative of David's escape for any signs presaging what is to come.

More than one writer faces the issue of David leaving Michal behind when he finds himself in danger. Samuel writes:

> I do not like that picture of David escaping into the night and leaving Michal to face the music. He must have been convinced that the situation was desperate; and he was at last beginning to find the king's explosions intolerable—two reasons why he should have hesitated to leave Michal behind, and two grim reflections of his failure to send for her at the first opportunity.[1]

In those sentences the writer expresses a negative judgment on David's commitment to Michal. A more neutral account, in which the episode is considered and told very much from the point of view of Michal is this:

> She could not flee with him, for she must stay behind to gain time; and there would be no place for her in the life which he must hitherto [*sic*; read 'henceforth'] lead as a hunted outlaw in the hills and the caves and the waste places.[2]

And here is an even more objective account:

> For a long time after this David remained an outlaw in exile from his wife's father. It would be almost impossible for a marriage to survive under such conditions.[3]

What these remarks have in common is a desire to explain what the text itself does not comment on, namely the significance of the single event for the narrative as a whole. They each evince a certain lack of ease with the narrative's silence; how can the narrator pass over an event of such moment without saying a word? The episode demands (does it not?) to be put into a wider context.

One attempt to find significance in the episode for the developing plot of the David story is the following:

---

1. Samuel, 'Three Wives', p. 275 [199].
2. Lofts, 'Michal', p. 240 [114].
3. Deen, 'King Saul's Daughter—David's First Wife', p. 142 [98].

Apparently Michal's false testimony implied David's repudiation of the marriage, and so Saul gave her to Palti(el).[1]

It is true that the next we will hear of Michal is, some six chapters later, that Saul had given Michal to Palti son of Laish (25.44); and to seek some connecting link between the two events is reasonable. What is hard to accept about this particular explanation is, first, that David's threat of violence against her can be understood by Saul as having this precise significance, and second, that it is that supposed threat rather than David's absence that brings the marriage to an end.

Is there anything else then in the narrative of the episode that could be thought to signal this wider concern? Consider the following:

In her reply to Saul's petulant question why she has helped David slip through his fingers, Michal says, 'He said to me, "Let me go; why should I kill you?"' It is not too surprising that in inventing words for the soldierly David she should have him threatening her with violence; this is a woman trying to talk gruffly and swagger like her man. But why should she say, 'He said, "Let me go"'? How could David have needed her to *let* him go? How could she have *prevented* him? She would not have been putting the words into David's mouth, I think, if she did not somehow realize that what is happening is not that she is saving David's life but that she is in fact, quite precisely, *letting him go*. She loves him, but he does not love her—not enough for it to be mentioned, at any rate; in escaping from Saul he escapes from his marriage. We know that, from the subsequent course of the narrative, for he never returns to Michal; Michal's words know that too, even if Michal herself does not yet quite know it.[2]

No one could be expected to pick up such a significance, if indeed the words can carry them, on the first reading; but in asking after the meaning of the episode as a whole we are programmatically probing beneath the surface of the text. What makes a comment interpretative is not whether the text explicitly supports it but whether it has some kind of anchor in the text. Whether the interpretative comment is right, or sound, is of course another matter, which is debatable.

1. Hugenberger, 'Michal', p. 205 [348].
2. D.J.A. Clines, 'The Story of Michal, Wife of David, in its Sequential Unfolding', pp. 131-32 below. The reader is invited to consider whether the fifth line of this quotation enshrines a male point of view, and, if so, whether the interpreter has managed to convey it as the narrator's point of view rather than his own.

7. What does Michal feel about her husband Paltiel?

We had better be clear at the outset that the biblical text is wholly reticent on the subject of Michal's feelings about her second marriage, to Paltiel (the short form of the name, Palti, is used in 1 Sam. 25.44; the long form appears in 2 Sam. 3.15). In 1 Sam. 25.43-44 we are told, after a long story about Abigail, who becomes David's wife, that David 'also took Ahinoam of Jezreel' as a wife; and the note is added that 'Saul had given Michal his daughter, David's wife, to Palti the son of Laish, who was of Gallim'. And in 2 Sam. 3.12-16 there is a narrative of how David reclaimed Michal, as part of a deal with Abner, Saul's general. Here we read that Ishbosheth, Saul's son and successor, 'sent and took her from her husband Paltiel the son of Laish' (3.15). In neither passage does Michal speak, and nothing is said by the narrator of her reaction to either event.

We readers, however, are intrigued by these episodes. We feel we are owed some explanation by the text; there are too many loose threads left hanging. First, we know that Michal loved David (18.20), so we want to know what she feels about Paltiel. Has she stopped loving David? Secondly, we know, as second-time readers, that the next time Michal's feelings for David are expressed it will be said that she 'despised' him (2 Sam. 6.16). Does this mean that she no longer loves him? And if so, when has this happened? Has it anything to do with Paltiel? The existence of two (apparently) contradictory statements about Michal's attitude to David, 'she loved him' and 'she despised him', requires us as interpreters to do some bridge work between the two. Thirdly, when Michal is taken from Paltiel, although not a word is said about her feelings, Paltiel's feelings are very vividly depicted: 'But her husband went with her, weeping after her all the way to Bahurim. Then Abner said to him, "Go, return"; and he returned' (3.16). This depiction makes us even more curious about Michal's feelings. Does the absence of comment on them mean that she has none, or none comparable to Paltiel's? Does she welcome the return to David?

This is certainly one of those

> key determinations concerning the characters about which the text leads us
> to speculate without providing sufficient information to draw any certain
> conclusions,

as Alter puts it.[1] I shall be concluding that we cannot know what Michal's feelings are about Paltiel, or how and when her feelings for David change. But I will insist that the text requires us to wonder— Alter says 'speculate'—about answers to these questions, and to stake out the ground around the interpretational possibilities. Our inability to arrive at a definitive conclusion demands, not that we abandon the question, calling all the suggested solutions equally 'speculations' and so without interpretational worth, but that we hold open all the possibilities for its solution. Such inbuilt indeterminacy at this crucial juncture will, if we recognize it, stealthily undermine our firmer conclusions elsewhere, and make everything more provisional than we might have hoped.

What possibilities of answers exist? Here is a case where being in the company of a plurality of interpreters is almost indispensable. For no matter how ingenious a commentator is, any individual commentator is likely to move toward some preferred reading of the story and to privilege one piece of information in the narrative over another. If we are interested in exploring the depth of the indeterminacy, we need to consider what answers a wide range of readers have put forward. Here are eight comments made by readers who appear in the present anthology; I append to each questions that might arise in the mind of a reader of these readers:

> (1) Palti. . . the weird little man for whom I have such an aversion—Palti the weeper. . . From what we have seen of Michal, and from what we shall yet see, we know that she was not forced into the marriage. She entered into it contemptuously, and if a sword lay between husband and wife in the night, it was she who put it there.[2]

Questions: Was she not forced into the marriage? What else is the significance of 'Saul had given Michal to Palti'? How much choice of a husband could a woman in this cultural setting have? And is there any sign of 'contempt' for Palti? Is this an implication from the fact that she does not weep when she is taken from him? If so, is it a fair inference?

1.   Alter, 'Characterization and the Art of Reticence', p. 118 [of the original publication, not reprinted in this volume].

2.   Samuel, 'Three Wives', p. 277 [202]. There is an implicit reference here to the Targum on Ruth 3.8, which speaks of 'the pious Paltiel, who placed a sword between himself and Michal. . . because he had refused to go in unto her' (see T.C. Eskenazi, pp. 158-59 below, and L. Ginzberg, p. 202 n. 1 [186 n.3]).

(2) Soon after that incident [David's escape], however, her ardor for David waned. Phalti, she thought, was making a better bid for royalty than he, and she would do anything to secure and hold the glamor of royalty. She knew how to charm men. She succeeded so well in Phalti's case that when she later left him in favor of greater glamor, he followed on behind, weeping all the way. But Michal did not weep. Personal pride and the love of prestige leaves no room for these emotions. David had in the meantime been crowned a king and had expressed a willingness to have her again as his wife. Why should not such a woman as Michal was, leave Phalti in the lurch, then, and go to reign as a queen in Hebron?[1]

Questions: Is there any hint that Palti has any designs on kingship? How do we know that her ardour for David has waned? How do we know that she charmed men? What is the evidence for 'love of prestige'?

(3) Michal's love for David waned. Where was the pleasure in being the wife of a man forced to spend his days a fugitive, hunted like a wild animal in the wilderness? Phalti of Gallem was a better catch, she thought, seeing he was on his way to royalty which she was eager to secure and hold. So Michal became the wife of Phalti. This was an illegitimate union seeing David was alive and was in no way lawfully separated from Michal.[2]

Question: In what sense could the marriage be illegitimate if the king had sanctioned it?

(4) Michal, last observed as a forceful initiator of action, now [in 1 Sam. 25.44] stands in contrast to the energetically active Abigail as an object acted upon, passed by her father from one man to another. The dubious legality of Saul's action is perhaps intimated by the use of the epithet 'wife of David'. . . What Michal feels about this transaction, or about the absent David and his new wives of whom she may have heard, we are not told. . .

As for Michal [in 2 Sam. 3], who has been living for years as Palti's wife, we have no way of knowing whether she feels gratitude, love, pity, or contempt for her powerless second husband.[3]

Question: Is it 'dubious *legality*' that the phrase 'wife of David' suggests, or is the narrator underlining the tragedy of her fate, and contrasting her with the two wives of David who have just now entered the picture?

1. Kuyper, 'Michal', p. 224 [110].
2. Lockyer, 'The Woman who Tricked her Father', p. 230 [109-10].
3. Alter, 'Characterization and the Art of Reticence', pp. 69-70 [121-22].

(5) Other stories came in too, less shocking to the general public in that age of polygamy, but no more welcome to Michal's ear. David had married again. . . It seemed that David had renounced his nationality and his wife and that Michal would be left to live out her days, years and years of days, as a lonely woman who was neither maid, wife, nor widow.

From such a fate her realistic, mundane, ordinary human nature saved her. . . She neither pined away from sorrow nor remained steadfastly faithful to her lost love, defying her father when he attempted to make a second marriage for her. Instead she married Phalti; and if she retained any mournful memories, any yearnings for her vanished young harpist, young hero, young husband, she hid them well, for Phalti was very happy with her, as indeed almost any man might have been. For although Michal was ordinary enough, she was intelligent and pliable of mind, a worldly creature at home in the world and happy in it, capable of setting her sail according to the prevailing wind. Such women are responsible for much of the happiness in the life of men.[1]

(6) It is probable that Michal had been happy with Palti. . . [2]

Questions: Where is the textual evidence for this 'realistic, mundane' nature of hers? Why should we agree that she was 'capable of setting her sail according to the prevailing wind'? Is there anything to the contrary in the whole Michal narrative? Is it reasonable to say that Palti was 'very happy with her'; is this a fair implication from his weeping as he follows her? Is it reasonable to say that Michal was 'happy with Palti'; from what would that be a fair implication?

(7) When I was first brought to his house, he touched his forehead to the floor and gasped out a whisper: 'My Lady'. He never stopped calling me that as long as we lived together. . . He wasn't told I'd been taken from David, and I never talked to him. He was simple, but I think he knew there were politics involved. . . I wouldn't let him touch me. I slept at his feet, but he never once tried to come to me.[3]

Questions: Is there any evidence that Palti would regard Michal as his social superior? Is it reasonable to infer that Palti is 'simple' from his following her weeping when she is taken from him by force?

(8) But Michal did not cry. In a way, it seems as if she had lost her active personality in this great crisis, acting no longer as a human being but an object, a chattel. . . . The parting from him [David]. . . and her being handed over to Palti ben Laish broke her spirit until she reached a point of

1.   Lofts, 'Michal', p. 241 [116].
2.   White, 'Michal', p. 286 [363].
3.   R.C. Ehle, 'The Grace of God', pp. 48-49 [57].

total detachment. This emotional detachment was partly an expression of her aristocratic nature. The nobility was superior; they did not make scenes or have stormy fights, nor did they destroy social structures. Michal did not rebel; she did not try to escape from the entanglement by some extreme means, such as suicide, as did her father. . . [I]nstead she broke, and what remained was the outer shell of a personality from which the heart was missing. From this point onward, Michal responded to everything that happened with total passivity, the passivity of one who is past caring.[1]

Questions: Is the assumption of 'emotional detachment' based solely on her not weeping when Palti does? Is this the only way this sentence can be read? Can the analysis of Michal's responding to everything with 'total passivity' be reconciled with her later behaviour toward David when he dances before the ark?

I notice that at this point, where the text is at its most reticent and tantalizing, many authors are at their most expansive, imaginative and speculative.[2] If these are faults, it is the narrative itself that is to be blamed, for being so very unforthcoming about 'key determinations' (Alter). But they need not be thought of as 'faults'. If the narrative itself is not determinate but gives rise to a host of possible readings, that is the kind of narrative it is, and the best reader is the one who is open to as many possibilities as the text will allow.

Let us review the possibilities summarily. Palti may be despicable because he weakly allows his wife to be taken from him, and makes no protest except to weep. Or he may be decent but 'simple', non-plussed by Abner's theft of his wife, but lacking any resources to resist. Michal may be delighted to be reunited with David, or she may be speechless with horror at the prospect. She may have retreated into passivity, and allowed herself to be treated as a pawn in men's political games. She may have forgotten her former love for David, or, if she remembered it, hid the memory from Palti. Or she may have lived in hope of a restoration of their marriage. These are all, in my view, interpretational possibilities. They cannot all be right, and I suspect that we cannot know with any kind of certainty which of them are right. On this key issue, then, the programme of comparative

1. Steinsaltz, 'The Princess and the Shepherd', pp. 282-83 [149].
2. See, for example, the treatment of this episode in the work of the modern authors—novelists and dramatists—dealt with in the articles by T.C. Eskenazi and A.P. Kapelovitz in the present volume.

interpretation leaves us with more uncertainty than we would have imagined necessary or possible; and the character of Michal becomes more than ever enigmatic.

Are there, finally, any readings that cannot be called interpretational possibilities? Yes. All the foregoing have some anchor in the text, but there are others that do not. There is no anchor for the idea that Palti had ambitions for kingship; there is nothing in his ancestry, his alliances, his behaviour or his personality to suggest it. It follows that we may not say, as interpreters of the text, that Michal married him in hope of regaining her queenly status. Nor is there any anchor for the idea that Michal was contemptuous of him. These ideas are possible *speculations*, as are the speculations that Palti had white hair or only one leg, but they hold no interpretational value.

8. Why does Michal reproach David when he dances before the ark?

Even though it may be incorrect to speak of a 'Michal story' since the story is no more than a string of somewhat disjointed episodes scattered through the David story, the final scene in which Michal appears functions very successfully as a climax to her story. For in it we witness the first encounter we have seen between David and Michal since their marriage has been resumed, and we are eager to know what passes between them. In it we also find a sentence that reads as a quite formal conclusion to the Michal story ('And Michal the daughter of Saul had no child to the day of her death'), a sentence that persuades us that we have learned all we are ever going to know about this woman, and therewith invites us to the task of reprocessing all we have learned so far in an effort to make sense of her enigmatic character.

Why does Michal reproach David? Here we are not short of textual evidence. There is the report of the narrator (6.16), Michal's own words to David (6.20), and David's reply (6.21-22)—the combination of which provides us with a stereoscopic view of the event. There is almost too much evidence of what passes between them, and yet we still feel that the text has not told us the whole truth, that we are meant to infer some deeper cause, some underlying agenda that Michal and David are addressing.

Let us sample some interpretations. To begin with:

> [I]t was not merely her woman's impatience of the absurd that made her 'despise him in her heart'. . . To appreciate her daring mockery, and the

cold anger of David's rejoinder, we must read them in the light of the
years that had passed. . . What wonder if the bitter reflexion that she had
indirectly facilitated the humiliation of her own family was coupled with a
suspicion that David had from the first regarded her merely as a means of
self-aggrandisement?[1]

This author passes over entirely the ostensible reason for Michal's despising David. According to the narrator, it is when David is 'leaping
and dancing before the LORD' that Michal despises him, and her sarcastic words tell us specifically what it is about his leaping and dancing
that she finds despicable: he has been 'uncovering himself today before
the eyes of his servants' maids'. David himself seems to have no doubt
about what she is referring to, for he retorts that he intends to go on
making himself 'yet more contemptible than this', however much his
behaviour is bound to make him 'abased in your eyes'. Nevertheless,
this author whom I have quoted, in common with almost all commentators, has his heart set upon finding some further unspoken reason.

Here is another such remark. This writer also so mistrusts the text
to be telling us the real story that he finds space in a brief encyclopaedia article of four paragraphs for the comment that

David detected in Michal's rebuke an underlying bitterness that God had
so established a dynasty for David rather than her father (v. 21).[2]

The writer's motivation may be sound, but the comment will hardly
stand. For it is hard to believe in this supposed bitterness of Michal's
that David is king. Had not the Michal of 1 Samuel 19 a shrewd idea
from the very beginning that her popular warrior hero of a husband
was destined for higher things? Had he never told her, on some
breathless evening when he was not off slaughtering Philistines, that
he had been anointed as Saul's successor by the prophet? Whence
comes this sudden bitterness? And in any case, now that both Saul and
Jonathan are dead, what future could there be in a Saulide dynasty?
And as for herself, is she any worse off being a wife of the king
David than being the daughter of the king Saul? The text may not be
telling us the whole truth, but underlying dynastic bitterness is not the
key.

Here is another attempt to bypass the text:

1. White, 'Michal', p. 286 [363].
2. Hugenberger, 'Michal', pp. 205-206 [348].

> When David brought the ark to Jerusalem, and performed the wild danc-
> ing associated with the Canaanite cult as part of the ceremony, Michal
> rebuked him.[1]

That is the entire remark of this writer on the subject. She is obviously so unhappy with the surface of the text that she must speculate—
there is no other word for it—that Michal's opposition is to the pagan
overtones of David's dancing. Not a hint from the narrator, though,
that there is anything remotely Canaanite about David's dance. David,
for his part, thinks he is dancing before Yahweh, and so does the narrator. Michal and David both agree that David is exposing himself,
though they disagree over whether that is disgraceful or not, or
rather, whether being disgraceful matters. But our commentator
knows better: Michal is speaking in code. She is not really against
David's lascivious dance in the eyes of his servants' maids; she is just a
stringent Yahwist who cannot abide Canaanite practices.

  More commonly, however, interpreters stand this explanation on its
head, and see in Michal's reproach a sure sign that her religious sensi-
bilities are the inferior of David's. David is quintessentially the pious
man, and if she reproaches David in the expression of his religion, it
is she who is at fault. Consider the following:

> For her there were no pious and affectionate feelings at the return of the
> Ark to Zion. Like her father, Saul, she had no regard for the Ark of God
> (1 Chron. 13.3).[2]

> As a Jewess, she had, perhaps, prayed to the Covenant God. But we
> know that she persevered in idolatrous practices from the fact that she kept
> an image in her house. Hence she was not in the least affected by the fact
> that the ark of God was returning to Moriah.[3]

> [A] woman of Michal's character could not but act like an icicle on the
> spiritual life of the household. She belonged to a class that cannot tolerate
> enthusiasm in religion.[4]

Everything about David's behaviour is magnificent; his religious
ecstasy is hugely attractive, if you have the taste for it; and if, like
Michal, you don't, what a poor, dispassionate, earth-bound person you
are:

1. Harvey, 'Michal', p. 204 [373].
2. Lockyer, 'The Woman who Tricked her Father', p. 232 [110].
3. Kuyper, 'Michal', p. 225 [110-11].
4. Blaikie, 'Michal in the Books of Samuel', p. 96 [96].

Michal, from her privileged place along the line of procession, looked down and saw the man she had loved, the king of Israel, behaving like a drunken man, his clothing disarrayed, his face distorted, dancing and shouting, oblivious to everything in the world save that the Ark, the only earthly manifestation of Israel's God, was coming in triumph into the city which God had given His people. Subject to no such spiritual afflatus herself, she looked at him dispassionately and thought that he looked like a drunken clown. Any observer of another person's complete abandon feels the same, especially if the abandon arises from an intoxication which the observer has never known. And Michal had never been religiously drunk. To her earth-bound eyes the Ark was just a little wooden structure being borne on two poles; and David's transport of emotion an hysterical, shocking lapse from dignity.[1]

Or, to put it another way:

David is utterly Yahweh's man, a fact Michal either cannot understand or refuses to acknowledge. . . David is established by this confident rhetoric which refutes Michal . . . In David's utter abandonment to dance and in his liturgic, social, royal extravagance, a new order is authorized, wrought out of unrestrained yielding and worship . . . Michal, who thinks she is in a position of strength, is dismissed by the narrative as barren and hopeless . . . David is indeed the one who humbles himself and who, by the power of God, is exalted.[2]

How could Michal have failed to see all this? How could she have allowed little things like royal dignity and sexual modesty to obscure the vision of humble, but royal, extravagance and the authorization of a new order, sustained by confident rhetoric?

Of course, it may not be a simple matter of Michal's lack of religious sensitivity; perhaps as well, and even worse, she is not really much of a wife:

Those who are deaf always despise those who dance. The deaf do not hear the music. And, on the other hand, those who do hear the music, they cannot understand those who can sit still. David could not understand

1. Lofts, 'Michal', p. 244 [120]. Cf. also John Eadie, *A Biblical Cyclopaedia; or, Dictionary of Eastern Antiquities, Geography, Natural History, Sacred Annals and Biography, Theology, and Biblical Literature, illustrative of the Old and New Testaments* (London: Charles Griffin & Company, 18??), p. 437: 'She was evidently an unprincipled woman. . . During David's exile Michal married another man, with whom she lived nine or ten years. . . As an evidence of her impiety, we are told that she despised David when she saw the expression of his gratitude and joy at the approach of the ark of the Lord, and was evidently filled with passion and contempt.'
2. Walter Brueggemann, '2 Samuel 6', pp. 122-23 [252-53].

how Michal could sit still that day. But Michal's ear had never been opened to the music of the ark. She had not been brought up to it, and it was not her custom to go up to the house of the Lord to sing and play like David. Had Michal been married in the Lord; had Michal reverenced her husband; had she cared to please her husband; had she played on the psaltery and harp sometimes, if only for his sake—what a happy wife Michal would have been, and David, what a happy husband![1]

Not then perhaps all Michal's fault, even though somehow she manages nevertheless to come out of the affair wholly blameworthy:

Being the woman she was, and having the husband she had, Michal could not but feel both scorn and affliction that day. But, when all is said for her, and all allowance made, she should not have spoken to David as it is recorded she did speak. She could not command her proud heart when she saw David dancing, but by the time he came home she should have had her tongue tamed and under a bridle. David was, no doubt, a great provocation and a constant cross to Michal. They were never made for one another. It was impossible they could ever be happy as man and wife, short of a miracle. David was all emotion, especially in divine things; whereas Michal was as proud and cold as if she had been a daughter of Lucifer, as indeed she was.[2]

indeed!
sexism

Strange how being an ill-matched couple from the beginning leaves him in the right and her in the wrong, is it not?

romance

But before we abandon altogether the idea that there is something deficient in Michal, let us try a reading that does not fall prey to the simple sexism of Whyte, a reading that is less judgmental and more romantic. Could this perhaps be the moment when Michal realizes she has never been the right woman for David?

Breathless, God-intoxicated, oblivious of everything but the vision, he sang that day, danced and sang, ascending the hill.

And Michal? Where was she? What part had she in the rejoicing, what understanding for the supreme moment in David's life, which was henceforth divided into two parts, that which led up to this glory and that which led from it? Of her who had kept idols in her room we read: 'As the Ark of the Lord came into the city of David, Michal the daughter of Saul looked out at the window, and saw king David leaping and dancing before the Ark; and she despised him in her heart. . .'

It was not the idolatrous strain in her that was revolted. It was the dethroned romantic realizing that she had never been the savior of this man

---

1. A. Whyte, 'Michal, Saul's Daughter', p. 288 [172-73].
2. Whyte, 'Michal, Saul's Daughter', p. 291 [178].

or the source of his strength. When she saw him whirling half-naked before the ark, her possessive soul felt itself disowned. It was more than she could bear. . . [1]

This is a reading harder to resist. It does not fly in the face of the text like those that put everything to the account of her idolatry; it is more subtle and not too novelettish. It is very fetching, that line about 'her possessive soul felt itself disowned'; for there is indeed something about David's character in general that is ungraspable, inconsequential and ultimately inexplicable that makes him infuriating and intriguing at the same time. If Michal too cannot seize him, is alienated by his eccentricity, his distance, his strange mixture of coldness and enthusiasm, we can be sympathetic and begin to understand the tragedy of the episode. But, however engaging, this reading also has no anchor in the text, and we must be firm in our resistance to it, and sideline it along with the other psychological speculations.

What is it exactly that Michal objects to in David's behaviour? When we have left aside the generalities and the character assassination, the sneers about her not dancing to David's music, her earthbound eyes, her perseverance in idolatry, what exactly is it about his cavorting before the ark that arouses her anger?

Is it his loss of royal dignity? This is an explanation favoured by not a few writers:

> Although she had loved him, risked her life for his safety, she now abhors him for his loss of royal dignity. Her haughtiness was shocked by David's participation in such an excitable demonstration. [2]

> In contrast to this modesty and circumspection, so characteristic of the aristocracy and nobility everywhere, at all periods of history, we find David. David did not stop to consider how he was dancing, how he was behaving, how he appeared to others. For Michal, the fact of exposure was less important than the humiliation—as she saw it—of cheapening himself before the masses, of descending to their level. She was injured by the fact that David did not treat his throne with respect, that he had no sense of the majesty of kingship, of being divinely chosen to lead. She was the daughter of the nobility contrasted with the man she actually regarded as simple, as a boor, as one who may have taken up the reigns of government but not the grandeur of the kingship. [3]

---

1. Samuel, 'Michal', p. 278 [205].
2. Lockyer, 'The Woman who Tricked her Father', p. 231 [110].
3. Steinsaltz, 'The Princess and the Shepherd', p. 284 [150].

She felt that it would hurt her queenly dignity to mingle with the common people. When she noticed that King David participated in the ovation as hilariously as any, and that he joined the daughters of Jerusalem's rabble as they danced their glee before the ark, she felt that she had been poignantly insulted. Why, it was a flagrant breach of etiquette, and, just as it would be to any woman who had no appreciation of essential virtues, a breach of etiquette was as terrible a violation as any Michal could conceive of.[1]

So it comes to this, does it? The daughter of the man Saul, whom we first met aristocratically hunting for lost asses and whose style of table manners did not forbid the hurling of javelins at dinner guests and musicians, has now come up in the world so far that her own queenly dignity is affronted by the thought of mingling with commoners in the street and she cannot find in it her to forgive her husband a breach of courtly etiquette. And even if it is his dignity that she cares about more than hers, and it saddens her to see him lacking any sense of the majesty of kingship, it is haughtiness and noble birth that drives her to it, and she cannot get out of her mind her opinion of David as a simpleton and a boor.[2]

1.   Kuyper, 'Michal', p. 225 [111].
2.   This idea of Michal's high birth in contrast to David's humble origins has been very pervasive in the literature. See, for example, the title of the piece by A. Steinsaltz in this volume, 'The Princess and the Shepherd' (pp. 280-84 below). And cf. also the epic poem of Y.L. Gordon who depicts her as having 'risked all for the love of a mere shepherd who was socially beneath her' (Eskenazi, p. 161 below), and the novelist I.A. Malkiely's portrait of Michal as a 'gentle but self-possessed princess who befriends David when he finds himself lost and uncertain in his new position at the palace' (Eskenazi, p. 161 below). Similarly, for the novellst Y. Goren, Michal is worldly and self-serving, while David is a 'naive country boy caught up in palace intrigue' (Eskenazi, p. 170 below). Much earlier, Gregory the Great had explained everything with his curt phrase about Michal, *adhuc ex tumore regii generis insana*, 'still mad with pride at her royal descent' (*Moralia libri, sive Expositio in librum beati Iob*, 5.27.46.77; J.-P. Migne, *Patrologia latina* [Paris, 1878], LXXV, col. 443; *Morals on the Book of Job*, trans. by members of the English Church (Oxford: J.H. Parker, 1844]). For Dante also, Michal's pride is a foil to David's humility: he is *l'umile salmista*, the humble psalmist, who *e più e men che re era in quel caso*, was then both more and less than king, while Michal, *effigïata ad una vista d'un gran palazzo*, figured [in the white marble carving gazed upon by Virgil and Dante] at the window of a great palace [her father's and her own, we have the feeling], looks on *sì come donna dispettosa e trista*, like a woman vexed and scornful (*Purgatorio* 10.65-69).

The real question about this interpretation, however, is not whether we find it to our taste but whether it has any rootage in the text. The answer, whether we like it or not, is that it does. It is very telling that Michal protests about David's uncovering himself 'in the eyes of the handmaidens of his servants'. If it had been in the eyes of freeborn citizens, of the gentry, of his courtiers, or even, of his servants or of his handmaidens, we suspect that things might have been different. But the *women servants of his servants*...It is not that David has been mingling with the common people, but with the lowest of the low, socially speaking, with women who are doubly subordinated, as Exum puts it, 'by sex, to all of David's male subjects or servants, and by class, to the royal couple'.[1] And it is not that the man David has been overcome with a sudden attack of *nostalgie de la boue*, but that 'the king of Israel' has. Michal's ironic turn of phase, 'How the king of Israel honoured himself today', shows unmistakably that she has some definite views about what constitutes royal dignity and what does not. And the 'vulgar' (RSV) and 'empty' fellows whose role David has been playing are obviously low-class types also. In the end, we will be forced to wonder whether this dignity of Michal's has anything to do with her staying indoors on the day of the procession. When 'all the house of Israel' is out there with David bringing the ark up from the house of Obed-edom (v. 15), and when 'all the people, the whole multitude of Israel' have been blessed by David and given portions, we are bound to worry about why Michal has kept herself secluded and is not out there in the street and at the altar. On that point we will gain no satisfaction from the text, but on the major matter, her 'haughtiness' (shall we call it?), the text seems to leave us in no doubt. Whatever else is wrong with David's behaviour, according to Michal, he is not behaving like a king, and that is what she expects him to be.

There is more to it than that, though. The text has all the clues we need. Even more prominent in Michal's reproach than her anger at his loss of dignity is her disgust at his sexual display, 'blatant sexual vulgarity'.[2] Evidently he is semi-naked, or intermittently naked, in the course of his dancing; he has been 'uncovering himself'. Now nakedness in Israel is generally regarded as shameful, but Michal does not profess herself troubled by the fact that men and women along the

1. Exum, 'Murder They Wrote', p. 194 [61].
2. Exum, 'Murder They Wrote', p. 183 [51]. It should be observed that Exum regards the sexual theme here as essentially a displacement of the political issue.

route of the procession have seen David naked, but that women have, that low-class women have, and that David has taken no pains to prevent it. It is important for our interpretation that David takes no steps to deflect this criticism; he too has been oblivious to the male bystanders and the more modest matrons who have kept their eyes averted. His interest is in being 'honoured by the maidservants of whom you have spoken'. It is of little consequence that he no doubt deceives himself into thinking that it is his religious ecstasy that everyone thinks so highly of; what he has been advertising to the maidservants of his servants is, it appears, his shamelessness and his sexuality.

What lies behind Michal's aversion to his sexual display is harder to determine. Her whole story has been so freighted with sexuality that it comes as little surprise that this issue rises to the surface as her relationship with David comes to a bitter end. But of what frustration, jealousy, disappointment, outrage, desire her outburst is compounded we can only guess. Once again, the story of Michal demands that we tell another story, a more causally integrated story of Michal, but refuses to lend us its sanction. No one motivation can account for the course of this episode. As Robert Alter puts it, her anger is 'overdetermined', containing within it all that has never been said but more than has been hinted about the relation between her and David. Only 'multiple interpretation' can address the complexity of the tale.

> With a fine sense of the tactics of exposition, the narrator tells us exactly what Michal is feeling but not why. The hiatus in explanation, which will in part be filled by the ensuing dialogue, again opens the gates to multiple interpretation. The scorn for David welling up in Michal's heart is thus plausibly attributable in some degree to all of the following: the undignified public spectacle which David just now is making of himself; Michal's jealousy over the moment of glory David is enjoying while she sits alone, a neglected co-wife, back at the provisional palace; Michal's resentment over David's indifference to her all these years, over the other wives he has taken, over being torn away from the devoted Palti; David's dynastic ambitions—now clearly revealed in his establishing the Ark in the 'City of David'—which will irrevocably displace the house of Saul. The distance between the spouses is nicely indicated here by the epithets chosen for each: she is the 'daughter of Saul,' and she sees him as the king. Michal's subsequent words to David seize on the immediate occasion, the leaping and cavorting, as the particular reason for her anger, but the biblical writer knows as well as any psychologically minded modern that one's emotional reaction to an immediate stimulus can have a complicated prehistory;

and by suppressing any causal explanation in his initial statement of
Michal's scorn, he beautifully suggests the 'overdetermined' nature of her
contemptuous ire, how it bears the weight of everything that has not been
said but obliquely intimated about the relation between Michal and David
(Alter).[1]

The Programme of Comparative Interpretation

Some of the principles that have emerged in this study may be worth
gathering together here.

1. The text, this text at any rate, demands gap-filling by its readers.
No text can spell out all that is implicit in its story-line or in its characterization; any interpretation of the story, any telling of it that is not
a mere verbal repetition of it, is bound to fill gaps in the original.

2. It is worth distinguishing between gap-filling and speculation.
While we are gap-filling we are engaged in interpretation; when we
speculate, about events or motives, we have stopped interpreting. For
interpretation is interpretation of the given text; when we speculate,
we are speculating about the characters as people or about events the
text might allow but does not require, and we have loosened our
attachment to the text.

3. The criterion for distinguishing gap-filling from speculation is
whether there is an anchor in the text for what we want to say. There
is often room for dispute over whether the text does or does not provide an anchor or support for a particular view, but any uncertainty
about the application of the criterion does not make the criterion itself
uncertain.

4. Speculation is the necessary foundation of any imaginative retelling or re-working of a story. If the story of Michal, for example,
is to be transformed into a novel or a drama, there must be an imaginative construction of the thoughts and words of the characters that
goes far beyond the biblical text. There is nothing wrong with such
speculative and imaginative re-tellings, so long as they do not mas-
querade as interpretation; looking at the diversity and richness even of
those re-writings represented in this volume tempts us to think of the
biblical story as little more than a sketch for innumerable orchestra-
tions or realizations of the story.

5. The act of interpretation benefits from reviewing all the readings

---

1.   Alter, 'Characterization and the Art of Reticence', p. 71 [123].

of it one can find, whether they are obviously 'imaginative' or not. For even the most determinedly imaginative telling of the story takes its rise from the biblical story and responds in some way or other to what lies on the page. Whenever the dramatist or novelist has formed an individual, nuanced and developed perception of a character in the story, for instance, the interpreter of the biblical text rarely fails to find illumination of the biblical text, assessing at every point how much of that characterization is authorized by the text and how much is not.

6. The distinction between gap-filling and speculation as the criterion for what may count as 'interpretation' collapses the distinction between 'scholarly' and 'unscholarly' readings of the story. For while 'scholarly' readings tend away from speculation and 'unscholarly' toward it, it frequently happens that scholars offer as interpretations readings that can only be called speculative, while novelists and other imaginative writers do not only create speculations about the story but also not infrequently draw attention to gaps in the biblical narrative that more 'scholarly' interpreters have failed to notice, and offer valuable suggestions about how they should be filled.

7. The programme of 'comparative interpretation' recognizes that all readers of the biblical text make their own readings of it. No one reads the text 'straight' and no one takes it 'neat'. All readings are to some extent, greater or lesser, relative to the readers and their concerns. But this does not make the readings bad; for it is this relatedness that makes readings possible. In our quest for interpretation we necessarily focus upon the readings that various readers have given of the text. And we do so, not in the expectation that we shall be able, by discarding most readings that have ever been made, to move ever closer to some one objectively correct meaning, but in the hope that by exploring the variety of readings that the text has engendered we may come to see our text as richer than we ourselves might have imagined, left to our own devices. Not all readers are equally good readers, of course. Some readers, we must recognize, do the text a disservice when they ignore the text as a whole or overlook any of its parts; and others, less reprehensibly, are less interested in the *text* than in the story that comes to expression in the text and so do not set themselves up as interpreters *of the text*. But on the whole, it is a good idea for us to read our texts in the company of other readers whom we can believe to be (almost) as clever and sensitive as ourselves. If

we can do that, we are well on the way to realizing one of the goals of
a feminist literary criticism, which has so transformed our way of
looking at texts:

> To suggest that there is one proper way to read the text results in an au-
> thoritarianism characteristic of phallocentric criticism—a position that
> feminist criticism rejects in its recognition (and celebration) of contradic-
> tion and multiplicity.[1]

To some of our questions about the text, the practice of comparative
interpretation will return us multiple answers—as to the question,
Why does Michal love David? To other of our questions, our comparative study of interpretations will offer us contradictory answers
which admit of no final resolution—as to the question, What does
Michal feel about Palti? And to yet other questions, the patient review
of the contradiction and multiplicity of previous interpretations can
suggest new possibilities which we ourselves will cling to. Whatever
happens, seeing our text from other people's angle of vision will open
us to new dimensions in the text (even if at times we think that other
people need new spectacles), and at the same time encourage in us renewed appreciation of our fellow-readers.

1.   Exum, 'Murder They Wrote', p. 177 [46].

Robert Alter

CHARACTERIZATION AND THE ART OF RETICENCE
(from *The Art of Biblical Narrative*)*

[114] How does the Bible manage to evoke such a sense of depth and
complexity in its representation of character with what would seem to
be such sparse, even rudimentary means? Biblical narrative offers us,
after all, nothing in the way of minute analysis of motive or detailed
rendering of mental processes; whatever indications we may be
vouchsafed of feeling, attitude, or intention are rather minimal; and
we are given only the barest hints about the physical appearance, the
tics and gestures, the dress and implements of the characters, the
material milieu in which they enact their destinies. In short, all the
indicators of nuanced individuality to which the Western literary
tradition has accustomed us—preeminently in the novel, but ultimately
going back to the Greek epics and romances—would appear to be absent from the Bible. In what way, then, is one to explain how, from
these laconic texts, figures like Rebekah, Jacob, Joseph, Judah, Tamar,
Moses, Saul, David, and Ruth emerge, characters who, beyond any
archetypal role they may play as bearers of a divine mandate, have
been etched as indelibly vivid individuals in the imagination of a
hundred generations?...

[115] In order to see how the Bible's artful selectivity produces both
sharply defined surfaces and a sense of ambiguous depths in character,
it will suffice to follow David's unfolding relationship with his wife
Michal, which also involves his relation to Saul, to his subsequent
wives, and to his men. Michal is introduced into the narrative shortly
after David, a young man from the provincial town of Bethlehem, has
made his debut as a military hero and won the adulation of the people
(1 Samuel 18). We have just been informed, in a pointed pun, that the

* Reprinted from *The Art of Biblical Narrative* (London: George Allen & Unwin,
1981), pp. 114-25. Used by permission of Unwin Hyman Ltd.

spirit of the Lord, now with David, has 'turned away' from Saul and that the troubled king has 'turned David away' from his presence by sending him into battle as a front-line commander. What follows is worth quoting at length because, as the initial presentation of David and Michal's relationship, it offers a small spectrum of nicely differentiated means of characterization:

> 14. David succeeded in all his ways, and the Lord was with him. 15. Saul saw that he succeeded remarkably and was afraid of him. 16. [116] Saul said to David, 'Here is my oldest daughter, Merab; her shall I give you as a wife. But you must be a good warrior for me and fight the Lord's battles.' And Saul was thinking, 'Let not my hand strike him down, let it be the hand of the Philistines'. 18. David said to Saul, 'Who am I, and what is my life, my father's family in Israel, that I should become the son-in-law of the king?' 19. But at the time Merab the daughter of Saul should have been given to David, she was given as a wife to Adriel the Meholathite. 20. And Michal the daughter of Saul loved David; this was told to Saul and he was pleased. 21. And Saul thought, 'I shall give her to him and she can be a snare to him, so that the hand of the Philistines can strike him down'. And Saul said to David, '[Through the second one] you can now become my son-in-law'. 22. Saul instructed his retainers, 'Speak to David privately in these words—"The king desires you, all his subjects love you, and so now become the king's son-in-law"'. 23. Saul's retainers repeated these words to David, and David said, 'Is it a little thing in your eyes to become the king's son-in-law, and I am a pauper, a man of little consequence?' 24. Saul's retainers told him, 'These were the words David spoke'. 25. Saul said, 'This is what you should say to David—"The king desires no bride price but a hundred Philistine foreskins to take vengeance against the enemies of the king"'. And Saul intended to bring David down by the hand of the Philistines. 26. His retainers repeated these words to David, and David was pleased by the thing, to become the king's son-in-law. [Before the time had expired,] 27. David arose and went off, he and his men with him, and killed two hundred Philistines, David brought back their foreskins [and counted them out] for the king in order to become his son-in-law, and Saul gave him Michal his daughter as a wife. 28. Saul realized that the Lord was with David, while Michal the daughter of Saul loved him. 29. Saul feared David all the more, and Saul was David's constant enemy. 30. The Philistine chieftains came out to do battle, but whenever they came out, David succeeded beyond all Saul's retainers, and his name became very great.

Now, in reliable third-person narrations, such as in the Bible, there is a scale of means, in ascending order of explicitness and certainty, for conveying information about the motives, the attitudes, the moral nature of characters. Character can be revealed through the report of actions; through appearance, gestures, posture, costume; through one character's [117] inward speech, either summarized or quoted as interior monologue; or through statements by the narrator about the attitudes and intentions of the personages, which may come either as flat assertions or motivated explanations.

The lower end of this scale—character revealed through actions or appearance—leaves us substantially in the realm of inference. The middle categories, involving direct speech either by a character himself or by others about him, lead us from inference to the weighing of claims. Although a character's own statements might seem a straight-forward enough revelation of who he is and what he makes of things, in fact the biblical writers are quite as aware as any James or Proust that speech may reflect the occasion more than the speaker, may be more a drawn shutter than an open window. With the report of inward speech, we enter the realm of relative certainty about character: there is certainty, in any case, about the character's conscious intentions, though we may still feel free to question the motive behind the intention. Finally, at the top of the ascending scale, we have the reliable narrator's explicit statement of what the characters feel, intend, desire; here we are accorded certainty, though biblical narrative, as the passage before demonstrates, may choose for its own good purposes either to explain the ascription of attitude or to state it baldly and thus leave its cause as an enigma for us to ponder.

With all this in mind, if we return to our passage from 1 Samuel 18, we can readily see how the writer, far from being committed to a monolithic or 'primitive' method of characterization, shrewdly varies his means of presentation from one personage to the next. Like many biblical episodes, the passage has a formal frame: David is said to be eminently successful, which is both proof and consequence of God's being with him, and immensely popular because of his success, both at the beginning of the episode and at the end; and if, as I would assume, this passage was written later than Genesis 39, the story of Joseph, another precocious high achiever in trouble, it probably alludes to that chapter from Genesis, which is similarly framed by verses at the beginning and end that stress the hero's success, God's being with him, and his popularity. In any case, the frame-verses here tell us something about David's divine election to the newly created throne of Israel, but nothing about his moral character, and one of the most probing general perceptions of the biblical writers is that there is often a tension, sometimes perhaps even an absolute contradiction, between election and moral character. But it is important for the writer to leave this tension under a shadow of ambiguity in order [118] to suggest a complex sense of David the private person and public man. David, then, remains a complete opacity in this episode, while Saul is a total transparency and Michal a sliver of transparency surrounded by darkness.

The means of presenting Saul are drawn from the top of our ascending scale of certainties. The narrator tells us exactly what Saul feels toward David—fear—and why he feels it—David's astonishing military success (in this instance, the parataxis of 'Saul saw...and was afraid' is a clear causal indication). We are given Saul's decorous public speech to David (verse 17), but his words are immediately commented on and exposed by a revelation of his inward speech in which he plots David's death. (In Hebrew these transitions from outward to inward speech are effected more elegantly and more pointedly because the same verb, *'amar*, is used to introduce both actual speech and thought or intention.) The next discussion of betrothal between Saul and David (verse 21) neatly reverses this order: first we get the interior monologue of the plotting king, then his decorous statement to the intended victim of his scheme. By the time we are given Saul's words to be conveyed by his henchmen, who are probably not conscious accomplices, to David, we know exactly what is behind those words.

As elsewhere in the Bible, attention is directed towards the use of language as a medium of manipulation. To make sure that we do not forget even momentarily just what Saul is up to, the narrator intervenes in his own voice in the second half of verse 25, after Saul's stipulation of bride-price, to tell us what the king's real intention is. The transparency of presentation might even be intended to imply a transparency in Saul's efforts as a Machiavellian schemer: he is a simple character, inclined to clumsy lunges rather than deft thrusts, and perhaps for that reason not *political* enough to retain the throne. Does David himself see through the king's scheme and decide to play along because he is confident he can overcome all dangers and bring back the gory bride-price? This is one of several key determinations concerning the characters about which the text leads us to speculate without providing sufficient information to draw any certain conclusions.

Michal leaps out of the void as a name, a significant relation (Saul's daughter), and an emotion (her love for David). This love, twice stated here, is bound to have special salience because it is the only instance in all biblical narrative in which we are explicitly told that a woman loves a man. But unlike Saul's fear, Michal's love is stated entirely without motivated explanation; this does not mean, of course, that it is inexplicable, only that the writer wants us to conjecture about it. The people [119] love David because of his brilliance on the battlefield; Michal might love him for the same reason, or for qualities not yet intimated, or because of aspects of her own character about which we will begin to guess only later. . .

The subsequent episodes of the David–Michal story consistently maintain this studied effect of opacity in the presentation of the warrior-king, and may be touched on more briefly. In the next chapter (1 Samuel 19), Saul sends his henchmen to David and Michal's house in order to ambush David when he comes out in the morning. In some unspecified way, the alert Michal learns of the plot and warns David in these urgent, [120] compact words: 'If you don't escape tonight, tomorrow you're a dead man' (1 Sam. 19.11). This is immediately followed neither by a verbal response from David nor by any indication of what he feels, but only by Michal's brisk action and David's emphatic compliance: 'Michal lowered David through the window and he went off and fled and escaped' (1 Sam. 19.12). These three verbs for the one in Michal's breathless instructions underline David's singleminded attention to the crucial business of saving himself.

Michal, meanwhile, is wily enough to cover David's escape by improvising a dummy in bed out of the household idols (*terafim*) covered with a cloth and a goat's-hair bolster for a head. This is obviously an allusion to Rachel, who, in fleeing with Jacob from her father (Genesis 31), steals Laban's *terafim* and hides them under the camel-pillow when he comes to search her tent. Perhaps the allusion is meant to foreshadow a fatality shared by Michal with Rachel, who becomes the object of Jacob's unwitting curse because of the theft (Gen. 31.32); what is certain is that the allusion reinforces our sense of Michal as a woman who has renounced allegiance to her father in her devotion to her husband. For when Saul, finding that David has slipped out of his hands, castigates his daughter for her treachery, Michal coolly turns around her own words to David and her actions of the previous night and pretends that David threatened her, saying, 'Help me get away or I'll kill you' (1 Sam. 19.17).

It is noteworthy that the only words purportedly spoken by David to Michal are merely her invention to protect herself. So far, their relationship has been literally and figuratively a one-sided dialogue. First we were told twice that she loved him while all that could be safely inferred about his attitude toward her was that the marriage was politically useful. Now she vigorously demonstrates her love, and the practical intelligence behind it, by her words and actions in a moment of crisis, while the text, faithful to its principle of blocking access to the private David, envelops him in silence, representing him only as a man in mortal danger who goes off, flees, and escapes.

David, after putting Saul's homicidal intentions to the test one last time with the help of his friend Jonathan, heads for the badlands, accompanied by a band of tough fighting men disaffected from Saul. Michal now disappears from the scene. Bare mention of her occurs only at the end of 1 Samuel 25, in connection with David's taking another two wives. The happily widowed Abigail, another of those extraordinarily enterprising and practical biblical woman, has just been seen taking off after David in a chain of verbs: 'Abigail hurried and got up and rode on her donkey, her five maids in attendance, and went after David's messengers and [121] became his wife' (1 Sam. 25.42). This is followed by an observation about David's matrimonial activity (probably to be construed as a pluperfect), which leads the narrator at last to inform us what has happened to Michal while David has been on the lam: 'David had taken Ahinoam of Jezreel, and so both of them became his wives, while Saul had given his daughter Michal, the wife of David, to Palti the son of Laish from Gallim' (1 Sam. 25.43). Michal, last observed as a forceful initiator of action, now stands in contrast to the energetically active Abigail as an object acted upon, passed by her father from one man to another. The dubious legality of Saul's action is perhaps intimated by the use of the epithet 'wife of David'; the motive, of course, for marrying off his daughter to someone else is political, in order to demonstrate, however clumsily, that David has no bond of kinship with the royal family and hence no claim to the throne. What Michal feels about this transaction, or about the absent David and his new wives of whom she may have heard, we are not told. The text is similarly silent about Palti's feelings—indeed, about his very identity—though he will later have his brief moment of memorable revelation...

[122] Michal returns to the story as a result of a series of decisive

political developments (2 Samuel 3). Saul has died, and after a bitter civil war, Abner, his commander-in-chief, is prepared to sue for peace with David, who makes it a precondition to negotiations that he be given back his wife Michal, 'whom I betrothed with a hundred Philistine foreskins' (2 Sam. 3.14). This bloody reminder is meant to stress the legitimacy of David's right to Michal, for whom he has paid the full bride-price stipulated by her father, and that emphasis suggests it is not any personal bond but political calculation—Michal's utility as a means of reinforcing David's claim to the allegiance of Saul's subjects—which makes him insist on her return.

His demand is promptly met by Saul's son (2 Sam. 3.15-16): 'Ish-Bosheth sent and had her taken from a man, Paltiel the son of Laish. Her man went with her, walking after and weeping, as far as Bahurim. Abner then said to him, "Go back!" and he went back.' The remarkable suggestiveness of the Bible's artistic economy could scarcely be better illustrated. This is all we ever know of Palti the son of Laish. He appears from the darkness to weep for his wife and to follow her, until he is driven back forever into the darkness by a man of power with whom he cannot hope to contend. He is called twice in close sequence Michal's man or husband (*'ish*), a title to which at least his feelings give him legitimate claim, and which echoes ironically against David's use in the preceding verse of *'ishti*, my wife or woman, to describe a relationship with Michal that is legal and political but perhaps not at all emotional on his side. The contrast between David, again speaking carefully weighed public words, and Palti, expressing private grief through publicly visible action, is pointed. As for Michal, who has been living for years as Palti's wife, we have no way of knowing whether she feels gratitude, love, pity, or contempt for her powerless second husband, though we may begin to guess that the feelings she now entertains toward David himself will be less than kindly.

The actual reunion between David and Michal is entirely suppressed, for the writer wants to leave us wondering a little longer while he attends to climactic political events (the murder of Abner, the end of the civil war, the conquest of [123] Jerusalem), and thus to reserve the revelation of what their mutual attitudes now are for a final confrontation between them. The writer's artful sureness of selectivity in the means he adopts to present character is evident in the striking fact that, until the final meeting between Michal and David, at no point is there any dialogue between them—an avoidance of verbal exchange particularly noticeable in the Bible, where such a large part of the burden of narration is taken up by dialogue. When that exchange finally comes, it is an explosion.

David, having captured from the Jebusites the mountain stronghold that will be the capital of the dynasty he is founding, settles his family and entourage there and then personally leads the Ark of the Lord in a festive procession up to Jerusalem (2 Samuel 6). Michal enters this picture as an unhappy spectator (2 Sam. 6.16): 'As the Ark of the Lord came into the City of David, Michal the daughter of Saul looked out of the window and saw King David leaping and cavorting before the Lord, and she despised him in her heart'. With a fine sense of the tactics of exposition, the narrator tells us exactly what Michal is feeling but not why. The hiatus in explanation, which will in part be filled by the ensuing dialogue, again opens the gates to multiple interpretation. The scorn for David welling up in Michal's heart is thus plausibly attributable in some degree to all of the following: the undignified public spectacle which David just now is making of himself; Michal's jealousy over the moment of glory David is enjoying while she sits alone, a neglected co-wife, back at the provisional palace; Michal's resentment over David's indifference to her all these years, over the other wives he has taken, over being torn away from the devoted Palti; David's dynastic ambitions—now clearly revealed in his establishing the Ark in the 'City of David'—which will irrevocably displace the house of Saul. The distance between the spouses is nicely indicated here by the epithets chosen for each: she is the 'daughter of Saul,' and she sees him as the king. Michal's subsequent words to David seize on the immediate occasion, the leaping and cavorting, as the particular reason for her anger, but the biblical writer knows as well as any psychologically minded modern that one's emotional reaction to an immediate stimulus can have a complicated prehistory; and by suppressing any causal explanation in his initial statement of Michal's scorn, he beautifully suggests the 'overdetermined' nature of her contemptuous ire, how it bears the weight of everything that has not been said but obliquely intimated about the relation between Michal and David.

There follow three verses which, leaving Michal in her fury at the window, describe in detail David's performance of his ceremonial functions as he offers sundry sacrifices, blesses the people, distributes delicacies. [124] Then David returns to his house to bless—or perhaps the verb here means simply to greet—his own family. . .

Michal, who at last must have her say with David, does not wait until he has actually entered the house but goes out to meet him (perhaps, one might speculate, with the added idea of having her words ring in the ears of his retinue outside). The exchange of whip-saw sarcasms between the two reflects the high-tension fusion of the personal and the political in their relationship. When Michal addresses David in the third person as the king of Israel, it is not in deference to royalty but in insolent anger at this impossible man who does not know how to behave like a king. She makes David an exhibitionist in the technical, sexual sense ('as some worthless fellow might indeed expose himself': apparently his skirts were flying high as he cavorted before the Ark), stressing that the hungry eyes of the slavegirls have taken it all in—an emphasis which leads one to suspect there is a good deal of sexual jealousy behind what is ostensibly an objection to his lack of regal dignity. David responds to the daughter of Saul with a sonorous invocation of the Lord who has chosen him for the throne instead of Saul and his heirs. As divinely elected king, David is to be the judge of what is a decorous celebration before the Lord: he seizes Michal's sarcastic 'honored', turns it into a defiant 'I will dishonor myself' (the opposed Hebrew roots suggest etymologically 'heavy' [*kabbed*], and 'light' [*qal*]); then, hurling back to Michal the idea of how he has shown himself in the eyes of other women, insists that he will be honored by these lowly slavegirls for the behavior his wife thinks degrading. In all this, the writer is careful to conceal his own precise sympathies. He does not question the historically crucial fact of David's divine election, so prominently stressed by the king himself at the beginning of his speech; but theological rights do not necessarily justify domestic wrongs, and the anointed monarch or Israel may still [125] be a harsh and unfeeling husband to the woman who has loved him and saved his life.

There is a strategically placed gap between the end of verse 22 and the beginning of verse 23. Michal, hardly a woman to swallow insults in silence, is refused the privilege of a reply to David, nor is there any indication of her inward response to this verbal assault. The breaking off of the dialogue at this point is itself an implicit commentary. David has the last word because, after all, he has the power, as he has just taken pains to point out to Michal. The daughter of a rejected royal house and by now a consort of only marginal political utility to the popularly acclaimed king, and the least favored of three or more co-wives, Michal can do nothing, and perhaps has literally nothing more to say, about her rage against her husband. Verse 23, the last one in which Michal will be accorded any mention, is a kind of epilogue to the confrontation, fastened to it with the special kind of ambiguity to which biblical parataxis lends itself. (Modern translators generally destroy the fineness of the effect of rendering the initial 'and' as 'so'.) The narrator states the objective fact of Michal's barrenness—in the ancient Near East, a woman's greatest misfortunc--but carefully avoids any subordinate conjunction or syntactical signal that would indicate a clear causal connection between the fact stated and the dialogue that precedes it. A theologically minded reader, and certainly any advocate of the divine right of the Davidic dynasty, is invited to read this statement as a declaration that Michal was punished by God for her presumption in rebuking His anointed king over an act of royal and cultic ceremony. A reader attending more to the personal drama that has been enacted between Michal and David might justifiably conclude that after this furious exchange, David simply ceased to have conjugal relations with Michal and so condemned her to barrenness. Finally, the paratactic link between the two verses leaves the teasing possibility, however less likely than the other two readings, that we may presume too much altogether in seeing here any definite relation of cause and effect: we cannot be entirely certain that Michal's childlessness is not a bitter coincidence, the last painful twist of a wronged woman's fate.

Zafrira Ben-Barak

THE LEGAL BACKGROUND TO THE RESTORATION
OF MICHAL TO DAVID*

[15] At the height of a long and bitter war between the House of Saul
and the House of David (2 Sam. 2.12–3.1) a singular episode claims
the attention of the biblical narrative:

> Then David sent messengers to Ish-bosheth Saul's son, saying, 'Give me
> my wife Michal, whom I betrothed at the price of a hundred foreskins of
> the Philistines'. And Ish-bosheth sent and took her from her husband
> Paltiel the son of Laish. But her husband went with her, weeping after her
> all the way to Bahurim. Then Abner said to him, 'Go, return'; and he re-
> turned (2 Sam. 3.14-16).

By way of a royal command Eshbaal[1] takes Michal, Saul's daughter,
from her husband Paltiel the son of Laish and gives her to David, in
accordance with the latter's demand.

This narrative passage gives rise to three fundamental questions:

A. *Why does Eshbaal agree to hand over Michal, who is under his
    authority, to his most dangerous adversary, David?*

The first question has a clearly political character. After the defeat at
Gilboa, with the death of Saul and his sons, Israel was divided into
two units. The first, 'Israel', included most of the tribes of Israel and
was under the rule of Eshbaal, the only remaining son of Saul (2 Sam.
2.8-10). The second unit, 'Judah', consisting of the tribe of Judah and

---

* From *Studies in the Historical Books* (ed. J.A. Emerton; Supplements to Vetus
Testamentum, 30; Leiden: Brill, 1979), pp. 15-29. Used by permission.

1. Eshbaal, the correct form, is preserved only in 1 Chron. 8.33; 9.39. Ishbosheth is a scribal alteration. See S. Loewenstamm, 'Eshbaal', *Encyclopaedia Biblica* 1 (Jerusalem, 1955), pp. 749-50 (Hebrew); E. Lipiński, "*šb'l* and *'šyhw*, and
parallel personal names", *OLP* 5 (1974), pp. 5-13.

tribal elements in the South, was under the leadership of David, who was crowned at Hebron (2 Sam. 2.2-7, 11). This political rift between 'Israel' and 'Judah' was accompanied by a civil war, in which superiority lay with David's forces (2 Sam. 3.1).[1] [16] David's motives for demanding the restoration of Michal are obvious, and fit in well with his aim of obtaining complete control over Israel. His marriage to a daughter of Saul king of Israel would bestow legitimacy upon his rule, and would act as a bridge between the two hostile factions.

There can be no doubt that all this was not lost on Eshbaal, who was well aware of the advantages to be gained from this marriage for an adversary who was going from strength to strength, and of the danger it heralded for his tottering rule. This was especially so since Eshbaal actually had no legal right to the throne, in view of the fact that in Israel the dynastic principle had not yet been established as a part of the institution of kingship.[2] Indeed, his ascent to the throne was unaccompanied by any act of sanctification (Noth, p. 169; E. tr., p. 183). One would therefore expect that he would strenuously resist any such union and spare no effort to frustrate the execution of an act so pregnant with danger not only for his kingdom but perhaps for his very life. It is thus all the more astonishing that he does not oppose the handing over of the king's daughter to David, and that he himself orders that David's request be complied with and sees to its execution.[3]

1. On 'Israel' and 'Judah' under David see M. Noth, *Geschichte Israels* (2nd edn, Göttingen, 1954), pp. 167-72 = E. tr. *The History of Israel* (revised edn, London and New York, 1960), pp. 181-6; J. Bright, *A History of Israel* (2nd edn, London, 1972), pp. 190-3; S. Herrmann, *Geschichte Israels in alttestamentlicher Zeit* (Munich, 1973), pp. 185-90 = E. tr. *A History of Israel in Old Testament Times* (London, 1975), pp. 145-9.
2. For the opinion that with Saul's reign the dynastic principle had not yet been established in Israel see J. Pedersen, *Israel, its Life and Culture III-IV* (London and Copenhagen, 1940), p. 58; R. de Vaux, *Les institutions de l'Ancien Testament* I (Paris, 1958), pp. 145-6 = E. tr. *Ancient Israel: Its Life and Institutions* (London, 1961), pp. 94f.; Bright, p. 191.
3. The response of Eshbaal to Abner in the matter of Saul's concubine (2 Sam. 3.6-8) demonstrates his great sensitivity to the stability of his kingdom and to anything that could endanger it.

B.   *How are Michal's marriage first to David and then to Paltiel and her remarriage to David to be explained?*

The second question is on the plane of social ethics. Twice Michal is given to a different man, in the lifetime of her husband, and on both occasions by the legal authority, the king. On the first occasion Michal, as David's wife, is given to Paltiel the son of Laish by King Saul (1 Sam. 25.44). On the second occasion Michal, as the wife of Paltiel the son of Laish , is given in his lifetime to David, at the command of Eshbaal king of Israel. This repeated offence against one of the sacred principles of society is in need of explanation. A [17] basic social principle in Israel, as in every ancient Near Eastern society, was the prohibition of any sexual relations between a married woman and another man. Its breach was an offence punishable with death, for both the adulterer and the woman.[1] The prohibition is laid down in the severest manner in a legal context—in the Ten Commandments two are devoted to the subject: Exod. 20.14, 17; and Deut. 5.17, 18 (cf. Lev. 20.10; Deut. 22.22). The same state of affairs, with punishment of equal severity, prevails in the ancient Near Eastern Law codes, e.g. the Code of Hammurabi, §§129-132;[2] the Middle Assyrian Laws A §§12-18, 22-24;[3] the Hittite Laws B §§197, 198.[4]

The biblical narratives provide us with detailed cases in which the offender incurred the most drastic penalty, no matter whether it was an ordinary citizen or the king himself. In the patriarchal narratives an adulterous relationship is seen as an offence also against God, which results in both individual and collective punishment, as in the traditions concerning Sarai and Pharaoh (Gen. 12.10-20), Sarah and Abimelech (Gen. 20), and Rebekah and Abimelech (Gen. 26.6-11; cf. Prov. 2.16-19; 5.3-14; 6.24-35; 7.5-27). The story of the marriage of Samson and the woman of Timnah (Judg. 14–15), which contains re-

1.   For the great severity of the prohibition against taking another wife see R. Patai, *Sex and Family in the Bible and the Middle East* (New York, 1959), pp. 80-91; de Vaux, pp. 62f. (E. tr., pp. 36f.); cf. S. Greengus, 'A Textbook Case of Adultery in Ancient Mesopotamia', *HUCA* 40/41 (1969-70), pp. 33-44.

2.   G.R. Driver and J.C. Miles, *The Babylonian Laws* I (Oxford, 1952), pp. 281-4; II (Oxford, 1955), pp. 50-3.

3.   G.R. Driver and J.C. Miles, *The Assyrian Laws* (Oxford, 1935), pp. 36-55, 386-97.

4.   A. Goetze, 'The Hittite Laws', in J.B. Pritchard (ed.), *Ancient Near Eastern Texts Relating to the Old Testament* (2nd edn, Princeton, 1955), p. 196.

markable parallels to the story of the marriage of Michal and David, describes the disaster which was caused as a result of the giving of a man's wife to another, albeit by her own father. To no avail were the father's attempts to minimize his deed, nor his willingness to give Samson his younger daughter. The consequences were terrible: the burning of the father and his daughter, the wife of Samson (Judg. 15.6). The episode of David and Bathsheba (2 Sam. 11–12.25) is a classic example of the outrage that results from the abduction of another man's wife.[1] The importance of this [18] example is manifold: it is based on historical reality, it is close in time to the events of the Michal and David episode, and the hero, David, is involved in both cases. From the outset it is emphasized that even the king did not dare openly to seduce the wife of Uriah the Hittite. He spares no effort to conceal what he is doing, and finally prefers murder of the husband to public exposure of his misdeed. The harsh reaction of the prophet Nathan and his condemnation of David shows that society would brook no compromise in matters of this nature (2 Sam. 12.7-12).

To return to the case of Michal, the reaction of her husband Paltiel the son of Laish is all the more astonishing by comparison. The story emphasizes the depth of his grief and his inability to take his leave of her, but at the same time his conduct shows that he accepts the decision. This is difficult to comprehend, for it is reasonable to suppose that he would appeal to the king or the leaders of the community, that he would put up a bitter and unyielding struggle, and that he would most certainly not accompany his wife on her way to another man. And no less incomprehensible is the absence of reaction of the community and its dignitaries, particularly in view of the fact that it took place within the sovereign territory of Israel and under the king of Israel.

C. *How can David's remarriage to his former wife Michal be reconciled with the law in Deut. 24.1-4?*

The third question is of a legal nature. The law expressly forbids remarriage where the wife has been married to another man in the interim:

1. On the story of David and Bathsheba see H.W. Hertzberg, *Die Samuelbücher* (Göttingen, 1956), pp. 245-55 = E. tr. *I and II Samuel* (London, 1964), pp. 305-17; P.R. Ackroyd, *The Second Book of Samuel* (Cambridge, 1977), pp. 99-115.

... Then her former husband, who sent her away, may not take her again to be his wife. ... [1]

The woman was thought to be impure to her husband and their conduct as a whole was considered an abomination before God and a defilement of the land (v. 4b).[2] Confirmation of this strict prohibition comes from Jer. 3.1:

> If a man divorces his wife and she goes from him and becomes another man's wife, will he return to her? Would not that land be greatly polluted?

[19] The presentation of this instance as an outstanding example of sin in a society is evidence that such a prohibition was well known to the society and was one of the principles whose breach it would not tolerate.

All the three significant questions have to be answered. Failure to resolve them, or even any attempt to explain them away, will call into question several of the basic principles of Israelite society at the beginning of the monarchy.

I

The passage 2 Sam. 3.14-16 discussed above is part of a scattered biblical account which centres on one story: 'the marriage of Michal daughter of Saul to David' (1 Sam. 17.25; 18.17-19, 20-29; 19.11-17; 25.44; 2 Sam. 3.12-16; 6.16, 20-23; 21.8-9).[3] The outstanding features of this story are its various stages and the vitality and dynamism of the narrative. Nonetheless, as some scholars see in some of the texts parallel or late traditions, it must be asked to what degree they are au-

1. See G. von Rad, *Das fünfte Buch Mose. Deuteronomium* (Göttingen, 1964), pp. 106-8 = E. tr. *Deuteronomy* (London, 1966), pp. 149f.; Z.W. Falk, *Hebrew Law in Biblical Times* (Jerusalem, 1964), pp. 154-7.
2. See M. Weinfeld, *Deuteronomy and the Deuteronomic School* (Oxford, 1972), pp. 269f.
3. For these writings see M.H. Segal, *The Books of Samuel* (Jerusaiem, 1956), pp. 134-58, 203, 248f. (Hebrew); Hertzberg, pp. 109-31, 162, 204-8 (E. tr., pp. 142-68, 205, 254-60); P.R. Ackroyd, *The First Book of Samuel* (Cambridge, 1971), pp. 136-58, 199f., and *The Second Book of Samuel*, pp. 39-44; H.J. Stoebe, *Das erste Buch Samuelis* (Gütersloh, 1973), pp. 312-65, 451, 460, and 'David und Mikal. Überlegungen zur Jugendgeschichte Davids', *BZAW* 77 (Berlin, 1958), pp. 224-43.

thentic and inter-connected, and by the same token how relevant are the questions which were raised above, since those problems arise only if the story itself is authentic and complete. Within the story, it is possible to distinguish the following stages.

Firstly, 1 Sam. 17.25: '. . . And the man who kills him the king will enrich with great riches, and will give him his daughter'.

King Saul's promise, then, signifies the start of the long chain of events.

The next stage is 1 Sam. 18.17-19, the marriage of Merab the daughter of Saul to David. According to the Masoretic text, Saul offers his elder daughter to Merab to David in marriage, on condition that David fight the wars of the Lord. At the end of this passage it is stated without any explanation that Merab is given as wife to another, to Adriel the Meholathite.[1]

The next stage, 1 Sam. 18.20-29, is the account of Michal's marriage to David. The motive for this marriage is Michal's love for David. The condition which is demanded of him this time for his marriage with Michal is a marriage-gift (*mohar*) of a hundred [20] foreskins. David fulfils the condition twice over, bringing two hundred foreskins. As a result, 'Saul gave him his daughter Michal for a wife' (v. 27).

The two stories of the marriages of David to Saul's daughters give rise to a number of reservations, the basic questions being whether we have before us a reflection of historical reality, i.e. that David was offered first the hand of one of Saul's daughters and later of another, or whether they are two versions of David's marriage.[2] In the view of most scholars the Michal narrative is authentic and reflects historical reality, while the Merab narrative is dismissed as a colourless imitation.[3] Even among those scholars who uphold the trustworthiness of the Michal narrative, however, there are doubts as to the tradition

1. Ackroyd, *The First Book of Samuel*, p. 153.
2. Hertzberg, p. 123, n. 4 (E. tr., p. 159, n. a.).
3. This view is in accord with Codex Vaticanus, which makes no mention of the Merab tradition (1 Sam. 18.17-19). Cf. Stoebe, *Das erste Buch Samuelis*, pp. 550f., and 'David und Mikal', pp. 224-43. In his view the whole question is one concerning the traditions about David's youth, in which are reflected the motifs of the patriarchal narratives, the marriage of Jacob to Leah and Rachel, the daughters of Laban.

which places Michal's marriage to David in the reign of Saul.[1] In our view, the account of Michal's marriage to David taking place in Saul's lifetime and at his initiative is rooted in historical reality. This story is linked in all its details to everything else that is written about the affair as a whole. It is not possible to understand any of the biblical passages on Michal's marriage to David, which are accepted as reliable by most biblical scholars, without the original passage in 1 Sam. 18.20-29, which indicates that the marriage took place in Saul's lifetime and at his initiative. A further decisive fact is that throughout Michal is explicitly referred to as David's wife: 1 Sam. 19.11; 25.44; 2 Sam. 3.14. Thus the words of Ahimelech clearly establish that the marriage took place in Saul's reign (1 Sam. 22.14).

The following stage is 1 Sam. 19.11-17, where Michal saves David's life. This incident shows that Michal is living in David's house, and emphasizes her devotion to her husband—she is the one who presses him to flee, and hides his escape. When rebuked by Saul, she does not hesitate to give a deceitful answer.[2]

The next stage is 1 Sam. 25.44, where Saul gives Michal the wife of David to Palti the son of Laish from Gallim. This piece of information [21] was apparently inserted at this point in connection with the account of David's other wives, and because it is related to the difficult solution in which David finds himself.[3]

The final stage is 2 Sam. 3.12-16, the restoration of Michal to David. This passage has also given rise to misgivings—is this a single narrative or two versions? But even if there were two traditions concerning the manner in which Michal was returned to David, it does not affect the historical fact that Michal was formally restored to David. She could return to him only by order of Eshbaal, the king.[4]

---

1. Noth, p. 170, n. 1 (E. tr., p. 184, n. 1); Stoebe, *Das erste Buch Samuelis*, p. 352, and 'David und Mikal', pp. 227f., 234f.

2. Hertzberg, p. 130 (E. tr., pp. 166f.).

3. Cf. J. Morgenstern, 'Additional Notes on "*Beena* Marriage (Matriarchat) in Ancient Israel"', *ZAW* 49 (1931), pp. 54f.

4. Two further passages may be seen as supplements to the story of the marriage of Michal and David. The first, in 2 Sam. 6.16-23, indicates the rift between Michal and David and the fact that she had no children. The second, 2 Sam. 21.8-9, is the handing over of Saul's offspring to the Gibeonites. Here are mentioned the five sons of Michal whom she bore to Adriel the Meholathite. See p. 87 below [original pp. 26-27].

The following three conclusions may be drawn from the discussion so far:

1.	The narrative of Michal's marriage to David is reliable and is based on historical reality, and its stages are consistent with one another.
2.	The fundamental questions which were posed at the beginning of this discussion are relevant, but remain unanswered. Proof of the authenticity of the narrative is what causes these questions to arise and serves to emphasize their difficulty.
3.	At the same time it has become clear from the discussion that the biblical source alone cannot provide the answers to these questions.

II

Legal documentary material from Mesopotamia reveals a remarkable practice which has significant implications for the case of Michal and David.

In the Laws of Eshnunna (paragraph 29, 19th century B.C.) we find the following law:

> If a man has been [*made prisoner*] during a raid/or an invasion, or has been carried off forcibly, (and) [*dwelt*] in another land for a l[ong] time, another indeed took his wife and/she bore a son—whenever he returns, he will [*take back*] his wife.[1]

The law[2] deals with the case of a man who is forcibly displaced by an enemy force and against his will lives for a considerable time [22] in a foreign country. His wife who is left on her own is allowed to remarry. A son is born of the second marriage. The first husband upon his return receives back his wife. The law is laconically phrased and important details are missing (cf. Yaron, p. 134).

Paragraph 135 of the Laws of Ḥammurabi (c. 18th century B.C.) informs us:

> If the man takes himself off and there is not the (necessary) maintenance in his house, (and) before his return his wife enters another man's house and then bears sons, (if) her husband afterwards returns and regains his

1.	This translation follows R. Yaron, *The Laws of Eshnunna* (Jerusalem, 1969), pp. 34f.
2.	Cf. Yaron, pp. 109f., 134f.

city, that woman shall return to her first husband; the sons shall follow
their (respective) fathers.[1]

This law, like that of Eshnunna, discusses the case of a woman
whose husband is taken by force and lays down the same ruling. However, it adds two important details: first the reason for the wife's second marriage, second the rule for children born of the second marriage.[2]

Paragraph 45 of tablet A of the Middle Assyrian Laws[3] deals with
the same case. But while the earlier sources from Eshnunna and
Babylon are brief and give only the main points of the case, the
Middle Assyrian tablet discusses the subjects at length, adds important
details and presents different aspects of the law:

If a woman has been given (in marriage), and her husband has been taken
by an enemy, (and) she has no father-in-law or son, she shall belong to
her husband for two years; during these two years, if there is not enough
to eat, she shall come and declare it. If she is a villager of a palace, her
[palace?] shall feed her, and she shall do its? work. If she is the [wife?] of
a *ḫupšu*, [.....] shall feed her, [..........]; and, [if she is a free woman?
and there is] a field and [a house at her disposal (?)], she shall come [and
declare it] saying: '[I have nothing] to eat'. (Then) the judges shall ask the
mayor (and) elders of the village whether the field and house belong in
that village, (and) they shall sell the field and house for her maintenance
during the two years, on her behalf (-*še*). She is 'in waiting' and they
shall write a tablet for her (to that effect). She shall complete two years,
(and) then she may be 'in waiting' for the husband of her [23] choice,
(and they shall write a tablet for her as if she were an *almattu* ('widow').

If, after a time, her lost husband returns to the land, he shall take (back)
his wife who was married outside (his household), (but) he shall have no
claim on any sons she bore to her later husband—it is her later husband
who takes (them). The field and house which she had sold outside (his
household) for her maintenance, if it? has not entered the. . . of the king,
he shall pay as (much as) was paid (for it before), and shall take (it back);

1.   This translation follows Driver and Miles, *The Babylonian Laws* II, pp. 52f.

2.   For this law see Driver and Miles, *The Babylonian Laws* I, pp. 284-90; II,
pp. 215-17; T.J. Meek, 'The Code of Ḥammurabi', *ANET*, p. 171.

3.   Cuneiform text in O. Schroeder, *Keilschrifttexte aus Assur verschiedenen
Inhalts* (Leipzig, 1920), I, col. VI, 46-88 (p. 10); Driver and Miles, *The Assyrian
Laws*, pp. 212-28, 256-66, 412-15; G. Cardascia, *Les lois assyriennes* (Paris,
1969), pp. 217-26; J.N. Postgate, 'Land Tenure in the Middle Assyrian Period: A
Reconstruction', *BSOAS* 34 (1971), pp. 496-520. For the date of the Laws see
Driver and Miles, pp. 4-12.

and, if he has not returned, (but) died in another land, the king shall give
(away) his field and his house wherever he wishes to give (it).[1]

From this document we are given to understand that the wife has no
father-in-law or sons who will provide for her or look after her in
her husband's absence. The tablet deals with three cases of women in
this situation, over two of whom it pauses only briefly, these being
women from the lower classes, the wife of a villager-dependant of the
Palace, whom the Palace is obliged to support in return for her
employment there, and the wife of a *ḫupšu*, who is also required to
work in return for her maintenance. The third case, which is the
central concern of the law, is that of a free woman whose husband
possesses an estate and who belongs to a higher social class than the
other two. This woman is not required to work for her living, and
thus she finds herself in distress. The judges, the mayor and the elders
of her village, sell her estate, and in return supply her needs (see Postgate, p. 506). She remains in this situation as a deserted wife for two
years, and then she is allowed to remarry. Finally, upon the return of
her first husband she goes back to him and her children remain with
their natural father. The tablet concludes with the right of the first
husband to redeem his estate.

The three sources discussed above, from Eshnunna, Babylon and
Assyria, reveal the existence of a similar custom.[2] The fact that the
sources are dispersed over a very long period of time and derive from
different peoples may be evidence that this practice was widely
accepted throughout Mesopotamia. Some development may be dis-
cernible in it: from the brief Eshnunna law through that of Babylon to
the Assyrian law which drew upon the two earlier laws and enlarged
upon them. It is possible from these sources to sketch a clear and com-
prehensive picture of the practice and to lay down the following principles:

[24] 1. The basis of the law and its essential condition is that the husband has been forcibly taken by an enemy and now is absent
from his home and his city against his will, by reason of
force majeure. This basic element is found in all three
sources and is what determines the law.

1. This translation follows Postgate, pp. 502f.
2. Cf. E. Szlechter, 'Effets de la Captivité en Droit Assyro-Babylonien', *RA* 57
(1963), pp. 181-92.

2. The wife is left without any means of sustenance and in need of assistance. This clause, which is lacking in Eshnunna, is expressly stated in the Babylonian and Assyrian laws. The Assyrian law brings to light the woman's situation and why she is left without means of maintenance even though she belongs to a high social class.

3. It is remarkable that in all the sources discussed there is no mention of the wife's father. It is reasonable to presume from this that after her marriage the wife belonged to her husband's household and her father was no longer obliged to look after her. The fact that the document does not mention the woman turning, in the hour of her need, to her father's house for help, but only, it would appear, to the local authority, shows that her father has ceased to be the source of her maintenance and protection. The matter is not made to depend on the social status of the father, nor on his economic status.[1]

4. The wife was obliged to make a declaration of her condition and thus came under the protection of the local authorities. This clause is lacking at Eshnunna and Babylon. It reveals the responsibility of the authorities towards the deserted wives especially the free woman from the upper class.

5. At least two years were set as the period during which the woman had to remain as wife of her first husband. This is according to the Assyrian law; the law from Eshnunna remarks only that the husband may be absent for a long time, while the Babylonian law makes no mention of the time involved.

6. After two years the woman received the status of an *almattu*, a 'widow'. The term refers to a woman who has not only lost her husband but also has no father-in-law or adult sons to maintain her, and thus is left without support from her husband's house. Only after receipt of a tablet confirming her as an *almattu* is she entitled to remarry. This clause is likewise

1. See Driver and Miles, *The Assyrian Laws*, p. 217, n.1. From the Mesopotamian custom of bestowing a *šeriktum* upon a daughter of the family on the occasion of her marriage we may conclude that this was her share of the parental estate, and that she had no right to additional claims thereafter.

only found in the Assyrian law.[1]

[25]7.   The woman marries a second time. This basic element is found in all the sources (cf. Szlechter, pp. 186-91).

8.   The woman has borne sons to her second husband. This clause appears in all the sources, and emphasizes that she was free to build a completely new life in the home of her second husband.

9.   With the return of the first husband, the woman is obliged to come back to him.

10.   The children that were born to the second husband remain with him. The law recognized that offspring belonged to the family of their natural father.

In summary, according to the sources from Eshnunna, Babylon and Assyria the law was in essence that a woman whose husband had been taken under constraint, i.e. by *force majeure*, and who was left without means of support was allowed to remarry. Nonetheless, from the legal point of view she belongs to her first husband and although her second marriage is lawful it is immediately and incontestably invalid upon the return of the first husband, and the woman returns to the latter.

III

The Mesopotamian practice discussed above is important for an understanding of Michal's marriage to David, for a closer examination will demonstrate the similarity of the Mesopotamian practice's principles, particularly the Assyrian law, to the biblical narrative.

David is forced against his will to abandon his home and flee for his life, to wander in the desert and go into exile in a foreign land. There appears *prima facie* a difficulty in comparing David's situation with the main principle of the law: while the Mesopotamian law is concerned with a man who has been taken by an enemy, David is said to have fled himself. We have already emphasized, however, that the law in question is based on a single criterion, namely whether the situation in which the man finds himself was imposed upon him against his will, by *force majeure*, or whether he created it of his own free will. In the

---

1.   See Postgate, p. 504. Cf. Driver and Miles, *The Babylonian Laws* I, p. 294, and *The Assyrian Laws*, pp. 212f.

case of David it is made abundantly clear that his departure was invol-
untary, by *force majeure* to no less an extent than that of a captive.
The narrative lays stress on Michal's initiative in smuggling David out
of the house (1 Sam. 19.11-12) and thus removes any similarity to
paragraph 136 of the Laws of Ḥammurabi. Likewise it cannot be compared with paragraph 30 of the Laws of Eshnunna (cf. Yaron, p. 136,
n. 105). On the contrary, this narrative [26] is a link in the special
complex of relations between Saul and David, wherein David continually shows feelings of loyalty, love and honour towards Saul (1 Sam.
24.6, 9-15, 22; 26.9-11, 17-20, 22-23), while Saul on the one hand
shows his love for David, raises him above the people and makes him
his son-in-law, and on the other seeks to kill him and pursues him (1
Sam. 16.21-22; 18.13, 17, 27; 19.11-15; 22.1-8; 23.13-21; 24; 26).[1]
So far as this reflects a conflict, one reason may be David's elevated
position (son-in-law of the king, hero of Israel and the person to
whom the people give precedence—1 Sam. 18.7), which defines it as a
court conflict over the succession to the throne.

Michal is left alone in her husband's house; she has no sons, and her
father-in-law, David's father, is forced to find refuge with the king of
Moab (1 Sam. 22.1-4). We might also suppose that David's household
could not afford to support her in a fitting way, in view of David's
sudden flight. Michal's status is similar to that of the free women of
the upper class whose only protector is the formal authority. It should
also be remembered that the woman no longer belongs to her father's
household; it is not clear, moreover, what the relations between Saul
and Michal were after she helped David to escape. At all events,
Michal, without father-in-law, and sons, was in the eyes of the law
without means of support and therefore entitled to marry another
man. The accounts of David's wanderings point to his being away
from home for years. According to the Assyrian law, which lays
down a period of two years for the time that a wife still belongs to her
first husband, Michal would be formally free to remarry. It is possible
to understand Saul's action as that of a ruler who is responsible for
her fate and assists her in remarrying, and not at all because he is her
father. It would be proper in the matter of a woman of the status of a
king's daughter that the palace should deal with it. His action must be
recognized as a customary official act and not as the arbitrary act of

1. See Pedersen, *Israel. . . II-IV*, pp. 50-7; and Bright, pp. 187-9.

Saul giving his daughter in marriage.

With the return of the missing first husband the wife was by law obliged to come back to him. In like manner David demands Michal.

One is not informed whether or not Michal had sons from her second marriage, except for the knowledge that she returned to David without sons (2 Sam. 3.16-17). It may be possible to conclude that she is from a piece of information that is the subject of dispute:

> [27] And the King took. . . the five sons of Michal the daughter of Saul, whom she bore to Adriel the son of Barzillai the Meholathite (2 Sam. 21.8).

It is usually thought that there is an error here, and that 'Merab' should be read instead of 'Michal', on account of the name of the husband, Adriel the Meholathite, who is referred to in 1 Sam. 18.19. It is difficult to accept that there was a mistake in the name of Michal, however, and possible that the mistake is actually in the name of the second husband (who is of secondary importance in the narratives), which should be Paltiel the son of Laish. Stoebe suggests that 'Adriel' and 'Paltiel' are the same name. 'Paltiel' is the Hebrew name, while 'Adriel' is Aramaic and has the same meaning: 'God is the saviour'. It would appear that there are several different versions of the name of Michal's second husband: Palti (1 Sam. 25.44), Paltiel (2 Sam. 3.15), Adriel (2 Sam. 21.8).[1] With the aid of the Mesopotamian custom one may explain the passage of events; Michal bore sons to her second husband and they remained with their natural father after the return of the first husband. It is for this reason that it is stated that Michal had no sons (2 Sam. 6.23).

The following is a chart comparing the principles of the Mesopotamian law to the Michal and David narrative.

Legal Principles	Eshnunna	Babylon	Assyria	The Marriage of Michal to David
1. Husband is absent from home and city by reason of *force majeure*.	x	x	x	x

1. See Stoebe, *Das erste Buch Samuelis*, p. 451, and 'David und Mikal', pp. 228-32.

2. Wife is without means be- cause she has no father-in-law or sons.	x	x	x	x
3. Two years (minimum) laid down as time she must wait for return of her husband.	x		x	x
4. Wife marries a second time.	x	x	x	x
5. Wife bears sons to second husband.	x	x	x	x
6. First husband returns and his wife goes back to him.	x	x	x	x
7. Children remain in house of second husband.		x	x	x

[28] Comparison of the Mesopotamian law and the biblical narrative thus shows that identical principles were involved. We may therefore conclude that the same practice that was widespread in Mesopotamia was known and followed in Israel, at least at the beginning of the monarchic period.

Conclusion

In the light of this conclusion let us now attempt to answer the fundamental questions which were raised from the biblical narrative.

A. The first question was: why does Eshbaal agree to hand over Saul's daughter Michal to David? David's demand for the return of his wife on the strength of his being her first husband rests on the basic law and custom of the society. Its breach was liable to tarnish the reputation of Eshbaal the king, marking him as a ruler who attacked the legal foundations of society, and in consequence as unconcerned for social order and lawfulness in his kingdom.[1] There can be no doubt that Eshbaal was especially sensitive to his name in this delicate period, when the very existence of his kingdom was in question. It is reasonable to suppose that he would try his utmost to prove to Israel that they were right in making him king. Thus his desire to create the image of a king who preserves law and order was balanced against his

---

1. It was an official preoccupation of oriental monarchs that their names should be synonymous with order, justice and preservation of the law. See D.J. Wiseman, 'Law and Order in Old Testament Times', *Vox Evangelica* 8 (1973), pp. 5-21.

fear of the advantages that a daughter of Saul would give to his adversary David. And the former considerations proved decisive. Only thus can Eshbaal's action be understood.

B. The second question is: how can we explain Michal's repeated remarriage? Only in the light of the Mesopotamian law can we understand not only that there was not a crass breach of one of the sacred principles of society, the prohibition against taking another man's wife, but that all the parties in this case were acting in accordance with law and custom. After Michal has been living for years in the house of her husband David who is absent, and has been without husband, sons, or father-in-law, she is married to her second husband Paltiel the son of Laish. Her remarriage to David is to be understood in the same way. With his return to his country David, Michal's first husband, claims his wife and received her in accordance with the law. Again, only by reference to the Mesopotamian law can the [29] conduct of her second husband be explained. From the beginning of their marriage Paltiel knows that, as long as there is no positive knowledge of her first husband's death, the latter retains a claim to his wife. When the time comes, he acts as a responsible citizen in accordance with custom, albeit openly showing his deep distress. This is the reason for the absence of any reaction from the leaders of Israel. Not only is it not to be expected that they will side with Paltiel the son of Laish, her husband, but as representatives of law and order in the society it is their duty to see that the transfer is carried out, even at the price of causing pain and suffering to a respected citizen. Their silence is to be taken as assent.

C. The third question was: how can David's remarriage to his former wife after her marriage to another be explained in the light of the express law in Deut. 24.1-4? In the Mesopotamian sources (Laws of Eshnunna paragraph 30; Laws of Ḥammurabi, paragraph 136) it is expressly stated that if a man leaves his wife and his city of his own free will and his wife marries another he has no further right to her and is not entitled to take her back. Thus in the biblical law (Deut. 24.1-4) it is expressly stated that the man sends away his wife of his own free will and at his own initiative and afterwards she marries another—contrary to David's case. The biblical law adds the fact that she married another man and is therefore forbidden to her husband, for whom it is a sin:

... after she has been defiled, for that is an abomination before the LORD,
and you shall not bring guilt upon the land which the LORD your God
gives you for an inheritance (Deut. 24.4b).

The language of this addition is clearly Deuteronomistic,[1] and evidently the law was not yet in force in David's time. Likewise the reference to this law in Jer. 3.1 as one of the customary laws is evidence for the lateness of the law and its connection with the Deuteronomist (cf. Weinfeld, p. 359).

In sum: the Mesopotamian law mentioned above contributes to our understanding of Michal's marriage to David and places it in its proper social and legal contexts. The biblical story, as a result, is seen to be based on a custom known and accepted throughout Mesopotamia as well as in Israel. Only in the light of this Mesopotamian legal practice can one adequately answer the questions posed at the beginning of this study.

1.   On Deuteronomic phraseology see Weinfeld, pp. 323, 340f., 359, 362.

Adele Berlin

CHARACTERIZATION IN BIBLICAL NARRATIVE:
DAVID'S WIVES*

[70] Michal was the first, and in some ways the most interesting of
David's wives. Robert Alter has given a vivid description of this character and the personal tragedy surrounding her, and it need not be
repeated here.[1] What I would like to add is the aspect of Michal's
characterization that emerges when it is compared with Jonathan's.
This comparison cries out to be made: both Michal and Jonathan are
the children of Saul who show more love and loyalty to their father's
competitor than to their father. The biblical author further invites the
comparison by juxtaposing their stories in 1 Samuel 18–20. The
results are surprising: the characteristics normally associated with
males are attached to Michal, and those usually perceived as feminine
are linked with Jonathan.

The first of Michal's unfeminine traits is found in the notice that she
loved David and made it known. It is recorded twice (1 Sam. 18.20,
28), and is the only time in the Bible that a woman seems to have chosen a husband instead of the usual pattern of a husband choosing a
wife.[2] (Of course the marriage could only take place because father
Saul approved, for his own ulterior motives.) David, on his part,
married Michal not for [71] love but because 'it pleased David well to
be the king's son-in-law' (18.26). His relationship to her is always col-
ored by practical considerations. He apparently did not (or could not)
object when she was married to someone else during his absence (1
Sam. 25.44), and his later demand for her return was motivated by

*   Excerpted from *Journal for the Study of the Old Testament* 23 (1982),
pp. 69-85 (70-72).
    1.   'Character in the Bible', *Commentary* 66/4 (Oct., 1978), pp. 58-65 (70-72).
    2.   The initiative taken by Naomi and Ruth is more complex and differently
motivated.

political reasons (2 Sam. 3.13-15). In this last incident Michal's feelings are not recorded, but her second husband appears somewhat effeminate as he tags along after her crying until Abner commands him to go back home.

The feelings of love and tenderness that David might have been expected to have for Michal are all reserved for Jonathan. Jonathan, too, like his sister, made known his warm feelings for David (1 Sam. 18.1; 19.1; 20.17), but in his case they were reciprocated. The parting of the friends in the field describes how 'they kissed one another and wept upon each other until David exceeded' (20.41). At their final parting David laments, 'I am distressed over you, my brother, Jonathan; you have been very pleasing to me—more wonderful was your love to me than the love of women' (2 Sam. 1.26).

David, then, seems to have related to Michal as to a man and to Jonathan as to a woman. It is not a question of sexual orientation here, but a subtle suggestion that this reflects something of the essence of these two characters. Michal is the aggressive and physical one. She saves David by physically lowering him out of a window,[1] and arranging the bed so as to appear that he is in it. She lies to the messengers, telling them that David is sick in bed, and then, after the ruse is discovered and Saul himself questions her, she brazenly fabricates the story that David threatened to kill her if she did not aid his escape (1 Sam. 19.12-17). Jonathan, too, saves the life of his friend, but it is never by physical means; it is through words (talking Saul out of killing him in 1 Sam. 19.4-5), and words with a coded meaning (the episode of the arrows in 1 Sam. 20.20ff.). Jonathan's most physical action is the shooting of the arrows for the pre-arranged signal—hardly a show of strength. The 'little white lie' that he told his father to explain David's absence from the new moon feast (20.28-29) had actually been concocted by David himself (20.6). Jonathan is just the messenger boy. His words and deeds are certainly much less daring than Michal's.

The last bit of information we have about Michal is that she never bore a child (2 Sam. 6.23). Not only is this the culmination of the disappointment in her life, and a hint that the [72] husband who never

---

1.   The lowering of a person through a window may be a motif connected with females; compare Josh. 2.15 where Rahab does the same. Nevertheless, Michal's actions throughout appear more physical and aggressive in contrast to Jonathan's.

loved her now stopped having marital relations with her,[1] but, in the light of the foregoing discussion, it suggests that Michal never filled a female role, or at least the role that the Bible views as the primary female role. Significant, too, may be the fact that Michal, unlike many women in the biblical narrative, is never described as beautiful. Far from being a typical woman, Michal has been cast in a most unfeminine role.

1.　Cf. Alter, 'Character in the Bible', *Commentary* 66/4 (October, 1978), pp. 58-65 (63).

W.G. Blaikie

MICHAL IN THE BOOKS OF SAMUEL
(from *The First Book of Samuel* and *The Second Book of Samuel*)*

[307]...Knowing her father's plot, Michal warns David that if he does not make his escape that night his life is sure to go.

Michal lets him down through a window, and David makes his escape. Then, to give him a sufficient start, and prolong the time a little, she has recourse to one of those stratagems of which Rebecca, and Rahab, and Jeroboam's wife, and many another woman have shown themselves mistresses—she gets up a tale, and pretends to the messengers that David is sick. The men carry back the message to their master. There is a peculiar ferocity, an absolute brutality, in the king's next order, 'Bring him to me in the bed that I may slay him'. Evidently he was enraged, and he either felt that it would be a satisfaction to murder David with his own hand when unable to defend himself, or he saw that his servants could not be trusted with the dastardly business. The messengers enter the house, and instead of David they find an image in the bed, with a pillow of goat's hair for his bolster. When Michal is angrily reproached by her father for letting him escape, she parries the blow by a falsehood—'He said unto me, Let me go; why should I kill thee?'

On this somewhat mean conduct of hers a light is [308] incidentally shed by the mention of the image which she placed in the bed in order to personate David. What sort of image was it? The original shows that it was one of the class called 'teraphim'—images which were kept and used by persons who in the main worshipped the one true God. They were not such idols as represented Baal or Ashtoreth or Moloch, but images designed to aid in the worship of the God of Israel. The

*   *The First Book of Samuel* (The Expositor's Bible; London: Hodder & Stoughton, 1898), pp. 307-309; *The Second Book of Samuel* (The Expositor's Bible; London: Hodder & Stoughton, 1898), pp. 95-96.

use of them was not a breach of the first commandment, but it was a breach of the second. We see plainly that David and his wife were not one in religion; there was discord there. The use of the images implied an unspiritual or superstitious state of mind; or at least a mind more disposed to follow its own fancies as to the way of worshipping God than to have a severe and strict regard to the rule of God. It is impossible to suppose that David could have either used, or countenanced the use of these images. God was too much a spiritual reality to him to allow such material media of worship to be even thought of. He knew too much of worship inspired by the Spirit to dream of worship inspired by shapes of wood or stone. When we read of these images we are not surprised at the defects of character which we see in Michal. That she loved David and had pleasure in his company there is no room to doubt. But their union was not the union of hearts that were one in their deepest feelings. The sublimest exercises of David's soul Michal could have no sympathy with. Afterwards, when David brought the ark from Kirjath-jearim to Mount Zion, she mocked his enthusiasm. How sad when hearts, otherwise congenial and loving, are severed on the one point on which congeniality is of deepest moment! Agreement in earthly tastes and [309] arrangements, but disagreement in the one thing needful—alas, how fatal is the drawback! Little blessing can they expect who disregard this point of difference when they agree to marry. If the one that is earnest does so in the expectation of doing good to the other, that good is far more likely to be done by a firm stand at the beginning than by a course which may be construed to mean that after all the difference is of no great moment. . .

[95] The last thing recorded of David is, that he returned to bless his house. The cares of the State and the public duties of the day were not allowed to interfere with his domestic duty. Whatever may have been his ordinary practice, on this occasion at least he was specially concerned for his household, and desirous that in a special sense they should share the blessing. It is plain from this that, amid all the imperfections of his motley household, he could not allow his children to grow up ignorant of God, thus dealing a rebuke to all who, outdoing the very heathen in heathenism, have houses without an altar and without a God. It is painful to find that the spirit of the king was not shared by every member of his family. It was when he was returning

to this duty that Michal met him and addressed to him these insulting words: 'How glorious was the king of Israel to-day, who uncovered himself to-day in the eyes of the handmaids of his [96] servants, as one of the vain fellows shamefully uncovers himself'. On the mind of David himself, this ebulition had no effect but to confirm him in his feeling, and reiterate his conviction that his enthusiasm reflected on him not shame but glory. But a woman of Michal's character could not but act like an icicle on the spiritual life of the household. She belonged to a class that cannot tolerate enthusiasm in religion. In any other cause, enthusiasm may be excused, perhaps extolled and admired: in the painter, the musician, the traveller, even the child of pleasure; the only persons whose enthusiasm is unbearable are those who are enthusiastic in their regard for their Saviour, and in the answer they give to the question, 'What shall I render to the Lord for all His benefits toward me?' There are, doubtless, times to be calm, and times to be enthusiastic; but can it be right to give all our coldness to Christ and all our enthusiasm to the world?

Richard G. Bowman

THE FORTUNE OF KING DAVID/
THE FATE OF QUEEN MICHAL:
A LITERARY CRITICAL ANALYSIS OF 2 SAMUEL 1–8*

The story of Michal's relationship with David is related through five
incidents in 1 and 2 Samuel. These incidents trace the relationship
from establishment through estrangement, from rescue and release
through return and restoration.

The first three incidents occur in 1 Samuel 16–31, which portrays
various facets of the tenuous relationship between David and Saul. As
a part of this relationship Saul gives Michal to David for a wife (1
Sam. 18.20-29). She in turn helps David escape from Saul's vengeance
(19.11-17). Saul then gives her to Palti (25.44). However, the death of
Saul (2 Sam. 1) inaugurates a new phase in the story of David as well
as a new phase in David's relationship with Michal.

This paper explores the literary portrayal of the David/Michal relationship as it is reflected in the final two incidents (2 Sam. 3.12-16 and
6.16-23). I shall analyze these incidents both as they function as in
their immediate canonical context and as they echo the earlier incidents. I argue that the fate of Michal is inextricably linked with the
fortune of David and that the vicissitudes in David's fortunes result in
the three-fold victimization of Michal.

In order to focus my analysis on the story of Michal and David, I
shall assert rather than argue a number of preliminary positions such
as the functioning of 2 Samuel as a discrete, coherent literary unit.
Given this assertion, one can observe several organizational schemes
which are employed by the narrator/redactor of 2 Samuel. Primary
among these is the use of two lists of court officials in 2 Sam. 8.16-18
and 20.23-26. These nearly identical lists function to divide the book

* Presented to the Narrative Research on the Hebrew Bible Group, Society of
Biblical Literature, Chicago, November 1988.

into three sections:

Section 1	1.1–8.15	The Internal, External, and Divine Crises of King David
Section 2	8.18–20.26	The Personal and Political Crises of King David
Section 3	21.1–24.25	A Retrospective on the Crises of King David

From a literary, canonical perspective the final two incidents involving David and Michal are integral components of the narrative unit defined as 2 Samuel 1–8. Within this narrative unit the use of the temporal phrase וַיְהִי אַחֲרֵי־כֵן in 2 Sam. 2.1 and 8.1 identifies its constituent narrative parts:

Part 1	1.1-27	Saul's Kingdom in Chaos
Part 2	2.1–7.29	David's Kingdom Established
Part 3	8.1-15	David's Kingdom Consolidated

The first part takes place after the death of Saul. It shows a defeated, scattered, and leaderless Hebrew nation in a state of chaos. The third part reports David's successful efforts to consolidate the nation. These two frame the central part which relates the process by which David moved the nation from chaos to consolidation.

It is within Part 2 that the David/Michal incidents occur. The narrator has organized this part into a series of four episodes:

Episode A	2.1–5.16	David Becomes King over Judah and Israel— Internal Politics
Episode B	5.17–6.11	David defeats the Philistines—External Politics
Episode C	6.12-23	David Transfers the Ark to Jerusalem—Divine Politics
Episode C′	7.1-29	The Dynastic Oracle—Divine Politics

Each episode deals in turn with an aspect of the political situation— internal, external, and divine—confronting David as he seeks to establish his monarchy. Common to each episode are cases where David learns or fails to learn the divine will, cases which govern the events that follow.

The final two incidents in the story of Michal and David occur in Episodes A and C. In Episode A Michal is involved in one of David's four attempts to secure monarchial authority: (1) moving his family to Hebron in Judah where the men of Judah anoint him king, (2) appealing for support from the men of Jabesh-gilead who were once loyal to Saul, (3) negotiating with Abner for control of the kingdom of Ishbosheth, and (4) negotiating with Ishbosheth for the return of Michal,

Saul's daughter and his former wife. David is immediately successful in the first of these attempts, an attempt which is clearly authorized by God. He initially fails in the second and third attempts which are not authorized by God. The result of the final, also unauthorized, attempt involving Michal remains ambiguous until Episode C.

One significant feature of these episodes is their portrayal of the characters of David and Michal. David's is a flawed but favored character, while Michal's is ever victimized but never vindicated.

Episode A (2 Samuel 2.1–5.16)
Internal Politics

The initial episode relates various aspects of the internal political situation surrounding David's acquisition of the throne of Israel and Judah. It has a complex structure with six elements in a modified chiasmus:

A		2.1-11	Potential Conflict
	B	2.12-32	Conflict Realized but Stalemated
	C	3.1-5	Summary and List of Sons
	B1′	3.6-39	Abner's Death; Stalemate Broken
	B2′	4.1-12	Ishbosheth's Death; Stalemate Broken
A′		5.1-5	Conflict Resolved
	C′	5.6-16	Summary and List of Sons

The chiasm can be visualized in this diagram:

There are two chiastically related sections. The narrative begins with a potential conflict in Part A and concludes with the conflict resolved in Part A′. The initial attempts at resolution end in a stalemate in Part B. Since there are two leaders in Israel, the breaking of the stalemate requires two narrative parts, B1′ and B2′, each focusing on the elimination of one of the leaders. Each of the chiastic halves then concludes with a parallel summary and list designated as Parts C and C′.

Part A. Potential Conflict (2.1-11)
The narrative in 2 Samuel 1 focuses on David's mourning the death of

Saul and Jonathan. However, it also shows that, as a result of these deaths, the kingdom is leaderless and in a state of chaos—which gives David the opportunity to secure royal authority.

Part A begins with a scene (2.1-4a) which shows David taking advantage of the situation and moving in to fill the power vacuum, but only after securing divine approval for his actions. After reporting David's divinely approved move to Hebron, the scene concludes with the decisive statement: 'And the men of Judah came, and there they anointed David king over the house of Judah'. David, however, has become king only of Judah; there are factional differences between David and the house of Saul, between Judah and Israel, differences which become apparent in a subsequent scene (2.8-9) where the narrator reports that Ishbosheth, specifically identified as Saul's son, becomes king over 'all Israel'. However, Ishbosheth's kingship comes about not at the initiative of God or with his approval but at the instigation of Abner, the 'commander of Saul's army'. Nor is it the people who anoint him king, but Abner. Clearly, the succession to Saul's kingship is as yet an unresolved issue.

The juxtaposition of these two scenes indicates the potential for conflict between David as king of Judah and Ishbosheth as king of Israel. The significance of this conflict is presented and emphasized by an intervening scene (2.4b-7) which reports David's direct appeal to the men of Jabesh-gilead, supporters of Saul, for political support. After learning that they were the ones who buried Saul, David sends messengers to them affirming his kingship over the house of Judah. He commends them for having loyally served their lord (that is, with חסד), even to the point of seeing that he received a proper burial. In return for that loyalty, David not only invokes divine reciprocity but also promises his own.

The scene shows David actively building support for his kingship. However, he invokes divine favour without first seeking it. The first scene showed David taking steps to become king of Judah, but he first sought and received divine approval, whereas in this scene he initiates action without first securing divine authorization. He does, however, assume divine favor since he promises it to the men of Jabesh-gilead in return for their support. The erroneousness of David's assumption is betrayed in the following scene which reports Ishbosheth's own coronation.

In these scenes we see, first, that David can and does act assertively and take advantage of situations. Second, they show that when David acts aggressively after securing divine approval, he succeeds. However, when he acts without it, he fails—a pattern we will encounter again.

Part B. *Conflict Realized but Stalemated (2.12-32)*
The potential for conflict between David and the house of Saul as portrayed in Part A is realized in this part of the narrative—but through an encounter between Joab and Abner, not David and Ishbosheth. Their confrontation concludes with a stalemate, each retreating to the headquarters of their respective kings, Abner to Mahanaim and Joab to Hebron.

Part C'. *Summary and List of Sons (3.1-5)*
The final part of the first chiastic pair reports that the conflict developed into a 'long war between the house of Saul and the house of David', in which 'David grew stronger and stronger, while the house of Saul became weaker and weaker'.

This concluding summary also records the sons born to David at Hebron. While David is in the process of establishing his monarchy, he is also creating the means by which it can be sustained after his death. Further connections must be drawn to the list of sons born in Jerusalem and to the notice about the barrenness of Michal in 2 Samuel 6.

Part B1'. *Abner's Death; Stalemate Broken (3.6-39)*
The stalemate reached in Part B is broken in two sequences of dramatic action which function as chiastic parallels. In each, one of the major leaders of Israel is assassinated. Part B1' relates the assassination of Abner, and Part B2' records the assassination of Ishbosheth.

The first half of the chiastic parallel, Part B1', is the most complex narrative in this section of the larger narrative. The action unfolds in three phases:

Phase 1	3.6-21	Abner Negotiates with David
Phase 2	3.22-31	Joab Assassinates Abner
Phase 3	3.32-39	David Laments

Phase 1. *Abner Negotiates with David*
The first phase of the narrative shows dissent with the house of Saul.

It is comprised of a chiastically organized sequence of seven scenes:

Scene I	3.6-11	Abner's conflict with Ishbosheth
Scene A	3.12-13	Abner and David
Scene BX	3.14	David and Ishbosheth
Scene C	3.15	Ishbosheth and Michal
Scene C′X	3.16	Abner and Paltiel
Scene B′	3.17-19a	Abner and the Elders
Scene A′	3.19b-21	Abner and David

Scene I. Abner's Conflict with Ishbosheth (3.6-11)
The introductory scene relates an emerging conflict within the house of Ishbosheth. Previously, as the war between David and Ishbosheth dragged on David grew stronger and Ishbosheth weaker. This scene begins with a similar comment about Abner: 'While there was war between the house of Saul and the house of David, Abner was making himself strong in the house of Saul'.

Abner's attempt to assert his authority by claiming Rizpah, Saul's concubine, provokes a censure from Ishbosheth. Abner's angry response to Ishbosheth reveals his belief that he deserved Rizpah because of his continuing loyalty (חסד) to the house of Saul as evidenced by his not giving it 'into the hand of David'. This statement hints that he possessed the means though not the inclination to betray the house of Saul to David. Since that loyalty has not been appreciated, he vows now to act against the house of Saul.

The scene concludes with the narrator's report that Ishbosheth did not answer Abner 'because he feared him'. His challenge to Abner's authority has not been successful.

Scene A. Abner and David (3.12-13)
Abner fulfills his threat and sends messengers to David, demanding that David make a covenant with him. In return for making the covenant with him, Abner vows to deliver to David 'all Israel': 'Behold, my hand shall be with you to bring over all Israel to you'— which is to say, a monarchy that David has not been able to acquire by his own efforts.

In the context of the larger narrative there is an irony in Abner's proposal. Abner claims that 'his hand' will be 'with (David)' to give him 'all Israel'. But at the conclusion of the episode (5.6-16), when David has been anointed king over Israel, the narrator observes that 'David became greater and greater because the Lord, the God of hosts was with him'. David will ultimately be established as king of Israel because God is 'with him' not because Abner is 'with him'. Abner further proposes that as a result of a covenant he will make with David, he will secure for him the kingdom. However, as the final episode, 2 Samuel 7, reveals David's kingdom is secure because of a covenant that God, not Abner, makes with him.

Having failed to establish ties with Israel through his own initiative, David agrees to Abner's proposal. However, David adds a curious condition. He demands that his wife Michal, 'the daughter of Saul', be returned to him. He says, 'Good (טוב), I will make a covenant with you; but one thing I require of you; that is, you shall not first see my face, unless you first bring me Michal, the daughter of Saul, when you come to see my face'. The importance of this condition is stressed by the repetition of the phrase 'see my face'.

By means of this condition, David makes yet another attempt to establish ties with the house of Saul. In seeking to regain Michal, Saul's daughter, he is attempting to legitimate his monarchial claims.

Scene BX. David and Ishbosheth (3.14)
Significantly enough, David does not wait for Abner to make the arrangements necessary to fulfill his condition to the covenant. Both the chiastic structure of the narrative and the fact that the request is made to Abner anticipate a scene in which Abner approaches Ishbosheth. Instead the narrator offers an anomalous scene, in which David himself sends his request directly to Ishbosheth.

The introduction to the scene shows that David has again taken the initiative. Whereas the previous scene began, 'And Abner sent messengers to David...', this scene begins, 'And David sent messengers to Ishbosheth, Saul's son...' Abner's message to David offered a proposal. David's message to Ishbosheth issues an order: 'Give me my wife Michal, whom I betrothed at the price of a hundred foreskins of the Philistines'.

The (re)introduction of Michal into the narrative at this juncture is significant as it echoes the earlier episode in 1 Sam. 18.20-29 in which David first established a link with the house of Saul. That episode began abruptly with the narrator's report: 'Now Saul's daughter Michal loved David'. In that Michal's love for David stands at the beginning, not the end of the episode, it is portrayed as generating the action of the episode, not as being the consequence of it.

Michal's love for David is reported to Saul, whose inner thoughts are reported by the narrator: 'Let me give her to him, that she may be a snare for him, and that the hand of the Philistines may be against him'. Because of her love for David, Michal will become a pawn in one of Saul's schemes to eliminate David.

The negotiations between David and Saul are recorded at length. David's initial response to Saul's offer protests that his humble family origins do not merit his becoming the king's son-in-law: 'I am a poor man and of no repute'. Saul apparently interprets this to mean that David cannot afford to pay a bride price, for he counters with this message: 'The king desires no marriage present except a hundred foreskins of the Philistines, that he may be avenged of the king's enemies'.

At this point, the narrator discontinues the dramatization of the negotiations through direct discourse to report from his omniscient perspective on the internal thought of each of the negotiators. Again stressing Saul's ulterior motives, he says: 'Now Saul thought to make David fall by the hand of the Philistines'. He similarly suggests David's ulterior motives when he says, 'It was pleasing in the eyes of David to become the son-in-law of the king'. Saul uses Michal's love for David as a covert means to assassinate him and David, for his part, does not return Michal's love but also uses it as a means by which he can become the king's son-in-law. In fact, the sentence reporting David's response to the bride price is a variant repetition of the one used earlier to report Saul's response to Michal's love for David. Michal's love for David is 'pleasing in [Saul's] eyes'; and Michal's bride price is 'pleasing in [David's] eyes'. Michal is thus portrayed as a victim twice over. She is at once the victim of Saul's desire to eliminate David and the victim of David's desire to establish ties with the royal family by becoming the king's son-in-law.

The narrator resumes the story with a summary report that David killed two hundred Philistines and gave Saul double the number of foreskins stipulated in the bride price. As if to emphasize the reason for the overkill, the narrator reports that David presented the king with the foreskins so that 'he might become the king's son-in-law'— not 'Michal's husband'. This is the fifth use of the phrase 'the king's son-in-law' in this episode. Twice it is used in speeches by Saul when he is inviting or perhaps enticing David to become his son-in-law. It is used once in a speech by David when he protests that he is not important enough to become the king's son-in-law. The narrator also uses it twice in reporting David's response to Saul's requirement of a bride price and David's fulfillment of it. The repeated use of the phrase suggests that expediency, not love, motivates both the actions of David and Saul. Michal may love David; but her father uses that love to manipulate David, and David uses it to manipulate Saul.

Saul honored his agreement and 'gave [David] his daughter Michal for a wife'. However, the narrator's choice of vocabulary suggests that Saul's honoring of the agreement is a mere formality. For the first time in the episode the relationship is referred to as a husband/wife relationship, not a father-in-law/son-in-law relationship. David does not become the king's son-in-law; instead Michal becomes his wife. The narrator supports this notion by again revealing Saul's inner thoughts: 'When Saul saw and knew that the Lord was with David and that Michal, Saul's daughter, loved him, Saul was still more afraid of David'. Saul is motivated by fear to honor his commitment to David. Saul is afraid of David because he perceives that Yahweh is with him and that his daughter loves him. These perceptions also foreshadow significant aspects of the larger narrative. Saul's plan to assassinate David covertly has failed because Yahweh is with David. It is Yahweh who will ultimately establish David as king of Israel as well as Judah apart from his own efforts to do so and apart from any attempt to thwart his assumption of the kingship. Furthermore, the fact that Michal loves David will prove to be a liability not a benefit as Saul once envisioned. The exploiter of Michal's love will in a future incident be exploited by it.

The episode then concludes with the narrator's comment that 'Saul was David's enemy continuously'. Saul's initial love for David has deteriorated to fear and hatred, though it is now replaced by Michal's love for him. Ironically, at the beginning of the episode Michal's love for David provided Saul with an opportunity to eliminate David. Now at the end of the episode Michal's love further occasions Saul's fear of David.

However, in the context of the present episode (2 Sam. 3.14) it is Michal's relationship with David, not Saul's, that is the focus of attention. Now that Saul has been killed by the Philistines, David is in a position to acquire political authority. One of the means by which he seeks to do so is to regain possession of his wife Michal, thereby reclaiming his status as the king's son-in-law and re-establishing his ties with the house of Saul. He justifies his request by stressing that he legitimately acquired her as his wife for the bride price of one hundred Philistine foreskins. Once again Michal's love for David is exploited and used as a means to a political end.

Echoing each other, these two episodes suggest that the fate of Michal is irrevocably linked with the ongoing fortune of David. As David's relationship with Saul deteriorates, Michal becomes a pawn in one of Saul's schemes to kill David. David, however, uses the scheme to establish political ties with the royal family. Once Saul is dead David invokes his relationship with Michal in an attempt to assert his political authority.

Scene C. Ishbosheth and Michal (3.15)
Though the previous scene concludes without giving Ishbosheth's reply, this scene briefly relates without further comment Ishbosheth's compliance with the request. Like the two previous scenes it begins with an exercise of authority. The narrator observes that 'Ishbosheth sent and took [Michal] from her husband Paltiel'. However, Ishbosheth's seeming assertion of authority is not an independent action but one taken in compliance with David's prior exercise of authority. The scene shows Ishbosheth submitting to the authority of David, another indication of the tenuousness of Ishbosheth's own monarchial authority.

This scene and the following scene, Scene C′X, function as the center of the narrative's chiastic structure. What is compositionally emphasized as central to David's quest for political power is the return of Michal. Even the reigning monarch of Israel is powerless to block this return.

Scene C′X. Abner and Paltiel (3.16)
This scene is also an anomaly within the structure of the larger narrative. Abner again becomes involved in the process but only after Michal's husband will not leave her. The narrator reports that he followed her, 'weeping after her all the way to Bahurim'. Abner, not Ishbosheth as might be expected, then orders him to return, and he complies.

Abner's successful intervention is a further indication of Ishbosheth's weakness as king of Israel. Even Paltiel does not recognize Ishbosheth's authority, though he does Abner's. Thus this scene and the previous one combine to portray the diminished status of Ishbosheth's authority in relationship both to David and to Abner. They also show David securing the return of Michal even though he must take her from a husband who mourns her loss.

These scenes which report the actual return of Michal to David also echo an earlier episode in 1 Sam. 19.11-17 in which David secures his release from the house of Saul. In that last of many overt attempts and covert plots to eliminate David, Saul sends messengers to watch David's house at night so 'that he might kill him in the morning'. Somehow Michal learns of these arrangements, and she takes the initiative to warn and rescue David, saying, 'If you do not save yourself tonight, tomorrow you will be killed'. That the narrator explicitly identifies her as David's wife, not Saul's daughter, suggests that she acts to protect her husband, not to profess loyalty to her father. This portrayal is consistent with the narrator's previous two statements that she loved David. This love now causes her to betray her father and to aid David in his escape from Saul.

The narrator does not give David's reply but only reports that she let him out through a window and that 'he fled and escaped'. Michal is here the assertive initiator of action and David the passive recipient of her efforts to save him from Saul. As the object of Saul's vengeance, David is without power or authority.

The story resumes with a scene which does not yet follow David's escape but which reports further on Michal's assertive attempts to facilitate this escape. In a scene dramatized by dialogue, Michal refuses to surrender David, claiming that he is sick. To support this claim she apparently shows Saul's messengers a bedded form actually made up of concealed teraphim and goat's hair.

When Saul finally uncovers this ruse, he confronts Michal: 'Why have you deceived me thus, and let my enemy go so that he has escaped?' She replies: 'He said to me, "Let me go; why should I kill you?"' Thus Michal not only arranges David's escape and deceives Saul's messengers, but she also lies to her father about the circumstances motivating her deceit.

Ironically, Michal acts to protect David, but she cannot protect herself. After Michal aids David in his escape from the court of Saul, he never returns. Michal is in a 'no win situation'. If she does not arrange for David's escape, Saul will kill him. If she does, David will in effect be forced by circumstances to desert her. Either way she loses him: to death or to desertion. Whether she acts or fails to act, she is the victim of David's deteriorating relationship with Saul.

The present episode (2 Sam. 3.15) shows Michal continuing to be the victim of David's changing relationship with the house of Saul. The death of Saul places David in a position to capitalize on his marriage relationship with the house of Saul. In re-establishing ties with the house of Saul, Michal is again useful to David. However, now that David desires a reunion, the once assertive Michal who rescued a passive David becomes the passive subject of David's aggressive manipulation. Just as she had once been a pawn in one of her father's schemes to eliminate David, she is now a pawn in one of David's schemes to assume authority in Israel.

Michal's progressive victimization is further documented by the pivot episode in the story of David and Michal. The episode in 1 Samuel 25 reports the story of David, Nabal and Abigail. As a fugitive from Saul, David seeks to provide for his own well being. He seeks assistance from Nabal, who refuses. An angry David then threatens to kill Nabal. Like Michal, Abigail intervenes and rescues David. However, she rescues him from his own vengeance rather than the vengeance of Saul.

The story resolves with the narrator's report that David 'sent and spoke to Abigail to take her as his wife'. Abigail willingly complies: 'And Abigail made haste and rose and mounted on an ass, and her five maidens attended her; she went after the messengers of David, and became his wife'.

The episode then concludes with the narrator's note that David also took Ahinoam of Jezreel, as well as Abigail, for his wife. Juxtaposed to this note is the statement: 'Saul had given Michal, his daughter, David's wife, to Palti the son of Laish who was of Gallim'. Like Michal, Abigail rescues David; but, unlike Michal who is given to another man, she remains with him to reap the benefits.

In the context of the larger narrative this note also foreshadows the fact that, with the acquisition of Abigail and Ahinoam as wives, David establishes for himself a potential political and dynastic power base independent of his marriage to Michal and apart from the house of Saul. This, however, is a topic which will be more appropriate for a later discussion. At issue now is the tragic irony that although Michal's love for David and her loyalty to him secures his release from Saul, it also occasions circumstances which allow David to establish an independent identity and authority. These episodes thus contribute to the portrait of Michal as the victim of David's relationship with Saul.

Echoing these previous episodes, the present episode further highlights this victimization. As David seeks to regain Michal, he does not 'send and speak' to her as he did with Abigail. Instead he order Ishbosheth to 'send and take' her. Whereas Abigail willingly came to David, the narrator does not reveal Michal's emotional response to David's reacquisition of her from Palti, just as he did not reveal her response to the transaction which gave her to him originally. Although her initial emotion for David was one of 'love' and her actions in rescuing him were motivated by this love, her subsequent feelings about David are as yet unstated. Instead, the narrator reports only on the distress of her second husband, Paltiel. The presence of information about Paltiel's emotions as well as the absence of information about Michal's feelings function to stress the passive role which she now plays.

Scene B. Abner and the Elders of Israel (3.17-19a)
Now that David's only condition to making an agreement with Abner is fulfilled, the narrator returns to the process by which the kingdom will be transferred. As the chiastic pair to Scene BX, this scene reports Abner's negotiations with the elders of Israel that David be made their king.

Scene A'. Abner and David (3.19b-21)
Paired with Scene A, this final scene reports Abner's return to David at Hebron. The narrator reports the result of the negotiations with Israel repeating the vocabulary used by David in his response to Abner's earlier overture to him. Israel also regards the negotiated arrangements as 'good' (טוב). David then welcomes Abner with a feast and sends him away in peace.

The next phase of the narrative (3.22-31) shows, however, that David's negotiations with Abner come to an abrupt halt. Joab intervenes and assassinates Abner. Thus his second attempt to obtain the kingdom of Saul also ends in failure, suggesting once again that David cannot obtain monarchial authority through negotiation though he will ultimately receive it as a divine gift.

Part B2'. Ishbosheth's Death; Stalemate Broken (4.1-12)
The second half of the chiastic parallel to Part B relates the assassination of Ishbosheth. Assuming that David perceives Saul as his enemy and therefore seeks vengeance upon his house, the two assassins bring him the head of the dead monarch. David, however, responds with an oath which identifies God, not humans, as his redeemer. He says: 'As the Lord lives, who has redeemed my life out of every adversity...' He continues by referring to the situation of the Amalekite in 2 Samuel 1 who also supposed he was bringing David 'good news' when he brought the announcement of Saul's death. David notes that the reward for such news was the execution of the Amalekite, and he then orders their own execution.

David's response to the two traitorous opportunists shows that, though he has not always consulted God, he still recognizes that divine authority plays a decisive role in his future as king over all Israel and Judah. It also shows that though he has assertively sought ties with the house of Saul, he regards assassination as an unacceptable means of acquiring power.

Part A'. Conflict Resolved (5.1-5)
As the parallel to Part A which initiated the conflict between David and the house of Saul, this part of the narrative resolves it. With the potential rivals from the house of Saul now eliminated, the tribes of Israel approach David at Hebron and invite him to become their king as well. That the initiative is theirs is stressed by two repetitions reporting their request as well as an account of it. The first repetition relates that 'all the tribes of Israel came to David at Hebron'; and the second variation relates that 'the elders of Israel came to the king at Hebron'. The variations emphasize that support for the overture comes from the people as well as the leadership. They also emphasize that the initiative is theirs, not David's. David is given the kingdom; he cannot and has not been able to seize it upon his own initiative. It is also significant that, in approaching David with their offer, the people of Israel perceive that a Davidic monarch is divinely ordained. They tell him: 'The Lord said to you, "You shall be shepherd of my people Israel, and you shall be prince over Israel"'.

The narrator concludes this part in summary fashion by reporting David's response to their initiative: 'King David made a covenant with them at Hebron before the Lord'. That the covenant between Israel and David is made 'before the Lord' suggests its legitimacy, in contrast with the two previous illegitimate attempts to form alliances between David and Israel which were initiated either by David or by Abner. In language that repeats the vocabulary of 2 Sam. 2.4 the narrator also reports that the elders 'anointed David king over Israel' just as he had previously been anointed king over Judah. The narrative tension pertaining to the war between David and the house of Saul thus appears to be resolved.

Part C'. Summary and List of Sons (5.6-16)
This part of the narrative is parallel to Part C which reported that after the initial confrontations the house of David grew stronger while the house of Saul grew weaker in the war between the two. It then concluded with a summary of the sons born to David at Hebron.

Now that the war is over, the earlier summary about the progress of the war is replaced by an expanded narrative relating the establishing of David's capital at Jerusalem. Whereas the previous part emphasized the narrator's perspective that David became 'stronger and stronger', this part emphasizes that David became 'greater and greater'. The success granted David in establishing a united monarchy supports this conclusion. However, the narrator also offers a theological reason for his success with the comment: 'And the Lord, the God of hosts, was with him'. For the first time in 2 Samuel 1-8, the narrator explicitly attributes David's success to God. David's achievements are as much the result of divine favor as they are the product of human skill and ingenuity.

The narrator also uses his omniscient perspective to report David's internal thoughts on his success. As such he notes that David himself attributes his success to God: 'And David perceived that the Lord had established him king over Israel and that he had exalted his kingdom for the sake of his people Israel'. At the conclusion of this episode, the narrator not only makes explicit the belief that divine mandate authorizes the establishment of David as king over Israel and Judah, but he also makes it clear that David himself recognizes the priority of this divine mandate.

The final part of the episode then concludes as did Part C by noting the sons born to David in Jerusalem. The two lists of David's sons, those born in Jerusalem and those born in Hebron, occur at strategic junctures in the narrative. As such they function to suggest that David has a progeny that can continue the monarchy after his death. This fact becomes important in a later incident dealing with the childlessness of Michal.

This episode thus portrays David as a flawed but favored character. As he seeks monarchial authority, David is shown to be flawed in his perception of the means by which he is to obtain it. To his credit, David will not seize it when it is illegitimately offered to him by opportunists courting his favor and when it violates his loyalty to Saul or the reigning member of his family. Yet neither can he attain it through usurpation as he attempts with the men of Jabesh-gilead, or through negotiation as he attempts with Abner, or finally (as will be shown in Episode C) through manipulation as he attempts with the repossession of Michal.

Though he is flawed, David is nonetheless the recipient of divine favor. As such, David receives monarchial authority when it is given to him as a gift by the men of Judah and when the people of Israel 'come' to David and offer him the monarchy of Israel. In different ways both instances stress that David attains power because of a divine mandate.

This episode also portrays Michal as the victim of David's changing relationship with the house of Saul. As David seeks to capitalize on the power vacuum created by the death of Saul, Michal becomes the object of a scheme to legitimate his authority. As such, she is the victim of David's flawed perception of how he is to acquire the kingdom—just as she had earlier been the victim of David's deteriorating relationship with Saul.

Episode B (2 Samuel 5.17-25)
David Defeats the Philistines—External Crisis

Whereas as the previous episode focused on the internal politics of establishing a Davidic monarchy, this episode focuses on the external politics of maintaining it. As such, it revolves about David's elimination of the Philistine menace which had plagued Saul's reign and eventually led to his demise.

The stylized structure of this episode emphasizes by repetition the success of David in handling the Philistine crisis. It also underscores his obedience to the divine will as the reason for his success. On two occasions the Philistines initiate an assault upon David. On each occasion, David consults God before responding, and on each occasion his counter-assault is successful.

This episode then functions as the second phase of the sequence through which the Davidic monarchy is established. Having stabilized the internal political situation, David now handles the external Philistine threat. Eliminating this threat paves the way for the final two episodes which relate David's handling of the divine political situation.

Episode C (2 Samuel 6.1-23)
David Transfers the Ark to Jerusalem—Divine Crisis

The third episode begins the final crisis David must face to secure his throne, i.e. the divine political situation. As such it reports on David's attempt to gain possession of the ark. The narrative is comprised of two parts:

Part 1	6.1-11a	Transfer of the Ark Begun
Part 2	6.11b-23	Transfer of the Ark Concluded

Each part has its own distinctive organizational structure and focus. The distinguishing feature which divides the narrative into two parts is the interruption of the transfer of the ark to Jerusalem in 2 Sam. 6.11.

Part 1. Transfer of the Ark Begun (6.1-11a)
This part of the narrative focuses on David's initial but unsuccessful attempt to move the ark to Jerusalem from its resting place in Baalejudah. It begins with the narrator's report that David gathered 30,000 people, identified as 'all the chosen men of Israel', traveled to the depository of the ark, and began a procession to return it.

Two features of this report are striking. First is the fact that David does not consult God before undertaking this mission. That David must secure divine authorization before he undertakes a successful action is a characteristic feature of each of the four episodes in this section of the larger narrative. David is again acting on his own initiative and without divine authorization, for the fourth time. The first instance, involving his appeal for support from Jabesh-gilead (2 Sam. 2.4b-7), proved unsuccessful. The second instance was his unsuccessful negotiation with Abner for the throne of Israel. The result of the third instance where he made a direct appeal to Ishbosheth for Michal has not yet been revealed, though its unsuccessful outcome is related in Part 2 of this episode. The unfolding story of this episode shows that David's unauthorized attempt to take possession of the ark also fails.

The other significant feature is the characterization of the ark of God. The narrator relates that it is 'called by the name of the Lord of hosts who sits enthroned upon the cherubim', reminding the reader that the ark traditionally represented the presence of God among the people and his protection of them.

So David, having secured the throne of Judah and all Israel and having subdued the Philistines, now attempts to guarantee the continuation of his reign by obtaining possession of the ark of God. Such possession would further legitimate his rule.

The story includes an account of a celebration which accompanies the procession. The festivities, however, are abruptly halted when the oxen stumble, and Uzzah, one of the ark's attendants, touches the ark, apparently to steady it. The narrator reports God's anger at this act: 'And the anger of the Lord was kindled against Uzzah; and God smote him there'.

The narrator makes no attempt to explain this seemingly irrational act. Explanations do not seem to interest him. What does interest him is David's response of anger 'because the Lord had broken forth upon Uzzah'. God's anger and subsequent action are matched by David's anger as a response.

David has attempted to take personal possession of the ark without first securing divine authorization as he had on his previously successful ventures. His attempt to legitimize his reign theologically fails. Whereas the narrative began with David initiating the ark procession, it concludes with him stopping it. David takes the ark not to Jerusalem but to the house of Obed-Edom the Gittite. There it remains for three months.

Part 2. Transfer of the Ark Concluded (6.11b-23)
The second part of this episode reports on the resumption of the procession of the ark to Jerusalem. It is comprised of five interrelated parallel scenes which shift the focus of the story:

Scene I	6.11b-12	David and God
Scene A	6.13-15	David and the People
Scene B	6.16	David and Michal

| Scene A´ | 6.17-19 | David and the People |
| Scene B´ | 6.20-23 | David and Michal |

After the introductory scene, the narrator alternately focuses attention on the festivities surrounding the successful resumption of the transfer and on Michal's critical response to them.

Scene I. David and God (6.11b-12)

The introductory scene begins with a report that God had blessed Obed-Edom and all his household. A similar report is made to David. He is told not only that God has blessed the household of Obed-Edom but he is also given the reason for the blessing: 'because of the ark of God'. David correctly interprets this as a sign of renewed divine favor. Having learned of God's intentions and received the authorization he previously lacked, David successfully resumes the transfer of the ark to the city of David.

Scene A. David and the People (6.13-15)

The narrator reports in some detail on the resumption of the celebration surrounding the transfer of the ark. It includes the note that David himself 'danced before the Lord with all his might'.

Scene B. David and Michal (6.16)

The focus of the narrative abruptly shifts with the reintroduction of Michal, specifically identified as the daughter of Saul. In Episode A David took assertive action to regain possession of her. Now in this episode, as the procession enters the city, she watches the proceedings from a window, observing 'King David leaping and dancing before the Lord'. Now we also learn of her emotional response: 'She despised him in her heart'.

Several features of this scene are interesting. First is the explicit identification of David as 'King David'. Second is the emphasis that the king is dancing 'before the Lord'. The dance is part of a worship ritual. Given this information, Michal's response is curious. The narrator implies that, as king, David has done nothing despicable, yet reports that Michal does, in fact, despise him. However, he withholds the reason.

Scene A'. David and the People (6.17-19)

The focus of the story abruptly shifts again, returning to the ark processional reported in Scene A. The ark is brought into the city and placed in a tent which David has prepared for it. David then offers burnt and peace offerings before the Lord, and he blesses the people in the name of the Lord. With the procession of the ark to Jerusalem and the attendant celebration completed, the people return to their homes.

Scene B'. David and Michal (6.20-23)
In the final scene the focus of the story returns to Michal and David. Having blessed (ברך) the people, David returns to bless (ברך) his own household. Ironically, he is not received as warmly at home as he is by the people. He encounters Michal who is again specifically identified as the daughter of Saul. She addresses him with the sarcastic contempt previously reported by the narrator: 'How the king of Israel honored himself today, uncovering himself today before the eyes of his servants' maids, as one of the vulgar fellows shamelessly uncovers himself'.

Michal apparently regards David's behavior as inappropriate. Instead of conducting himself like a king, David shamelessly cavorts before his servants' maids. David, however, justifies his actions just as the narrator has previously done. He tells her that he danced 'before the Lord'. He then reminds her that it was the Lord who chose him over her father and all his house and that it was God who appointed him as a prince over Israel. He replies to her accusations: 'It was before the Lord, who chose me above your father, and above all his house, to appoint me as prince over Israel, the people of the Lord—and I will make merry before the Lord'. He continues by promising her that 'I will make myself yet more contemptible than this, and I will be abased in your eyes; but by the maids of whom you have spoken, by them I shall be held in honor'.

The scene then concludes with the narrator's terse report that Michal, again identified as the daughter of Saul, 'had no child to the day of her death'. That he gives no reason for this has led interpreters to speculate on one. Some suggest that God prevented her from having children, while others suggest that David no longer desired a sexual relationship with her or she with him. The actual reason, however, remains unstated. Apparently it was not consistent with the narrator's purpose to divulge one. As a result the emphasis rests on the fact that she was childless, not on the reason for it.

This fact refocuses attention upon the two previous lists of David's children. The significance of their prominent place in the structure of the narrative now becomes apparent. David may not have children from the daughter of Saul, but he does have an abundance of other children who can succeed him. The royal lineage of Saul has come to a conclusion, but the royal lineage of David is just beginning.

That David's confrontation with Michal occurs in an episode which reports on his initially abortive but ultimately successful attempt to bring the ark to the city of David is not without significance. It is likely no coincidence that the result of his attempt to regain possession of Michal also reaches resolution in this episode.

David's earlier request for the return of Michal invites comparison with his efforts in this episode to obtain the return of the ark. First, both attempts are undertaken on David's own initiative without prior divine approval. Second, both efforts have the potential benefit of legitimizing David's monarchy. Possession of the ark would theoretically guarantee him divine presence and protection, and possession of Michal would guarantee him the presence of a representative from the house of Saul and protection from further revolts by that faction. Third, both efforts result in failure so long as David is acting upon his own initiative. Whereas God eventually authorizes David's regaining possession of the ark, he apparently does not authorize his regaining possession of Michal. The narrative contains no story of birth to this barren woman, a story typical of the Hebrew scriptures.

This suggests that God himself will legitimate the monarchy of David. Legitimization will not come through an alliance with the house of Saul, nor will it continue through its progeny. As such, this incident foreshadows the final episode of this part of the narrative in which God establishes an eternal Davidic dynasty through an unconditional covenant with David.

The present episode thus continues to develop David's fortune in terms of an ongoing pattern of success and failure relative to David's consultation with the divine will. It shows the divine rejection of two more of David's unauthorized initiatives to secure and legitimize his kingdom. David cannot guarantee either a present or future monarchy by seizing possession of Michal. David is, however, given the monarchy, despite his flaws, because of divine favor. Its continued existence depends upon his own progeny, not upon any any who might have resulted from his opportunistic marriage to Saul's daughter.

David is again portrayed as a flawed but favored character. He is flawed in his understanding of how to establish his monarchy. Acting upon his own initiative and without divine authorization, he seeks to align himself with the legitimizing political and religious traditions. He negotiates for the return of Michal, his wife and Saul's daughter, and he inaugurates an expedition to regain possession of the ark. He initially fails in both efforts. Yet he is ultimately successful, as a result of divine favor. Divine favor, not his own human faithfulness, allows him to complete the transfer of the ark to Jerusalem. Favored not by Michal but by God, David has also procreated sons who will continue his monarchy.

Michal, however, is portrayed as a victimized but not vindicated character. She is the victim of David's flaws but has no share in his divine favor. This episode casts her not only as the victim of one of David's unauthorized attempts to legitimize his monarchy but also as the concomitant victim of the divine will for David. David's dynasty is ultimately authorized only by divine favor, not through a humanly initiated alliance with the rejected house of Saul. Hence her victimization by David's fortune in relation to Saul is not even vindicated by Yahweh. And she is further victimized by David's fortune in relation to Yahweh.

Michal's hostile response to David also echoes an earlier scene in 1 Sam. 18.6-9 which reports Saul's response to David following his introduction into Saul's court. Both father and daughter respond to David with hostility following a celebration in which David is praised and receives the attention of women.

Earlier (1 Sam. 18.6-9), Saul's love for David turned to hate when he heard the women of Israel sing, 'Saul has slain his thousands and David his ten thousands'. Angered by such prowess accorded David, Saul thinks, 'What more can he have but the kingdom?' Now that David has in fact acquired Saul's kingdom, Michal in turn despises David because he does not exhibit appropriate kingly decorum but instead exhibits himself before his servants' maids. In this she is her father's daughter. Neither father nor daughter ultimately tolerate either the behavior David inspires in other women of Israel or the self-proclaimed, divinely inspired behavior which he displays before them.

Whatever love Saul once felt for David was replaced by hatred and fear. Whatever love Michal once felt for him is now replaced by contempt and disdain. As a courtier, David did not fulfill Saul's expectations. As king, David does not fulfill Michal's expectations. Like her father before her, she acts upon her feelings and expresses them to David.

Although she could not control the previously portrayed situations in her relationship with David, she does have a measure of control in this one. Her estrangement from David is in part the result of her own actions and on her initiative. This then is her only protest against victimization by the fearful vengeance of her father, by the manipulative opportunism of her husband, and finally by the providential prerogative of her God.

Episode C' (2 Samuel 7.1-29)
The Dynastic Oracle—Divine Politics

In spite of Michal's hostility toward him, David has acquired a position of status in the eyes of the people. Even more importantly, David, unlike Saul, is the recipient of divine favor.

The final episode then resolves David's quest to establish, legitimize, and ensure a monarchy. It also is the final stage in the victimization of Michal.

David faithfully inquires whether to build a temple for the ark. Yahweh replies through Nathan that David will not build a house, i.e. a temple, for Yahweh, but that Yahweh will build a house, i.e. a dynasty, for David. This dynasty will, of course, be sustained by sons born to a wife of David other than Michal. Not only is Michal not the means by which David establishes his monarchy, but she will also not be the mother of his sons through whom his monarchy will become a dynasty.

These episodes in the narrative life of David and Michal show that the fate of Michal is inseparable from the fortune of David. David is portrayed as a humanly flawed but divinely favored character. He is flawed in his perception of how he is to achieve monarchial authority; yet he is divinely favored in his quest for it. Michal's fate is, for her part, to be portrayed as an ever victimized but never vindicated character. She is victimized by David's deteriorating relationship with Saul. Saul's vengeance initially unites her with David, but ultimately separates her from him. She is further victimized by David's own flawed ambition. This ambition reunites her with him as he attempts to legitimize his monarchy, but it also finally estranges her from him. Finally she is victimized by David's relationship with Yahweh, who favors David but will not allow David to determine the course of events on his own initiative and apart from the divine will. Divine will apparently ordains that the dynasty of David be established and sustained apart from any connections with the rejected house of Saul. Hence Michal, though ever victimized by the vicissitudes of David's fortunes, is never vindicated.

Walter Brueggemann

2 SAMUEL 6
(from *First and Second Samuel*)*

[251] The abrasive note of verse 16 [2 Sam. 6-16] prepares us for this last scene. We move from a public display to a private domestic conversation, a conversation between husband and wife. David had won Michal from Saul (1 Sam. 18.25-27). He had lost her (1 Sam. 25.44) and then claimed her a second time (2 Sam. 3.13-16). Michal is obviously important to David. As Saul's daughter she gives David legitimacy in the eyes of the old Saul party.

This is also a conversation between the voices of two conflicting factions. The narrator treats this conversation as part of the public account of power that has important implications for the future of governance in Israel. Michal is not only David's wife but is also something of a competitor as a Saulide. We do not know why Michal despises David. Perhaps his behavior is too reminiscent of Saul's behavior when he also was out of control (1 Sam. 10.9-13; 19.20-24). Perhaps Michal does not want a husband who is out of control in public.

The situation of being out of control, however, may be crucial to the function of the narrative. Flanagan suggests[1] that this out of control is the liminal point of transition between the restraints of the old tribal order and the possibilities of the new royal order.

> [The scene was] a period of release from usual constraints and an occasion for creative response. It was here that the structures of the former state no longer held sway and the new state of Davidic dynasty had not yet

* *First and Second Samuel* (Interpretation. A Bible Commentary for Teaching and Preaching; Louisville: John Knox, 1990), pp. 251-53.

1.   J.W. Flanagan, 'Social Transformation and Ritual in 2 Samuel 6', in C.L. Meyers and M. O'Connor (eds.), *The Word of the Lord Shall Go Forth* (Winona Lake, IN: Eisenbrauns, 1983), pp. 361-72 (368).

been fully established. The dialogue between Michal and David made explicit that the issue was the legitimacy of his house as leader of Israel.

The exchange between Michal and David is carefully crafted. She speaks sarcastically about 'the king' (v. 20). Perhaps she suggests that because she is the daughter of a king, she knows how a king should act, in contrast to David, who acts unworthily. Michal speaks with authority, with an assumed voice of strength. Her speech concerns 'honor' (glory), 'the [252] maids', and 'uncovering shamelessly' (v. 20). Her words drip with sarcasm and anger. David's response to her contains the same three elements, 'contemptible', 'the maids', 'honor' (glory) (v. 22). Michal believes David has forfeited the respect he must have to be ruler. David refutes her judgment by saying he may be contemptible in her eyes, but in the eyes of the maidens (and therefore of political opinion) he is more honored.

In the center of the exchange (v. 21), David makes the claim that establishes his preeminence and dismisses Michal and the entire Saulide claim. That verse begins and ends with 'before the LORD'. The words pile up to establish David's claim of legitimacy: 'Yahweh chose me...above...above...to be prince over...[over]'. David's 'dishonor' consists in glad yielding to the gift of Yahweh. David is utterly Yahweh's man, a fact Michal either cannot understand or refuses to acknowledge. The rhetoric of David's response (vv. 22-23) evidences complete reliance on Yahweh and, at the same time, a disdainful dismissal of Michal and an end to any reliance on Saulide legitimacy. The rhetoric thus succeeds in driving an irreversible wedge between Yahweh (and David) and the Saulide patrimony now expressed by Michal. It is almost inevitable that in verse 23 the narrator finally, tersely, and without pity dismisses Michal. The future now lies with David, who has broken with this Saulide attachment.

The entire exchange moves toward the Yahwistic claim at the center:

```
Michal:   honor
              maids
                 shamelessly
David:              before Yahweh
                       chose me above...above
                          prince over
                       before Yahweh
                    contemptible
                 maids
              honor
```

In the end, David is established by this confident rhetoric which refutes Michal. David uses Michal's words to dismiss her. Michal has no future, no claim on Israel, no prospect for life. In David's utter abandonment to dance and in his liturgic, social, royal extravagance, a new order is authorized, wrought out of unrestrained [253] yielding and worship. avid is freshly legitimate. The narrative of chapter 6 concerns a shift in power, a risk of worship that embraces Yahwism and permits new order. Popular use of this text to justify liturgic dance is quite beside the point, unless liturgic dance is seen as a means whereby power is reconfigured and new political legitimacy is received. The exchange with Michal reflects a total inversion. David, who is thought to be despised by Michal, is in fact honored in Israel and by Yahweh. Michal, who thinks she is in a position of strength, is dismissed by the narrative as barren and hopeless. There is something here of the exalted being humbled and the humbled being exalted (Mt. 23.12; Lk. 14.11; 18.14). David is indeed the one who humbles himself and who, by the power of God, is exalted. The text remembers and enacts the strange singing of Hannah (1 Sam. 2.7-8).

David J.A. Clines

X, X *BEN* Y, *BEN* Y:
PERSONAL NAMES IN HEBREW NARRATIVE STYLE*

[266] Abner is sometimes called Abner, sometimes Abner b. Ner; Jeroboam appears both as Jeroboam and as Jeroboam b. Nebat; Gideon is usually Gideon or Jerubbaal, except for three places where he is called Jerubbaal b. Joash. Shimei is four times Shimei b. Gera, and fourteen times simply Shimei, but Sheba is invariably Sheba b. Bichri on the eight occasions he is mentioned by name. Similar variations occur in the names of other personages in the historical books. Judging by the lack of attention this phenomenon receives in the commentaries one must assume that the choice of the name-forms 'X' or 'X *ben* Y' is generally thought to be arbitrary.

This view may be questioned, however. While it is impossible to be certain that one has correctly identified the reason for the use of one of the name-forms in a particular passage, it will become clear from the present study that a number of factors that influence the narrator's choice of name-form may be distinguished. That is, when both 'X' and 'X *ben* Y' are in use for an individual, it can be observed that the long form 'X *ben* Y' is used:

    a.   for clarity, to distinguish e.g. X *ben* Y from X *ben* Z
    b.   for reasons of narrative form
        (i)   to introduce a new character into a narrative[1]
        (ii) to introduce a new scene in which the character appears
        (iii) when a speaker mentions a character for the first time (an extension of (i) and (ii))

* Excerpted from *Vetus Testamentum* 22 (1972), pp. 266-87 (266, 269-72). Used by permission.

1. This, the most obvious reason for the full name-form, is the only one recognized even by I. Lande in her valuable *Formelhafte Wendungen der Umgangssprache im Alten Testament* (Leiden, 1949), p. 80.

   (iv) in initial or concluding summaries
 c. for formality
   (i) in legal formulations
[267] (ii) in prophetic oracles
   (iii) in other formal and official phrases
   (iv) in stereotyped formulas, e.g. royal synchronisms
 d. for contextual significance
   (i) where the relationship (of X to Y) is meaningful in the context
   (ii) where the name Y has some significance for the narrative

Each of these offers a quite natural occasion for the use of the long form, and most could be readily paralleled in modern English usage. What is noteworthy is that the use of the 'X *ben* Y' form can be reduced to so small a set of contexts. It is of course obvious that a clear distinction between the uses mentioned above cannot always be maintained: thus it could well be argued that the 'X *ben* Y' form in legal formulations is motivated by a need for clarity rather than for formality, but the analysis will, it is hoped, prove useful practically.

It needs to be remarked that the long form 'X *ben* Y' is not always employed when one of the situations analysed above arises; one can only hope to show why 'X *ben* Y' is used when it *is* used, and one cannot usually speculate about why it is *not* used...

[269] *Michal.* The name-forms used for Michal, daughter of Saul and wife of David, are particularly instructive:

1 Sam. 14.49 'The names of (Saul's) two daughters were these: [270] Merab the first-born and Michal the younger' (genealogical, contextually clarified, hence 'X' form).

18.20 'Michal daughter of Saul loved David'. This is doubly significant: on the one hand, David has been cheated of Merab, the elder daughter (v. 19), but now looks likely to succeed with the *other daughter of Saul*; and on the other hand, ch. 18 has been concerned with Saul's growing disenchantment with David, and in that setting it is dramatically promising that David falls in love with—the *daughter of Saul*. So this is type *d* i.

18.27 'Saul gave him his daughter Michal for a wife'; to 'Michal' there is added the determinative 'his daughter' because the relationship is significant. 'Daughter of Saul' is obviously impossible because 'Saul' already appears in the sentence.

18.28 'Saul saw and knew that Yahweh was with David, and that the daughter of Saul loved him, and Saul became yet more afraid of David'. 'Daughter of Saul' in a sentence of which 'Saul' is the subject would appear to annul the last observation made on the previous verse. But it is virtually certain that ומיכל בת־שאול is an orthographical error for וכי כל־ישראל,[1] for the MT presents the following difficulties: Saul already knew that Michal loved David (v. 20), and Michal has done nothing more to prove her love for him (though it could be argued that David's double bride-price proved *his* love for *her*), so nothing can be inferred from the emphatic 'saw and knew' (וירא וידע); why should Michal's love for David make Saul *afraid* of David? It could have been a further ground for his *hating* him, but Saul obviously fears a threat to his throne. Verse 28 emended in fact summarises the material of ch. 18 in reverse order: 'Yahweh was with David' recapitulates v. 14 (and perhaps also David's success with the Philistines, v. 27), while 'all Israel loved him' recapitulates vv. 6-8.

19.11 'Saul sent messengers to David's house to watch him that he might kill him in the morning. But Michal, David's wife, told him. . .' Here at the beginning of a new episode Michal is introduced in the form usual for mentioning a married woman: 'X wife of Y' (cf. e.g. [271] 'Deborah wife of Lappidoth', Judg. 4.4; 'Abigail, wife of Nabal', 1 Sam. 25.14). Thus we have an analogy to type *b* ii. However, it may be significant in the light of 2 Sam. 6, to be discussed below, that when Michal is attempting to defend David from Saul she is called 'wife of David' (thus possibly a further example of *d* i). In any case, the narrative 19.11-17 continues with just 'Michal'.

25.44 'Saul had given Michal his daughter, David's wife, to Palti b. Laish'. The relationships indicated by both long forms (which are functionally equivalent to 'XbY') are relevant to the story (type *d* i).

2 Sam. 3.13, 14 David agrees to make a covenant with Abner on condition that Abner brings 'Michal daughter of Saul' with him. David then sends messengers to Ishbosheth to say: 'Give me my wife

---

1. Older commentators occasionally saw that some explanation of the full name-form is called for, though their explanations were beside the point, e.g. '*Michal* is expressly called *Saul's daughter*, not thereby to characterize her as lacking in true-hearted piety (Keil), but to distinguish her in comparison with David's other wives, as highest in position' (C.F.D. Erdmann, *The Books of Samuel*, ed. C.H. Toy and J.A. Brooks [New York, 1877], p. 419); or, 'as king's daughter, she valued her royal dignity' (R. Payne Smith, *II Samuel* [Pulpit Commentary; London, 1906], p. 147).

Michal'. Why does he call her 'daughter of Saul' when speaking to Abner (through his messengers), but 'my wife' when speaking to Ishbosheth? For these reasons: he has no quarrel to pick with Abner and so avoids the technical legal question of whether Michal is the wife of David or Paltiel. It is a purely business arrangement between David and Abner, so David uses a neutral, and not an emotive, term for Michal. That may be sufficient explanation of the fact that he does not refer to her as 'my wife', but it may be asked: why does he call her 'daughter of Saul'? Surely Abner does not need to have spelled out for him who the Michal is whom David has an interest in! She is after all Abner's cousin's (or nephew's) daughter. The long form is not for clarity (type *a*). Conceivably, the sentence has the formality of a legal contract (type *c* i), or, perhaps, this is a simple case of the use of the long form when a person is first mentioned in conversation (*b* iii). But most probably this is a further instance of type *d* i: David will know that Abner has turned his back on Ishbosheth for good when he brings with him *Saul's daughter*; that will prove that Abner assents to David succeeding to Saul's throne.

In v. 14, on the other hand, David is saying in effect to Ishbosheth: she is *my* wife, not Paltiel's, and the responsibility for her being now with Paltiel is *yours,* since you are son and heir of your father who gave her to Paltiel (1 Sam. 25.44). (This explains, incidentally, why Ishbosheth is here called 'Ishbosheth son of Saul' [type *d* i] while elsewhere in the chapter he is simply 'Ishbosheth' [vv. 7, 8, 11, 15].) 'Michal daughter of Saul' would be ludicrous in this context, and 'Michal' alone would not beg the question so emphatically as David's well-chosen phrase does.

[272] 6.16 'Michal the daughter of Saul saw King David leaping and dancing before Yahweh, and she despised him in her heart'.

6.20 'David returned to bless his household, and Michal the daughter of Saul came out to meet David, and said: How the king of Israel honoured himself today...!'

6.21 'And David said to Michal: It was before Yahweh...'

6.23 'And Michal the daughter of Saul had no child to the day of her death'.

Here the normal pattern of name use is broken in two ways: first, Michal is called 'daughter of Saul' rather than 'wife of David', which one would expect for a married woman, especially since the episode concerns an altercation between man and wife; and secondly, the

'XbY' form is used three times, contrary to the usual practice of beginning a narrative with 'XbY' and continuing with 'X'. The reason for both these abnormalities is clear: Michal is not behaving as David's wife (contrast 1 Sam. 19) but as his opponent: she is acting like a true daughter of Saul,[1] and the narrator has spelled this out by writing 'Michal daughter of Saul' in the two places where her criticism of David is expressed (vv. 16, 20). Verse 23 presumably means: 'Here is the punishment for an opponent of David the divinely chosen king', and perhaps also: 'So David fails to legitimise his succession to Saul's throne through Michal'.

If it is correct that Michal's relationship with Saul is being emphasized by the use of the 'XbY' form (type *d* i), one may well wonder why it is not employed also in v. 21. The answer can only be that purely literary factors outweigh the significative value of 'XbY', e.g. one may sense that the narrative here gathers pace, which the long form would slow down, or perhaps preferably that attention now focusses on David, who is the subject of the sentence, and that it is therefore beside the point to stress the role that Michal is playing.

21.8 The reference here to Michal daughter of Saul as having borne five sons is almost universally agreed to be an error (cf. 6.23) for Merab (so LXX[L]).

---

1. Cf. e.g. S.R. Driver, *Notes on the Hebrew Text. . .of the Books of Samuel*[2] (Oxford, 1913), p. 352; J. Mauchline, *1 and 2 Samuel* (Century Bible; London, 1971), p. 302. J.J. Glück ('Merab or Michal', *ZAW* 77 [1965], pp. 72-81) alone retains 'Michal' at the cost of an unconvincing emendation of 'Adriel b. Barzillai the Meholathite' to 'Paltiel b. Laish'.

David J.A. Clines

THE STORY OF MICHAL, WIFE OF DAVID,
IN ITS SEQUENTIAL UNFOLDING*

I began to write this response by reading, not the estimable papers of our colleagues, but the whole of the biblical story of David, from the interest point of view of Michal. I felt like Tom Stoppard researching *Rosencrantz and Guildernstern are Dead*. It was an interesting novelty to review the totality of the David narrative from the perspective of a minor character, and it was rewarding to speculate on that character's personality and psychology.

But I had some misgivings about what I was doing, about what I was *meant* to be doing, about what—to be blunt—this session was meant to be doing. For I could not see that the *text* authorized me to take this myopic viewpoint, focusing so sharply on her that all the rest of the characters blurred, more or less, into a fuzzy background. Why, when there is an upfront David demanding attention for his posturings and declamations was I—like all of us here—standing, as Cheryl Exum puts it so well, in the street outside, watching her, inside, watching David.[1] There *is* a David story, but there is *not* a Michal story. What was I doing pretending there was a Michal story, solemnly reading the David story *as if* it was really only a Michal story?

I decided that this would have to be a *reading against the grain.* When you stroke a fabric against the grain you are surprised at its texture, it reflects light quite differently, it looks a different colour. When you plane wood against the grain, it takes more effort, but you make faster progress and dig deeper. Either way, with fabric and with

* Presented as a response to other papers to the Narrative Research on the Hebrew Bible Group, Society of Biblical Literature, Chicago, November 1988.
1. J. Cheryl Exum, *Arrows of the Almighty: Tragedy and Biblical Narrative* (Cambridge: Cambridge University Press, forthcoming), ch. 4.

wood, you have to end up by stroking or planing with the grain—for a good finish. A reading against the grain is what you do when you are a bit bored with the text and its textures and want to idly roughen it up a bit to see if it has any other textures or colours. A reading against the grain is what you do when you are feeling that your progress with the text is yielding diminishing returns and you want to bite deeper and more crudely by being insensitive to it for a little. But in the end, I know that I should not let my reading of David from Michal's point of view be determinative for my reading of David; I will have to end up with a reading *with* the grain, that reduces Michal back to a more proportionate size and that restores a David seen from as many different perspectives as the story offers. It *is* insensitive to the David story, isn't it, to imagine that it can be recast as a Michal story; but who says we have to be sensitive all the time? Cannot horseplay be a form of intimacy?

At any rate, this is an attempt to read the Michal story for Michal's sake and from her point of view, not David's.

1. Michal first enters the David story in a chapter where there is a veritable surfeit of love for David. 1 Samuel 18 opens with Jonathan loving David like his own soul, at its centre has all Israel and Judah loving David, proceeds to have Michal love David and concludes with Saul recognizing that Michal loves David. I would not say, with Richard Bowman, that the episode 'began abruptly' with the report of Michal's love for David (p. 103 above); I would see rather Michal's love as jostling for position among all the loves with which David is overwhelmed—none of which, incidently, he reciprocates. She is the only woman in Hebrew narrative who loves a man sexually,[1] and she is not loved by him first, not even at all. It takes some courage to step so far out of line, but what does it mean? Rather surprisingly, there is not a feminist among us who will argue that she sees what a good match David is and well judges that she is falling in love with the next king of Israel; that is to say, that her love is but the outward sign of an inward determination for political power and success. But if Saul is capable of urging the marriage in order to trick David to his death, why should his daughter not be capable of planning the marriage in order to set herself on the throne of Israel? But no; women are simple and loving; it is men who are devious and ambitious. That is the

1. Robert Alter, *The Art of Biblical Narrative* (London: George Allen & Unwin, 1981), p. 68 [118].

familiar stereotype perpetuated by the text, as Exum points out: 'men are motivated by ambition, whereas women respond on a personal level'.[1]

Well, perhaps that is true. And perhaps also the old romantic, and sexually stereotypical, interpretation was right, which I read in my old *Temple Dictionary of the Bible*: Michal was 'attracted...by the heroism and chivalry of the young soldier, a love reciprocated, if we may judge from the liberal fashion in which the strange dowry was provided', she quietly murmuring, no doubt, as she counts up to 200, 'He loves me, he loves me not'. (It is an even number, by the way.) What we cannot doubt is that, *whatever the motivation*, Michal loves David, and not as a brother. This is the leitmotif of the whole Michal story, and is, in my view, the neglected key to their last and cryptic exchange in 2 Samuel 6.

2. Only one scene elapses (19.1-7) before Michal has an opportunity to show whether she loves David or not. In the bedroom scene (19.11-17) that follows, Michal takes an utterly reckless action, breaking family loyalties and risking Saul's unpredictable anger, just because she is in love. All the other assessments that the commentators make are correct also: she *is* loyal to David, autonomous, and so on, no question. But they are wrong if they screen the basic motivation of the bride.

There is another line in this episode which no one remarks on, but which injects a troublesome note. Replying to Saul's petulant question why she has let David slip through his fingers, Michal says, 'He said to me, "Let me go; why should I kill you?"' It is not too surprising that in inventing words for the soldierly David she should have him threatening her with violence; this is a woman trying to talk gruffly and swagger like her man. But why should she say, 'He said, "Let me go"'? How could David have needed her to *let* him go? How could she have *prevented* him? She would not have been putting these words into David's mouth, I think if she did not somehow realize that what is happening is not that she is saving David's life but that she is in fact, quite precisely, *letting him go*. She loves him, but he does not love her—not enough for it to be mentioned, at any rate; in escaping from

1. J. Cheryl Exum, 'Murder They Wrote: Ideology and the Manipulation of Female Presence in Biblical Narrative', in A. Bach (ed.), *The Pleasure of her Text. Feminist Readings of Biblical and Historical Texts* (Philadelphia: Trinity Press International, 1990), pp. 45-68 (50; p. 82 in this volume).

Saul he escapes from his marriage. We know that, from the subsequent course of the narrative, for he never returns to Michal; Michal's
words know that too, even if Michal herself does not yet quite know
it.

3. Just one scene later, David is back at Gibeah for three days, con-
versing with Michal's brother Jonathan, and taking a tearful farewell
of him (20.41). But neither of them mentions Michal. They kiss one
another, which is more than David and Michal have ever done. David
is still respectful enough of Saul to have Jonathan give his apologies
for his absence from the dinner table (20.6), and uncertain enough
about Saul's real intentions toward him to lurk around Gibeah for
three days while Jonathan finds out. Where then is Michal in all this?
Does she know that David is within a bowshot of her bedroom window these days and nights? Where is the gallant lover? What goes
down a rope can just as easily go up. But David has no more business
with Michal. She will have to manage with the teraphim and the goat's
hair.

4. The very next scene finds David at Nob with Ahimelech the
priest, demanding the holy bread. David is a considerable liar, of
course, but there is a ring of truth about his speech when he maintains
that he and his young men are perfectly entitled to eat the holy bread
because they assuredly[1] always keep clear of women (fountains of impurity, he might have said), when they go on a military expedition.

Only one question now needs to be asked: When is David *not* out on
a military expedition? We first met him in ch. 16 as the armour-
bearer of Saul (16.21), saw him in ch. 17 as the slayer of Goliath, and
read in the following chapter that David 'went out [to battle] and was
successful wherever Saul sent him' (18.5), that he was feted by the
women as the slayer of ten thousands, that he led his warriors into
battle over and over (he 'goes out and comes in before them', 18.13;
cf. 18.16), that he killed two hundred Philistines (18.27), and that as
often as the Philistines came out to battle David had more success over
them than all the other servants of Saul (18.30). And we hear in the
next chapter that there was war again and we see David once more out
and about fighting Philistines (19.8).

You can't, under these circumstances, be a great warrior *and* a

1. *kî 'im*, 'with the force of an oath' (S.R. Driver, *Notes on the Hebrew Text
and the Topography of the Books of Samuel* [Oxford: Clarendon Press, 1913],
p. 174).

great lover. The king's daughter must have known this when she first set her sights on David; but there would still have been a conflict between her ideals and his. David has resolved the conflict by deciding against Michal; male bonding is his preference, and it has the decided advantage that it carries no ritual impurity with it.

I observe, incidentally, that this narrative, in which Michal is not actually present, had better be regarded nevertheless as an important element in the Michal story.

5. In the *next* chapter David has accepted that he will have to live outside the confines of the land of Israel for a time. In a rare glimpse of David as son, we find him sequestering his parents with the king of Moab until he should know what God has in store for him (22.3). Michal obviously does not qualify as one of the family, even though there is evident danger to her from Saul but none that we know of to David's parents. In no way can I consent to Richard Bowman's view that David is 'forced by circumstances to desert her' (p. 108 above); there are no circumstances that David cannot rearrange to his own advantage here. Michal has simply dropped out of David's reckoning.

6. David has not dropped out of Saul's reckoning, however. In the next chapter Saul is still getting reports of all David's movements, and is obsessively seeking him 'every day' (23.14). Jonathan manages to keep up contact too, visiting him at his hideout in Horesh (23.16). But there are no messages for Michal.

7. In the next chapter Saul and David get close enough for David to cut Saul's robe, and Saul admits that David is set fair to become the next king of Israel (24.20). Given that recognition, Saul's first move is to beg David to swear that he 'will not cut off Saul's descendants after [him]' (24.21). This includes Michal. From which we infer that Saul too knows how it stands with David and Michal. In every chapter since she was last mentioned, Michal has been present in her absence.

8. Perhaps it is not so very surprising that in the next chapter after this recognition that Michal is to David nothing more than a member of the house of Saul David encounters his next woman. Abigail takes a risk associating with this outlaw, even if Saul sees in him the next king; but after Nabal she can hardly do worse for herself, and with alacrity (25.42) accedes to David's peremptory wooing: 'David has sent us', say the messengers, 'to take you to him as his wife' (25.40). Perhaps Abigail's eagerness to ally herself with David would have been tempered somewhat had she realized that she was entering a

ménage à trois, of which the narrator breathlessly informs us. She
went after the messengers of David, says he, and became his wife,
we'et 'ahino'am laqach david, as if to say, and so did Ahinoam; and
the two of them, *sh'teyhen*, became his wives, not one after the other
or each in her own right, but the two of them, like a couple of clogs.

This is the time, is it not, for setting the record straight on Michal.
By this point, Saul had given Michal to Palti, says the narrator
(25.44). It is not that 'her romantic affection of early days was probably undermined by David's marriages with Abigail and Ahinoam';[1]
for her marriage to Palti is almost certainly prior to David's to his
two new wives. Nor is it, as S.R. Driver wrote, betraying his sex and
his age, that here we have a hint of the reason why David remarried:
he had been 'deprived of Michal'.[2] Not so; David has deprived *himself*
of Michal.

At the juncture, then, at which David sets himself up with two wives
as a man of class and property (which he can afford to do now, on
Abigail's money), Michal's fate is worth only a footnote. Her last reported deed had been the risky act of lying to her father in order to
save David's life; but since then David has done nothing but ignore
her.

9. Michal's ghostly presence may be glimpsed again in ch. 27
where David and his men move to Gath, 'every man with his household and David with his two wives, Ahinoam of Jezreel and Abigail of
Carmel, Nabal's widow' (27.3). Why are we being told this?, we
wonder. We know well enough who David's two wives are, and where
they come from, classy districts. Are we being reminded that when
David last moved house, to Moab (22.3), no wife accompanied him
then?

10. Three chapters on, and David's two wives make another slightly
cryptic appearance. Here they have been taken captive from Ziklag by
the Amalekites (30.5). Robert Alter spots the oddity:

> David's reaction is reported with the most artful ambiguity: 'David and the
> people with him cried out and wept until they had no more strength to
> weep, David's two wives had been taken captive, Ahinoam the Jezreelite
> and Abigail, wife of Nabal the Carmelite. And David was greatly dis-
> tressed, for the people wanted to stone him, for all the people were embit-

---

1. W. Ewing and J.E.H. Thomson, 'Michal', in *The Temple Dictionary of the
Bible* (London: J.M. Dent & Sons, 1910), p. 175 [463].
2. Driver, *Notes on Samuel*, p. 204.

tered over their sons and daughters' (1 Sam. 30.4-6).

First there is the public expression of grief, the long fit of weeping, in which David naturally participates. Then we are informed that his two wives are among the captives, and in the paratactic flow of the verses, with no sentence divisions in the original text, it is easy enough to read this as cause and effect: 'David's wives had been taken. . . and David was greatly distressed'. The idiom I have translated as 'distressed' (*vatetzer le*) can refer either to a feeling of distress or to the objective condition of being in straits, in physical danger, and the next clause, 'for the people wanted to stone him', pirouettes on the ambiguity and turns around to the second meaning. Where we thought we had a spontaneous expression of David's grief over the loss of his wives, we are again confronted with David the political leader in a tight corner, struggling to save both himself and the situation. . . It is not that we are led to infer any clear absence of personal feeling in David. . . [1]

No clear absence of personal feeling, hmm? At any rate, David rescues 'his two wives' (30.18). But I cannot help but think 'Michal' when I hear 'wife' for David; why can I not let the past be buried?

11. David's wives next appear in 2 Samuel 2, in another house-moving incident, this time to Hebron. Why do we read, '. . . and his two wives also, Ahinoam of Jezreel, and Abigail the widow of Nabal of Carmel' (2.2)? Is there some uncertainty about who precisely his two wives are? I keep thinking of the happily married man who loves to introduce his wife as his 'first wife', playing with the possibility that she is his ex-wife in order to savour the fact that she is not. Is the reader not being nudged, when reading of David's 'wives', into saying, 'Ah, yes, *those* wives'—which implies, not some other wife. Perhaps Michal is not so far from the narrator's thoughts as she is from David's.

12. In the next chapter, still located at Hebron, we stumble across a list of David's six sons born there, a list that tells us more than we want to know about David and his women, a list that puts in new perspective the story of Michal, even though she is not so much as mentioned. What is never pointed out in the scholarly literature about this list of sons is that they all have different mothers. This does not show that David has six wives, but that he has six wives *one after the other*. They remain his wives, so he is technically polygamous; but if he were a sincere polygamist, and not a serial monogamist, his wives

---

1. Alter, *The Art of Biblical Narrative*, pp. 121-22 [in the original publication, not reprinted in this volume].

would on average be producing more than one son each.

I conclude that David has difficulty, as they say, in forming stable relationships with women. He is keen on acquiring them and using them, but, unlike Solomon, he does not *love* them. I blame the male bonding, but probably that is just the symptom, not the cause. He doesn't get tired of Jonathan, not even of Saul, and certainly not of Absalom. Michal is more unlucky; she is a woman.

13. As if to subvert my point, in this very chapter David demands to have Michal back, first from Abner and secondly from Ishbosheth, her brother and king over all Israel except Judah. To Abner he refers to her as 'Saul's daughter' (3.13) and to Ishbosheth as 'my wife' (3.14). But the real question is, Who *is* Michal to David now? What is it that he wants back?

When David calls her 'Saul's daughter', it is not a case of his help-fully making clear to Abner which of the many Michals of the land he requires to be brought to him; Abner would not be in any uncertainty. *Which* is Michal is not the question; *what* is Michal *is* the question. For this juncture in the story she is *Saul's*. Abner has just offered to defect from Saul to David, so it is not remarkable that David should require him to bring with him, as a token of his good faith, a piece of Saul's property.

And in calling her 'my wife', David immediately makes clear in what sense he understands that term: she is 'my wife, whom I bought with the bride price of a hundred Philistine foreskins' (the other hundred being a makeweight, apparently). She is not only Saul's property, she is David's property; on both grounds he is entitled to her.

It would be counterproductive to demand her *from Ishbosheth* on the ground that she is Saul's daughter. Ishbosheth cannot be so stupid as to mistake the symbolic significance of David possessing Michal, but if David doesn't make it too blatant, he can afford to ignore it. What he cannot deny is the truth about ownership; and so he accedes to David's demands (3.15). With Abner, on the other hand, the question of David's ownership of Michal is neither here nor there, since the matter at hand is whether Abner genuinely intends to come over to David, and what needs to be made clear is that Abner must steal something from Saul for David.

So those commentators are correct, in my opinion, who see David's demand as a political move to reinforce his claims to the kingship. McCarter, I see, thinks that the narrator wants to disassociate David from any such ambition and that what he wants from Abner is nothing more than a proof of good faith. But that does not explain why it is *Michal* that David demands of Abner. McCarter also thinks that the narrator wants to present David in the best possible light, arguing, for example, that in some way David's remarriage to his first wife cannot be a breach of (Deuteronomic) law.[1] But the facts are a little more complex; for, while the narrator obviously wants to absolve David of responsibility for the *death of Abner*, he takes no trouble at all to disguise David's appalling treatment of his women.[2]

14. It is only three chapters later that Michal has her showdown and shootout with David, out in the street, for all to see and hear (6.20-23). The conflict that began in the bedroom ends in the street. 'It doesn't take a psychologist', as Cheryl Exum puts it so nicely, 'to recognize that David's attire, or lack of it, is not the real issue.'[3] Quite. But what is? Not, I submit, the kingship, as Exum would have it. That is *David's* perspective; that is how *he* would like this altercation to be regarded, as a conflict between the king that *is* and the representative of the king that *was*. For on that score David is assured of an easy victory over Michal, and Michal would be under a misapprehension if she thought that there was any mileage left in the defunct kingship of her father. No, *Michal's* perspective is different.

Michal indeed addresses David as 'the king of Israel', not 'you', but that doesn't make kingship the topic; it simply points up the irony that a king can be so common. The weight of her criticism lies entirely in the fact that David has 'uncovered' himself in the sight of 'the maid-servants of his servants'. Since we know that David is clad only in a

---

1. P. Kyle McCarter, Jr, *1 Samuel* (AB, 8; Garden City, NY: Doubleday, 1980), p. 115. Zafrira Ben-Barak, 'The Legal Background to the Restoration of Michal to David' (pp. 74-90 above), argues that David's remarriage to Michal is perfectly legal. She adduces Mesopotamian texts where a man, captured in war and forcibly exiled, eventually returns home and finds his wife remarried. He may reclaim her, though any children of her second marriage remain those of her second husband. It is hard to believe that David's fleeing from Saul is regarded in the narrative as anything comparable, even if we could believe that these Mesopotamian legal texts are likely to reflect Israelite custom of the time of David or of the author of 1 Samuel.

2. Even McCarter, who has something of a soft spot for David, can speak of his 'increasingly problematic relationships with the women in his life' (*1 Samuel*, p. 188).

3. Exum, 'Murder They Wrote', p. 184 [52].

skimpy loincloth (6.14), we can be pretty sure that David is exposing himself, and not just 'some part of his thighs or legs', as Matthew Poole's commentary of 1685 had it.[1] It is not the whirling and leaping that is offensive to her, and not merely her 'woman's impatience of the absurd' that makes her despise him.[2] Her disgust is not aesthetic, it is sexual. She cannot bear to see the man she has loved flaunt himself as sexually available—presumably, that is, to anyone but her. His self-exposure earns the acclaim of the bystanders, but is in fact a humiliation to him, if only he could recognize the fact; and it is a humiliation to her as well, because it proclaims David's indifference in matters of sexual loyalty. It is David's 'sexual vulgarity'[3] that she is protesting against, certainly; but it is more than that: it is his neglect of her.

There is another element in Michal's reproach: it is that David is flaunting himself 'in the eyes of the maidservants of his servants'. Whom is she thinking of? Perhaps, she means, any hapless lass who is stood watching the procession; but is there not here rather the implication that David is attracted by common women? McCarter for one does not hesitate to see an aristocratic tone here, as if Michal thinks no one but a king's daughter is good enough for David. This may be so, though we may well wonder whether there was a lot of aristocratic hauteur around at the rustic court of King Saul. It is enough to see in Michal a woman who has truly loved but who is now well and truly scorned, a woman therefore who is contemptuous of the other women who think they have a secure place in this man's affections. The only dignity left to her lies in her superior knowledge of what kind of man this David is.

David does not mistake Michal's meaning. On the one hand, he tries to deflect it by maintaining that there was nothing sexual about his self-exposure: 'It was before the Lord', he says, which means to say: it was a purely religious dance, and I am not going to be told by anyone I cannot throw myself into ecstatic religious activity. 'I *will* make merry before the Lord', he cries, as if to say, 'whether you like it or not'. But on the other hand, David meets the criticism head on, roundly affirming that if this is self-humiliation, Michal hasn't seen anything yet: 'I will make myself yet more contemptible than this, and

1.   *A Commentary on the Holy Bible* [r.p. London: Banner of Truth Trust, 1962], I, p. 598.
2.   N.J.D. White, 'Michal', p. 286 [363].
3.   Exum, 'Murder They Wrote', p. 183 [51].

be even more despised by you'—but I don't care. As long as he is esteemed by the maidservants of whom Michal has spoken he will be happy, no matter how contemptible Michal finds him. So his dancing is not just before the Lord, it is not just a matter of personal religious ecstasy. David finds religious ecstasy a good way of impressing women, and it matters very much to him whether they admire him or not. Michal has announced that she doesn't admire him, but David can get along quite happily with those 'maidservants', if that is what she likes to call them, who do admire him.

Michal is childless to the day of her death, at least childless by David. As is often observed, the text makes no causal connection between David's riposte and her childlessness, and the question is often debated whether it is David or God who keeps her childless. I was surprised not to find any commentator arguing that it is Michal herself who refuses David, and I ask: is it likely that a woman who so despises a man is going to bear his children? And in any case, even if it is David who refuses Michal and not Michal who refuses David, is it reasonable to speak of David's retaliation as 'giving her "no child"'?[1] Was her childlessnesss really one of the 'tragic consequences for Michal'[2] of her quarrel with David? Is she not better off to have no child of hers locked in unlovely struggle for the throne, to put no son to the risk of an untimely death at the hands of power-crazed stepbrothers? If it is really true that women without children were dishonoured (how many had Esther, or Vashti, or the dark lady of the Song of Songs?), how serious can that dishonour have been compared with the double dishonour Michal has already suffered, of being a deserted wife, who is then ripped from her second husband to be kept as property under virtual house arrest?

15. It is a pity that we shall never know whether the last word on Michal has been said by the end of 2 Samuel 6 and whether the reference to her in 21.8 and to her five sons slaughtered in the end by David is in fact a scribal error for her sister Merab. The reference to the father as Adriel b. Barzillai the Meholathite, whom we already know from 1 Sam. 18.19 to be the husband of Merab seems to clinch the matter—unless perhaps the explanation of the Targum and Jerome, followed by the KJV, that Michal brought up Merab's child-

1.   D. Harvey, 'Michal', p. 204 [373].
2.   J. Cheryl Exum, 'Michal', in *Harper's Bible Dictionary* (ed. P. Achtemeier; New York: Harper & Row, 1985), p. 634.

her days childless, thanks to none other than the philoprogenitive David.

16. The dynamics of the relation between Michal and David can be reconstituted to a surprising degree, given the paucity of our materials. Perhaps in the end they cast a needed light—or rather, a shadow—on the character of David. I should like Richard Bowman's assessment of the two to be opened up to further discussion: is it true that Michal is 'ever victimized... [but] never vindicated' (p. 120 above), or is not her dignity and her sarcasm sufficient vindication, in the eyes of readers at least? And is David a character who is 'flawed but favored', or is he not rather a truly nasty piece of work who has too many lucky breaks?

Edith Deen

KING SAUL'S DAUGHTER—DAVID'S FIRST WIFE
(from *All the Women of the Bible*)*

[96] Though a woman of exceptional fortitude in time of trouble, Michal, King Saul's daughter and David's first wife, lacked a genuine appreciation of her husband's religious zeal. It is to her credit, however, that she aided David in his early struggles long before he became king of Israel.

Her older sister Merab had first been promised by her father to [97] David after he returned victorious over Goliath, the giant champion of their enemies the Philistines. She was to be his reward for the victory. But King Saul failed to fulfill his promise. He gave his daughter Merab to Adriel, the Meholathite.

Next, we learn from the Scripture, 'Michal Saul's daughter loved David' (1 Sam. 18.20). She was the younger daughter. It is easy to suppose that she and David had often met when her brother Jonathan, a great admirer of David, had brought him home. And to a king's young daughter the brave and strong David became a great hero.

Michal must have had a gentle mother. Her name was Ahinoam. But her father Saul was an obstinate, jealous, and murderous man. He disliked David and began to plan how Michal might be the stumbling block to David's promising career.

As he began a plot against David, Saul sent the flattering word by servants to David that he wanted him for his son-in-law. Humble as he was at this time, young David sent word back to King Saul that it was no light thing to be a king's son-in-law.

Then it was that Saul said David could have Michal if he would go out and kill one hundred Philistines and bring back the foreskins to him. Saul was sure that David would be killed himself, but David sur-

* *All the Women of the Bible* (New York: Harper & Bros, 1955), pp. 96-100. Used by permission.

prised him. He brought back the foreskins of two hundred Philistines. And Michal became his wife.

Saul, however, did not cease plotting against David. One day, as his unsuspecting son-in-law sat entertaining him with music, a tall spear sped like lightning from Saul's hand toward David. But it missed its aim and went harmlessly over his head. David fled and escaped.

Michal, probably distraught at her father's continued efforts to take her husband's life because she was still in love with him, began to plan how she could save him. Messengers had already come to her house telling her that they would slay David in the morning.

Warning David of his approaching danger, Michal let him down [98] through a window, and he escaped. When her father commanded David to come to him, she sent back word that David was sick, but her father, still persistent, asked his messengers to deliver the sick David on his bed.

David was already well on his way to safety when Michal, to appease her father's wrath, took a large image resembling a recumbent figure, put it in David's bed, and then made a pillow of red goat's hair. The bed with what appeared to be a sleeping figure was taken before her father, and when he discovered the trick his daughter had played on him he asked why she had deceived him.

Clever woman that Michal was, she evaded her father's question, telling him that David had said to her, 'Let me go; why should I kill thee?' (1 Sam. 19.17). When Michal dared to defy a madman king like her father in order to save her husband, she must have possessed real courage.

We have no record that Michal had David's faith in God's protecting power. She no doubt believed in idols. When she placed the image in David's bed, to resemble his recumbent figure, it appear that she had other idols near at hand. Commentators, however, question the size of Michal's idol that she placed in the bed. It had to be large, in order that it might resemble a reclining figure. And teraphim, like the one Rachel had carried away from her father's house, were small enough to be put in a saddle bag. There is some discrepancy in this passage of Michal's idol but enough evidence to lead us to think she was not a believer in David's God of strength and mercy.

For a long time after this David remained an outlaw in exile from his wife's father. It would be almost impossible for a marriage to survive under such conditions. After some time had passed, King Saul arranged for Michal to marry Phalti, also called Phaltiel. Michal probably went with him to live in his town of Gallim.

Evidently some years passed before David and Michal ever met again. These were polygamous times, and David married Abigail, [99] the woman of good understanding and a stanch believer in God. He also took another wife, Ahinoam of Jezreel.

When David became Saul's successor as king, he demanded that his wife Michal be returned to him. This was done. As he marched up to Jerusalem with the ark of the Covenant accompanied by 30,000 chosen men of Israel, Michal looked from a window and saw David, girded in a linen ephod, leaping and dancing before the newly restored ark. Not understanding David's religious zeal, Michal thought her husband was acting in an undignified manner.

When David saw that the ark was set in the tabernacle prepared for it, he returned to bless his own household. Then Michal came out to meet him and mocked him scornfully, saying, 'How glorious was the king of Israel today, who uncovered himself today in the eyes of the handmaids of his servants, as one of the vain fellows shamelessly uncovereth himself!' (2 Sam. 6.20).

Because David obviously wore nothing but the ephod, a custom not uncommon in these times, Michal 'despised him in her heart' (2 Sam. 6.16). We might also infer that David's acts had reflected on his wife's queenly dignity because he had mingled so freely with the common people.

There must have been other reasons, too, for Michal's resentment of David. When he demanded her back after he became king, she did not forget that he was taking her away from a husband with whom she must have spent several years. This husband, Phalti, we learn, wept as he followed Michal to Bahurim, where she was taken from him (2 Sam. 3.16). But as king, David could demand whomever he chose, even a former wife who had married again.

The final record of the Michal–David love affair comes when David curtly tells Michal that he does not care for her opinion about the ephod and that he trusts the common sense of the maids and their loyalty to understand his motive. There then follows the phrase, 'Therefore Michal the daughter of Saul had no child unto the day of her death' (2 Sam. 6.23).

[100] A rather conflicting passage appears later, in 2 Sam. 21.8, when the five sons of Michal are mentioned. Scholars seem to be con

vinced that this is a scribal error, that these were not Michal's sons but the sons of her sister Merab, and that she reared them as her own after her sister's death.

Summing up the Bible portrait of Michal, first we see a young, beautiful, loving, courageous girl. But at the end we see a disillusioned, bickering woman with an inner poverty of spirit, one oppressed with many tragedies.

Not only had she been torn from two husbands, but if she lived long enough she had seen the five sons or nephews she had reared hanged in revenge for her father's wickedness. Also she had seen her father rejected by God, troubled by an evil spirit, and then killed by falling on his own sword. And his head was sent among many villages of the Philistines.

How could there be any happiness for his daughter Michal, who, like her father, had rejected God in her life?

Robert C. Ehle

THE GRACE OF GOD*

[56] *The following story is told by the daughter of the biblical King
Saul. She was David's first wife, given to him by her father before
Saul went mad and began his plots against David's life. She is telling
her story as an old woman, during the reign of Solomon, the son of
David and Bathsheba.*

> Listen to the voice of the old woman,
> Hear her song, you strong men of Zion:
> You are a great nation,
> A mighty folk feared and sung
> in kings' halls and town squares.
> Let the lion watch for the snare
> and the wolf beware
> the shepherd's sling.
> Let them learn the rabbit's fear
> and the doe's frail hope.
> Listen to the plaint
> of the barren old woman.

When I came back, he said to me, 'Was Paltiel a good man?'
'A good man? Yes', I said. 'But he was not a blessed man.'
'But he was pious', my husband said, 'which is all the Lord re-
quires.' He was old enough now for a beard, and very handsome.

A madness fell on my father, as it did on us all, when the shepherd
boy sauntered out of Bethlehem, still stinking of sheep shit, but
auburn-haired like a noble. When David appeared in the Valley of
Elah, God fell for him like a schoolgirl; and I, the schoolgirl, found a

* In *Tikkun. A Bimonthly Jewish Critique of Politics, Culture & Society* 3/4
(July/August 1988), pp. 56-60. Used by permission of the publisher, *Tikkun,* 5100
Leona St, Oakland CA 94619, USA.

false god. To kill a giant with one stone! He said he'd seen coyotes bigger than that back home.

I watched him play the harp before my father. He played the hill songs. Saul would begin to sing with him, because they were songs he'd known himself growing up. They were both hillbillies. They would sing songs together none of the rest of us had ever heard of. They were such bumpkin tunes; only a king or a shepherd could have sung them. They sang one song about secret lovers and perilous meetings, with a chorus that twanged over and over again, 'Where is my duckling, my rabbit, my rock-dove? Her father has hid her in the wine cellar.' They sang so seriously, but the rest of us did all we could to keep sad faces. I was too young to pretend, and I finally began to giggle. When I saw others begin to smile, I laughed out loud and finally stopped the song.

'Oh, I'm so sorry, but really, I—Father,...'

But he didn't look at me. He looked at David. The boy had turned away, blushing. And this is how my father showed us we were in love.

* * *

Four new wives were brought to Solomon today. They were all from Endor, in the north, a poor village. Their marriage to the king will bring wealth and honor to their families, and very likely there is a baby brother or sister somewhere who will now have enough to eat. They will each spend one night alone with the king, and after that they will live like very comfortable nuns. I myself have gained back a certain measure of respect among some of the palace women. They come to me for counsel. Before he died, David requested that his son build me a house outside the new city. It is very small and made of clay, not stone, but it is a good place for an old woman. I have never had an audience with Solomon. We never spoke together when he was a boy.

They say my brother's love for David was like a woman's. Saul would have loved him like that if Saul had not been king. My brother saw what all Israel knew as soon as David brought down the giant— we had asked too soon for a king.

The two of them rode into battle together, David carrying my brother's standard and Jonathan shouting, 'Hail, Philistines! Israel salutes you with a gift of a giant's [57] bane!' They were young and strong and terrible. The two of them would scatter a legion only by shouting their names.

My brother and I took turns saving his life after my father went mad. I said to Jonathan once, 'You know what the people are saying'.

'They want David to be the next king.'

He was older and seldom took anything I said seriously, but at this time he was quiet. Then he said, 'I can see you love him. I love him, too, but you will be the blessed one, because you will bear his child. In him, the lines of David and Saul will be joined. It will be a great dynasty.'

'You wouldn't give up the crown!'

'How would I reign over the Lord's Anointed?'

David and I began to walk together. In the fields outside Gilgal, he showed me how to tell when there were jackals close by.

'Are you ever afraid?' I asked him.

'The hand of the Lord has always been with me', he said. 'I will only fear when he withdraws his hand.'

My father began to take Jonathan with him to war, and to leave David behind. I went to David one day and told him to take me riding. 'You've only ridden with my brother', I said. 'Today the enemy will hear "David and Michal"'.

We rode together on my father's mare and David said nothing as we rode out from the town, farther and farther into the wilderness. The land rose, and finally in the distance we could see Jericho, the great city.

'I've never seen it before', I said. 'Is it true the walls fell merely at the sound of the trumpets?'

'They fell at the Lord's command.'

I leaned back into his arms and he cradled me as gently as a mother lion. He began to rock, and he hummed 'Hear Us, O Shepherd of Israel'. It was late in the day, and the sun was low on the hills behind the city. We watched it go down, and, as it disappeared, we turned back to Gilgal. When we were back at the king's gate, it was dark. He turned my face to his and kissed me.

'You will be my wife', he said. 'And I will be the next king of Israel.'

* * *

When my father was sure David wanted me for a wife, he thought up a scheme to rid himself of his rival. To marry a king's daughter, David would have to slay one hundred Philistines. My father was too silly to be a king. He thought the boy would die in battle. The boy who had not died using a slingshot against a giant, whom women made up songs for at wells, whom men fell on swords for rather than fight. He could have brought down fifty alone just by walking over to Gath and shouting his name.

But you slew them like a true zealot. For a man who could play the harp so well, who had such a gift for words, you had a gift for garish display as well. Into the great-house you strode with a satchel of some kind of game; you looked like you'd come back from nothing more than a hunt. The Spirit of the Lord was so much upon you, you never thought about what the real idea had been. You marched up all sweaty—smiled and in front of the king dumped out what looked like a lot of bloody little mouse hides.

'*Two* hundred!' you shouted, and turned beaming to face all of us. My father bent down close to the skins and when he saw what they were, he blanched and covered his mouth and ran out of the hall. It was a gift for the Lord. You'd circumcised each of the fallen.

While I was still a young bride, my father stole me back from David's house. He felt he'd traded a daughter without a return, and because he was king, he was allowed to reconsider. Although I was still David's wife, I was now betrothed to Paltiel, the Pious. It was the first time I knew what it is like to be born a woman, to grow up and never be treated like anything but a child. To hope, at least, to be a wealthy child. But Paltiel was not wealthy. He was a poor farmer, an old friend of my father's, chosen as my new husband for his loyalty and absolute lack of influence. His wife of forty years had died not long before I'd come, and you could see by the expression on his face when he looked at me that she had not been a pretty woman—it had been a long time since she'd been young.

When I was first brought to his house, he touched his forehead to the floor and gasped out a whisper: 'My Lady'. He never stopped calling me that as long as we lived together. And the corners of his mouth didn't stop twitching, either. I insisted on bringing my hand-maid and a cook. Even these women he bowed to and called 'Lady', and although at first they looked down on him for it, calling him an old hill donkey behind his back, his country manners gradually won them over. I think he knew he was my cook's uncle. He wasn't told I'd been taken from David, and I never talked to him. He was simple, but I think he knew there were politics involved. The king's business was the king's. He was an unfortunate man, a man who had prayed, I'm sure, for another wife to share his old age. He was given a royal shrew.

I wouldn't let him touch me. I slept at his feet, but he never once tried to come to me. Early in the mornings he would get up and say his prayers, as my husband [58] had done, but he never woke me. In the evenings before supper, he would recite what he knew of the laws and after supper he would interpret them.

I lived seven years with him. Of course, by the end we had begun to talk. One night, after supper, I asked, 'Was your first wife as much of a shrew as I am?'

He laughed much more easily than he ever had. He said, 'She was a rock badger, my wife. She was fierce and fat and she got the best prices at the market because she scared the merchants to trembling. I once had to hold my little niece in my arms for an hour, because Zillah had told her that the next time the little girl stole a piece of bread from the hotstone, she would gobble off her hand like it was a chicken wing!

'And she wasn't religious either. Her mother was an Ammonite. She had no use for a god she couldn't see, and the ones she could see seemed silly to her! She would go with me once a year to Shiloh to sacrifice, only so she could trade the next day. Oh, such a woman! But we loved each other, My Lady. We grew old together happy.'

He smiled and stopped, and as he looked at a guttering lamp and kept smiling, the silence came back into the house like a draft. Except for prayers, he had not said so much at one time to me while I'd lived with him. He wondered, I knew, whether he'd said too much. Or had sounded too happy.

'Mickele', he turned to me, bold and forgiving, 'I have had a good life, little child.' He would have touched my hand, I think, but finally turned his face back to the flame and patted the side of his chair. 'And your life will be happy again, too, someday.'

After my father died, his general, Abner, tried to make a deal with David. He came to Paltiel's house one day as Paltiel was working in his field and said I was to come with him. I was to be restored to my rightful husband. When Paltiel heard he had been living with another man's wife, he plucked his beard and said it couldn't be true. I mounted a donkey and he ran up to me, crying, 'Sweet Lady, Lady Michal, my evening star! No, Mickele!' But as he reached out to my robe, a soldier struck him broadside with his sword.

As we rode away from the village, we heard shouts behind us and turned to see Paltiel running in his torn cloak. Blood ran down the side of his face, and he shouted 'Don't do this to an old man!'

He followed us as far as Bahurim, shouting all the way. The people of Bahurim took him for an old mumbler and stopped him in their streets when we shouted back to them. The last I saw of him, he was sitting in the dust, with a few children and dogs staring at him. He rocked and rocked with his hands held in front of his face, as if to beg or ward off blows.

* * *

It was not easy after I was brought back. I had lived too long away from him, I think, and now he was the king of Israel. He had many wives, not like my father, Saul. I had been his wife for two years when he was a rebel soldier and had been Paltiel's wife for seven.

His heart was a cluttered room. He would sing in the morning and kill in the afternoon and make love to a woman in the evening. He talked with the priests or the generals late into the night. Humility and craft were mixed in him thoroughly to make him a great king. He made the Lord's name famous throughout the world; he gave us our great city, Jerusalem; he knew the greatness of Israel could be found most purely in himself. I didn't live easily with him.

When they brought the Ark of the Covenant into the city, he shamed me. At the front of the procession, he threw off his clothes and danced like a wild man. He shouted and whooped. He wiggled his royal buttocks before the women of the street and wagged his tongue and shouted things we were afraid to understand. Despite what they say, I was not the only one who turned her head in shame. It was something no one understood and only the rabble enjoyed.

At the palace I said, 'I see the king has joined the circus today'.

When he didn't reply, I said, 'You shamed all Israel'.

'I shamed only myself, and for the sake of the Lord. He chose to

fall on me today in front of slave girls to confirm his choice of me as
the king of Israel. If he has chosen me, and not your father's house, is
that a concern of mine?'

'You are a trickster, David. You throw mud on my father's name,
but you prophesy with the commoners as he did. If you prophesied
truly, how can anyone tell? We didn't understand a word. I only know
my father was a prophet, and should never have been anything else;
you are a king, and a very cunning one.'

'Think what you want to think', he told me, 'but the throne of Israel
is not for your father's house.' After that day he stopped taking me to
his chamber.

* * *

Solomon is building a temple for the Lord. We've never seen such
wealth in the city. Great logs from Lebanon, blocks of marble and
granite as big as houses. There are men here, too, that we have never
seen the likes of. Tall soldiers, with skin as black as a mynah's coat.
They stand by hundreds of covered wagon loads. Some say it is gold,
but that is hard to believe. So much gold!

[59] This is the temple David had wanted to build.

We had, for the rest of his life, a royal marriage. When I'd come back
to him, the king had two other wives, and he soon had five more. Almost all of the wives were gentiles, daughters of neighboring kings.
Abigail and I were the only women he had married for love, but his
love for me withered soon after my return.

His love for Abigail I didn't begrudge him. She was a good woman,
we got on well together. His betrayal came later, and it was not one of
love but of honor. A betrayal of my father, really. Did it start with
the plaited beard, the poetry? He began wearing his mail at court and
singing ditties to court sycophants. He became a gentleman-king. Look
at his son, Solomon, the aesthete, and you see the direction in which
he was heading. He took up the royal 'we' of the neighboring kings:

He said, 'We will see the minister of the harvests'.

He said, 'Is our horse waiting?'

He said, 'Tell us what you thought of our last psalm'.

'Your Highness', I said to him once, 'How many of you are there
now?'

He told me the king and the land are one.

'You sound like a Canaanite', I told him. 'You are beginning to act, Your Multitude, more and more like those lesser than yourselves.'

*   *   *

The defeat at Rabah was the first one Israel had suffered since David had been on the throne. He had ruled almost twenty years and had made people as far away as Nineveh talk about us with fear and wonder. He stopped going into battle himself after seventeen years, and no soldier begrudged it of him. He had fought longer than all but the oldest of them.

When he took a new wife after the defeat, I didn't even think about it. But others did. The first, of course, were the younger wives. Bathsheba, the new wife, did not appear in our chambers after the wedding. David had married a third time for love. But the young women spoke not just with envy, but with rage. They said this marriage was under a curse. The happiness in it would die as fast as it had been born. To have this woman, the king had put bloodguilt on his head.

After the wedding, he appeared nowhere without Bathsheba at his side. She was a beautiful woman, a woman it was easy to see a man would kill or die for. I don't know if she had a brain, but she had the eyes of a stallion, and David himself found it hard to look long at her. She had been the wife of a lieutenant in the king's army. The man had been killed at Rabah.

The king became more and more remote.

*   *   *

When it was clear what David had done I sent a court boy to the king's chamber with a request to speak with him that evening. 'Remember the wife of your youth', I told the boy to say.

He was sitting at the hearth, and by the way he didn't move when I came into the room, I knew he'd been sitting like that a long time. Bathsheba stood at a far wall and when she turned her face to me her eyes were wet. Oh, Lady, you were more beautiful in grief than you were in happiness. We could have been sisters, you and I.

I asked her if I could have a few minutes with my husband, and she left the room.

'How have you been?' he asked me.

I didn't answer and finally he looked up at me.

'She's a beautiful woman', I said. 'I think you have finally found your queen.'

'I wouldn't have married her if it had been only her beauty. She has the heart of a ruler.'

'And the eyes, yes.'

'Oh, you've seen that too? You know, Michal, she is the only woman I have not been able to look at? It makes me feel foolish. But she looks through me.'

'It doesn't surprise me. That you can't look at her.'

'She's made me a different man.'

'Such a curse.' He was used to my tongue, but looking at him now I knew that I had touched him. He turned once more to the fire, and I saw a tear on his face. 'She's God's chosen, David. God uses man's folly for his own good purpose, isn't that right? She'll bear you a son.'

'Michal. . .'

I sat down beside him, like a man. 'Ah, David. It's not easy, this tarnish, is it? It's something to learn to live with, though. My father never did—he never learned to live with his sin. It drove him howling.'

'There are lines on my heart I have never seen before.'

I smiled, but what he'd said made me sad. It was something a man his age should not have waited so long to discover about himself. 'You should write that down', I said. 'You say better than you see.'

He reached for my hand. When he'd touched it, I said, 'I heard you ordered her husband to lie with her.' He took his hand away.

'You have a devil's tongue', he said.

'Devils. What can I say? They run in the family. They frolic.'

'Why did I marry you? Why did I think I could redeem what God had discarded?'

I looked at him, long and hard, with the eyes now not of a schoolgirl, but of some crazed, old necromancer, looking, looking. He was the handsomest man in Israel. [60] Brave as a feist and sly as a fox. Was that enough, then? My father had stood a head taller than any other man in the land. Was David just a little braver? A little more handsome?

'But it was an order not even my father would have thought to give.'

'It's time for you to leave.'

'I want to know, David. Why did God choose you?'

'Today I wish he hadn't. Today I wish I were an old shepherd in Bethlehem.'

'You're lying, my friend. You exult in your sufferings as much as in your victories. You and your Jebusite wife are the stuff great tragedies are made of.'

'What are you talking about?'

'Saul. You and my father. You ordered Uriah to lie with his wife, but your soldier was as zealous as you'd been. He wouldn't do it. Not while his men were fighting. Which left a difficult problem. I mean, he may have been only a foot soldier, but he knew as well as anyone: it takes one and one to make three. His wife was getting plumper by the day, so what were you to do? What to do?'

'Do you remember the hunt, David?'

'What hunt was that?'

'The price you paid my father for me. Two hundred Philistines. Those little foreskins—I thought they were mice at first.'

He'd been quite sullen, but at this he laughed.

'You are a strange girl, my Mickele.'

'You aren't the first one to throw a problem into the ambiguity of the battlefield.'

He was quiet for a moment.

'Yes, beloved. You had God in your pocket at the time. You didn't see much beyond your own sheen. Saul thought you would die fighting them.'

'The Philistines.'

'Yes', I said.

'You were a carrot hung over a cliff.'

'Yes', I said. 'And it could have been done. You know that better than anyone.'

He looked at me without speaking.

'He only needed to have his most loyal men fighting close to you. In the front lines. For a while.'

'For a while', he said.

' "When the fighting is worst, withdraw from him." Is that what you said?'

'You shouldn't be saying these things to me, Michal. Not tonight.'

I didn't know, of course, that Nathan had already rebuked him. Weeks ago. By this time everyone knew not only the sin, but the sentence; but I wasn't in the court any more. I thought I was making the first, grand confrontation.

'Who else should be saying them to you? I don't understand it, David. Why were you chosen? What made you better equipped for kingship than my father? Your bravery? Or your blue eyes? Certainly not your heart, my shepherd boy, not your heart. You did in your sound mind what Saul did in his madness, and if I don't call down every curse on you for it, it's only because I don't have the gift of words.'

As I traced a stone with my finger, I said, 'But heaven should punish you for this, David. For this, if for nothing else.'

He held his face in his hands now, a gesture I found a trifle melodramatic.

'But I'm not', I said, 'a great believer in heaven's justice. At least I don't claim to understand it well. I've not gotten along well with anyone, least of all your and my father's God. I don't trust him much. That's why I came here tonight. The Lord gets weak-kneed around you, David, and doesn't know when you need a talking to. Who else would have made you taste the gall if I hadn't come?'

He looked at me. A smile came on his face that I had not seen since I'd looked at my father; it was a smile you would see only on a king's face, and I understood again the Lord's weakness.

'I've tasted much gall already tonight, Michal. The baby died today.'

*   *   *

Today I am walking the streets of Solomon's city, the brightest in the world. He is the second son of David and Bathsheba. A poet. A half-Jew. My handmaid stops me to buy some candles, and a rabbit for supper.

'Have you been to see the building of the temple?' she asks.

The old woman says:

> The grace of God falls on the world
> in eddies and swirls.

His goodness is like the snows
of the mountain ranges.
Tell the goat to climb down to the meadows.
Tell the hyrax to find cover.
An old woman, blessed with life
but not with youth,
here requests to die.
Bury her beneath the snow.

Tamara C. Eskenazi

MICHAL IN HEBREW SOURCES[1]

Different kinds of voices have retold Michal's story in Hebrew. Ancient rabbis, modern poets, playwrights, novelists and scholars have contributed their interpretation. A brief survey of some representative readings testify to the interest and variety of meanings that the biblical account of her fate have engendered.[2]

The earliest re-interpretation of Michal's story in Hebrew is 1 Chronicles 16. Chronicles retells Israel's story by recasting material from Samuel and Kings. In its account of David, Chronicles characteristically omits disparaging references to David and glosses over David's problematic domestic affairs. Hence the story of David's adultery with Bathsheba is ignored. She, like the other wives who bore David's children, is mentioned only in the genealogies (1 Chron. 3.1-9). Michal, however, appears in Chronicles' account of the return of the ark to Jerusalem: 'As the ark of the covenant of the Lord came to the city of David, Michal the daughter of Saul looked out of the window, and saw King David dancing and making merry; and she despised him in her heart' (1 Chron. 15.29). Given Chronicles' otherwise limited attention to David's 'private life', this reference is at first surprising. It could indicate an oblique criticism of David. More likely, however, it serves to emphasize David's greatness, a typical theme in Chronicles. The book records neither dialogue between the king and the queen nor quarrel, and makes no mention that she had no

1. I thank the poet Ruth ben Itzhak for her invaluable help. In particular, I appreciate her willingness to locate necessary sources at Ben Gurion University.
2. The purpose of this sampling is to present the English-speaking reader with versions of Michal not otherwise accessible. This essay is descriptive rather than critical, representative rather than exhaustive. At a late date I had been advised that some recent Israeli poets have written on Michal. Unfortunately I was unsuccessful in locating such work.

children. Nowhere does Chronicles say that Michal is David's wife. Instead, Michal functions essentially as 'the daughter of Saul'. She is a silent witness and foil to highlight David's success against the backdrop of Saul's failure.

Michal has very different kinds of roles in the vast rabbinic literature. This body of writings which combines legal, homiletic and midrashic traditions shows a marked appreciation of Michal as a positive and impressive figure. Rabbinic literature thrives on some of the incongruous details in the Michal material, and seeks to smooth inconsistencies and fill in the gaps. By its very nature, this literature cannot produce a coherent picture of Michal—or of any other figure—because the scope of rabbinic literature is immense, spanning centuries and stemming from disparate regions. But whereas the portrait cannot be coherent, the point of view and attitude seem surprisingly consistent. In their readings of Michal, the rabbis generally praise her and sympathize not only with her but also with her second husband Palti. They describe her as both beautiful and accomplished. Indeed, Michal had been able to wear *tefillin* (phylacteries), as men do in prayer.[1] Such a privileged obligation normally belongs to those who study Torah. By inference, the rabbis credit Michal with the study of sacred texts.[2] It is especially fascinating that the rabbis, in a literature famous for its love of debate, do not disagree as to whether Michal wore *tefillin*. They only argue whether or not some sages protested against her wearing them (*Pesiqta Rabbati* 29.11).

Three aspects of the Michal stories in the Bible perturb the rabbis: (1) The legal implications of her marriage to both David and Palti; (2) David seemingly marrying two sisters when both are alive; (3) the reference to Michal as the mother of five children (2 Sam. 21.8). The first of these concerns grows from the fact that David's reclaiming of his wife from Palti conflicts with Deut. 24.1-4 which prohibits a man from taking his wife back once she had been given to another. The rabbis are able to exonerate David from a seeming violation by concluding that Palti never consummated his marriage with Michal. Palti

---

1. See L. Ginzberg, 'The Family of David', from *The Legends of the Jews*, p. 142, esp. note 2 (reprinted in this volume, pp. 201-203 below).

2. The rabbis invoke Michal as an example in a debate concerning the education of the young. Should only sons be taught Scripture or daughters also? They agree that Michal wore *tefillin*, which means that she studied Torah. Michal sets an important precedent for moderns who claim an equal share for women in Jewish worship.

they say, placed a sword between himself and Michal to protect her from his own cravings. They praise him for his restraint. The rabbis resolve the second problem by concluding that Merab, Michal's sister, died before David married Michal; hence David did not violate the levitical injunction against marrying sisters (*Sanhedrin* 19b). This explanation allows the rabbis to solve the third problem as well. They suggest that Michal raised Merab's children once Merab had died and that Michal's devotion to them was so deep that they were deemed to be her children. Some rabbinic texts also conclude that Michal gave birth on the day of her death. Thus Midrash on Numbers declares: ' "Unto the day of her death", implying that she had one (child) on the day of her death' (*Numbers Rabbah* 4.20). Others claim that she already had some children (those listed in 2 Sam. 21.8) but that there were no others from the day of the quarrel with David (*Sanhedrin* 21a) and certainly no children by David. Michal's criticism of David's dancing is ascribed by the rabbis to modesty. She berates him for indecent exposure in public. 'O', she taunted, 'that it had at least been in private! But no; he has debased himself in the eyes of the servants' handmaids.' In her father's household no one had ever exposed even a heel or toe, so modest was Saul (she, then, not David, initiates a comparison between David and Saul). David's reply, according to the same Midrash, plays (among other things) on the words 'handmaids' and 'mothers' and thereby links Michal's accusation with her subsequent fate. 'He said to her: "Those daughters of Israel whom you call handmaids [*amahoth*] are not handmaids but mothers (*immahoth*) . . . " Because Michal had spoken thus she was punished, as you see from what follows in the Scripture: "*And Michal the daughter of Saul had no child unto the day of her death*" ' (*Numbers Rabbah* 4.20).[1] (For a detailed summary of other aspects of rabbinic sources, see L. Ginzberg, 'The Family of David', from *The Legends of the Jews,* in this volume.)

In modern Hebrew literature Michal appears as a heroine in a long epic poem by one of the great poets of the Jewish enlightenment, Y.L. Gordon (1831–1895). Gordon's *The Love of David and Michal*[2] provides an eloquent and elaborate testimony to the depth of the relation-

---

1. English translation from *Midrash Rabbah: Numbers* (trans. J.J. Slotki; London: Soncino Press, 1939), pp. 135-36.
2. *Ahabat David uMikal*, in *Kitbe Yehudah Leb Goren: Shirah* (Tel Aviv: Debir, 1964), pp. 53-87.

ship between David and Michal. It recreates the youthful romance of David and Michal and traces its transformation through time. Like many other expressions of nineteenth-century European romanticism, this historical poem essentially celebrates the power of love. It elevates Michal, more than David, as the true examplar of undying love.

Gordon evokes his characters and their love by interweaving biblical phrases and imagery, especially from Song of Songs and the Psalms, and by molding these images into new poetic forms in order to sing of the love of David and Michal. Theirs is a great love, both doomed and death defying. Its nature unfolds in great detail through over 450 stanzas, each of at least four lines and organized into twelve cantos. The love of David and Michal blossoms in their youth, amidst the flowers of palace gardens, yet it is never far from the harsh reality of war. The most exquisite flower is Michal herself. Her beauty shines like the sun after stormy clouds, casting brilliant golden rays everywhere. Gordon lavishes much attention upon the loveliness of her skin, her cascading raven-black curls, her neck like an ivory tower and her melodious voice. But it is her character that evokes the highest praise. David's looks and charm are also praised, but these descriptions pale somewhat next to those of Michal. David's love for Michal propels the young hero to greatness and encourages him to face his nation's enemies. It is for her sake that he defies danger and saves his people.

Having introduced the lovers, Gordon traces their relations by following the general contours of the book of Samuel. An occasional epigraph sets the tone for some cantos. The heading 'Love as strong as death' (Song of Songs 8.6) in the Fourth Canto, for example, heightens a contrast with Saul's mad jealousy and simultaneously evokes the passion that permeates the love lyrics of Song of Songs. In the Fourth Canto, as in 1 Samuel, David is forced to flee. The lovers separate at dawn with a display of affection that the biblical text reserves for David and Jonathan. For Gordon, the tender farewell between David and Jonathan in 1 Samuel finds its passionate counterpart in that of David and Michal. With trembling arms Michal embraces David; his fiery lips kiss hers, and soon he vanishes like a passing shadow.

Subsequent Cantos follow the transformation of a loving youth into a seasoned warrior. David's house, David's 'shoot', grows from the ashes of Saul. When Saul and his sons descend into the grave, the crown returns to David and with it returns Michal, David's wife whom David's soul so deeply loves.

The poet has taken nine Cantos to develop the drama of the lovers' separation and to describe their constant longing for each other against the backdrop of wars and danger. The Tenth Canto begins with a promise of a happy ending. A reunion is at hand, promising the culmination and fulfillment after a long and forced separation. Gordon once again praises Michal's beauty and honor; but most of all, he praises her fidelity. Having risked all for the love of a mere shepherd who was socially beneath her, Michal had fearlessly defied her father and her second husband. But the years have not been kind to her. Trapped in Paltiel's house, Michal longed not only for David but also for the kind of freedom that he possessed. Yet she faithfully remained his, chaste and unyielding. She protected her youthful vow of fidelity to David by keeping a sword near, in order to kill herself should she be coerced to betray that vow. At times she despaired enough to think of killing herself, but nevertheless she clung to hope in David and in their future. Here at last, in the Tenth Canto, the couple is about to reunite. The nation turns to David and asks him to rule. He, however, refuses the crown, demanding only that Michal be restored to him. She, not the crown, is most precious in his eyes.

As we come near to what appears like a happy ending, a chorus of praise multiplies images and sounds of joy. The chorus (the poet? the daughters of Jerusalem from Song of Songs?) exhorts Michal to forget her sorrow and invites the king to go forth to meet his beloved. Young women are to greet the reunited couple with a dance. Thus the Tenth Canto ends on a festive note, a most fitting conclusion to a love story.

The poem could have ended here; nevertheless it continues. A foreboding line from Ecclesiastes, 'A time to embrace and a time to refrain from embracing', opens the Eleventh Canto. We never witness the lovers' reunion, their long-awaited embrace. Instead, we 'hear' the poet's lament over the ravages of time. Time has touched David's heart and turned it from flesh into stone. Why?, asks the poet. Was David disappointed with Michal? Have her furrowed forehead and fading beauty taken his kindness away, causing him to shame her when she spoke up? Gordon's answer is interesting. No. David does not despise Michal. She remains as dear to his soul as before. But the king's soul no longer belongs to him. It serves his people. David no longer heeds his own feelings. Personal happiness is dwarfed beside the urgent need to provide an heir for the kingdom. A king's duty replaces a lover's passion. David reins in his love and sacrifices his heart. He takes many women and sires many children. But the violence done thereby to the barren Michal will haunt his house. Michal herself remains silent and forlorn. She spends her days in sadness, isolated and broken by her loss.

The Twelfth Canto begins with an epigraph, '...beloved and lovely, in life and in death they were not divided'. In 2 Sam. 1.23, this line was part of David's lament over Saul and Jonathan. Here it will speak of David and Michal. Aged David is shrunken and bent. His enemies and children had sought to trap him only to fall into the trap themselves. His crown now rests uneasily upon snowy white hair. David devotes his time to God. His psalms rise up, penetrating heaven. It is the night of his final song. Far away, under the oak tree where she swore to love David forever and where she now spends her time alone, Michal cries out and collapses. Her soul greets his at the heavenly gate. In death, the lovers David and Michal are joined again at last.

The most extensive, complex and poignant study of Michal as the central character is a drama by A. Ashman, entitled *Michal, the Daughter of Saul* (1940).[1] The cast of characters is small: Michal, Rizpah (Saul's concubine), Palti, Yephuneh (Michal's devoted servant), Azan (a conniving traveling merchant), and messengers from the king. David himself never appears.

The three-act drama recreates Michal's life just before David, as king, reclaims her from Palti. A brief introductory scene sets her years of waiting for David against the backdrop of an earlier scene, when Michal had first rescued David by using ropes and *teraphim* to send him to his freedom. The villain in Ashman's play is Rizpah, who plots against David but whose real victim, instead, proves to be Michal. As in the biblical text, Michal is a pawn in the schemes of others, this time in Rizpah's need to avenge the shame and death of her beloved Saul. Rizpah, a devoted concubine, has sworn to remain faithful to Saul's memory. His head, which used to rest on her shoulder, has last been seen stuck upon the wall, eyes bulging, dripping blood. She refuses to forget. She, she alone will prove loyal and extract vengeance, whatever be the cost.

1. *Mikal bat Sha'ul* (Tel Aviv: Yavneh, 1940).

In the opening scene Michal is still at the window. She has just sent David away and now alone must face Saul and the even more pernicious Rizpah who, in Ashman's telling, is an enemy masquerading as a friend. Michal, who is charged with violating the natural bond between father and child when she sided with David against her father, is condemned to violate the very bond that ties her to David. Saul gives her to another man, Palti son of Laish. Horrified, Michal nevertheless complies with the decree as the opening scene closes.

The play proper opens ten years later. Michal's life with the wealthy but miserly Palti is a form of living death. She languishes in Palti's house and pines for the one man she loves. She remains cold and unyielding to Palti's ardent attempts to consummate their marriage and to give him an heir. It is a touching figure of a frustrated man that Ashman creates in Palti. Michal contemptuously rejects this husband, yet he never forces himself on her. Honoring her wish, he waits—much as she waits—for love. Although she accuses him of capturing her like booty in battle and of having made her a prisoner, he reminds her that her father Saul was so enraged at her deceit that he had intended to kill her but relented only upon Palti's intercession. Palti is thus her savior, not her enemy.

Palti is wealthy and stingy. At first a despicable character, he soon comes to engage the audience's sympathy. He begs her for her love and for an heir to inherit his vast possessions. He refuses to take other wives in her stead, even though she encourages him. He resists forcing himself upon her. In every way, Palti seeks to win Michal's affection and consent.

Palti, more tragic than Michal, is wholly devoted to Michal. Having rescued her from her father's house, he appears as the only man ever to care for her, not simply to use her. He pours out his sufferings before her: his love which he restrains for her sake, and his desperation to have a child and to cease to be an object of ridicule. When Michal begs him to let her leave to join her sister or brother and thereby release him from the pain of her rejection, Palti confesses that he could not live without her. 'My heart is bleeding', he says. 'You are the knife that is thrust into it. If the knife be removed I shall fall and rise no more.'

But Michal's eyes are on the David who is away from her. David has been crowned in Hebron. He now has several wives. Rizpah intervenes in the hope of entrapping David through Michal. Rizpah urges

Michal to send a message to David to declare her love for him and inform him about her chastity. Michal resists. She refuses to be remembered simply for old time's sake. She hopes that David will come for her out of love, not guilt.

When Azan, the travelling merchant, reveals to her that he has been to David's palace in Hebron, she inquires about the other wives. The conniving merchant vividly conjures up these beautiful women, Michal's competitors: 'Ahinoam—milk and honey are her cheeks, and her eyes blue like the flowers in a field blessed by God...Abigail, a fiery woman, her hair black like the tents of Kedar, her teeth white as milk, and her shape under her gown is that of ripe pomegranates...'

Having heard of David's lovely wives and having at last come to appreciate Palti's genuine devotion, Michal's feelings towards Palti soften. She begins to suspect that David will never require her and that her future may lie, after all, with Palti. Some acceptance of that future looms. At long last she begins to waver.

Michal slowly starts to respond to Palti's ardent devotion. She begins to consider the possibility of love and joy, even though not in its ideal form with David. Perhaps the vivid descriptions of her competitors in David's house have released her from an illusion of reunion and opened her sealed heart to other possibilities of life and love with the one who is near and whose only happiness so deeply depends on her and on her alone. Compassion replaces romance. She even promises him that yes, someday she will be his.

Rizpah sabotages their possible union and shatters both Palti's dreams and, one suspects, Michal's only chance for happiness. Alarmed by Michal's changed attitude, Rizpah is determined to prevent Palti and Michal from consummating their marriage. She worries that David will no longer want or need Michal, and hence the trap that Rizpah is setting will prove to no avail.

Ostensibly helping Michal, Rizpah in fact plots against David. She sends messages to David in Michal's name, unbeknown to Michal. She wants David to reclaim Michal, convinced that this will inevitably lead to his death. Either he will be killed when he comes for Michal or he will die in the battle unleashed by opposition to him, first from powerful Palti and then from the other tribes.

Yet Rizpah is not simply a heartless vindictive woman. In Ashman's sensitive treatment, she too is a victim of an undying love. Her vengeance grows out of a single-minded devotion to Saul who himself had been betrayed by all those around him, but especially by David. She, however, remains true. Since David was responsible for Saul's misery and death, he must pay.

Once Michal's longings for David begin to wane, she also loses her will to live. Left to embrace only memories, she imagines David playing with—romancing—his other women who steal the love that rightfully belongs to her. She clings to the *teraphim* and the rope that she had used to save David, emblems of their last moment together. She discovers, alas, that the *teraphim* are gone (stolen, the audience knows, by Rizpah to be used as signs to David from Michal). At night, Michal once again addresses the absent David:

> And I stand by the window. . . Whether I come or go, whatever else I
> do, I am always standing by the window. O my beloved, my love, my
> man, why have you forgotten me? For whom do I treasure my beauty?
> For whom do I keep my youth? Cursed are you, my beauty, if David does
> not desire it!. . . Let my arms wither if they are not to embrace David's
> neck. Open your gates, Sheol of the shadow of death, if the gates of his
> heart are closed to me. . . (p. 44).[1]

As she bemoans her empty life, Michal reaches for the old rope. She had used it to save David and let him down through the window to freedom. She will now hang herself with it and be free of her misery. But the merchant interrupts her by bringing news about David. Messengers from David are on their way, he tells her. They are coming for her.

Upon hearing the news, Michal once again longs for life. Dazed by this sudden fulfillment of her dreams, she is overwhelmed with joy, revived by the hope of setting aside her garments of living death.

Messengers from David are indeed on the way to fetch Michal, lured by Rizpah's deception. Michal's restoration is but a fraud, of which she remains ignorant. But Michal and Palti are not the only victims of Rizpah's plot. Rizpah herself becomes one when she learns from the messengers that Saul's own brother is now in league with David. Feeling doubly betrayed, Rizpah accelerates her efforts. She lies to Palti, telling him that Michal had sent messages to David asking for her restoration; that Michal, not Rizpah, had sent the *teraphim* as tokens of love to David, to inform him of her fidelity and devotion. Palti nevertheless begs Michal to stay. Way should she join David and

---

1. Translations of Hebrew sources in this chapter are by T.C. Eskenazi.

be a seventh wife, a plaything in David's entourage? 'There you will be but a king's wife', he tells her. 'No. Not even a wife, more like a concubine or a maid. Here you are queen. You rule—over property and life. Command and it will be done. I am your servant, bonded to your very word' (p. 56). But Michal refuses to hear. David's summons is a new dawn, the rising of the sun. Even if the sun were to blind her by its brightness or consume her with its flame, she will go.

In desperation, Palti accuses her of sending messages to David, of begging David to rescue her, from a disgusting Palti whom she never permitted to come near to her. When his fields are set on fire (at Rizpah's instigation), Palti finally explodes. Rizpah fuels his rage and urges him to pour his wrath on Michal: he should rape and kill Michal, divide her corpse and send the pieces to the tribes of Israel as a rallying call to battle against the abominations perpetrated by David, who seized another man's wife (a direct reference to Israel's civil war in revenge for the rape of the Levite's concubine in Judges 19–21).

Knife in hand and blinded by passion and fury, Palti finally approaches Michal. This time she does not resist; she does not withdraw. With tearful eyes closed and a smile on her lips, Michal stands ready to accept death. Palti loses his courage and his rage. The knife slips to the ground and he lets her go. As Michal begs his forgiveness Palti musters power from his unrequited love and relinquishes her to seek her dream and pursue the happiness that she craves. 'Go in peace', says Palti. 'You made peace with death because of your love for David, and I will make peace with death because of my love for you.' As Michal steps towards the gate he trails behind her, mourning that he has lost her and mourning, too, over the child he will never have. His broken voice repeatedly cries out, 'Tomorrow your face will radiate peaceful joy—good; let it be—go in peace; go. . . Tomorrow your lips will drip the sweetness of love—go. . . As for me, what I have lost, lost, lost. . . Oh, Michal. . . Michal. . . Michal. . .'

With these words the drama ends. Palti's lament evokes other laments, most poignantly that of David's lament over his most beloved son. Only the audience, not Michal, nor Palti, knows what is ahead. Palti's loss is also Michal's. The life that she hopes to resume with David will deepen her isolation and cut off her future. She has just lost the only person who truly cared for her and the only future she could have had.

Works such as Gordon's epic poem and Ashman's play, where

Michal occupies the center, are relatively rare in modern Hebrew literature. Most often Michal appears not in her own right but, as in the Bible, only as a figure in David's story. Two recent Israeli novels (written, it seems, for popular readership) chart a range of possible recreations of Michal. Each fills the blank spaces of the biblical text with concrete but contrasting portraits of Michal.

In I.A. Malkiely's lengthy historical novel about the beginning of kingship in Israel, *A King's Heart*,[1] Michal is a strong, caring woman whose life from beginning to end is governed by concern for others.

Michal enters the story and David's life as a gentle but self-possessed princess who befriends David when he finds himself uncertain in his new position at the palace.

> 'May I come in, my young friend?' A soft and pleasant voice reached his ear. It was Michal, the younger daughter of the king. Excited, David rose up.
> 'Please. Do come in, my lady. . . I am honored', he said.
> 'Really?' Michal smiled. She hastened to close the door behind her.
> 'Where did you learn to sing?', she asked, 'and to play so beautifully?' (p. 136).

David tells Michal about the simple pleasures of a shepherd's life, of freely roaming the land. They banter, exchange confidences, and fall in love. David comes to prefer Michal over her older sister Merab. Both sisters are in love with David but when Saul offers Merab to David as victory prize, Merab rejects him for her sister's sake and paves the way for the marriage of Michal and David. The lovers are thus fortunate to see their hopes fulfilled.

As in the biblical tale, Saul's persecutions soon force David to flee from his newly wedded wife. Michal alerts David to the danger and helps him escape. Little is told about Michal for a long time after this. She re-emerges when Saul's general Abner enlists Paltiel to help kill an enemy and promises Michal to Paltiel as a reward. When the soldiers kill Saul's opponent and leave his five children orphaned, Michal takes pity on them and brings them home.

We next see Michal in Paltiel's house where she has been for years. She mourns over her life and her losses. In particular, she wonders about David. Has he forgotten her? Does he even know she has been given to another? Will he forgive her? Has he given her up? Should

1. *Leb Melek* (Tel Aviv: Amihai Press, 1977).

she inform him that she is still waiting? Her brother Ishbosheth
arrives and interrupts her musing. He reports that David wants her
back and assures her that he himself supports such a plan. Ishbosheth
confesses that he is glad to transfer the burden of the kingdom from
his shoulders to David's. These revelations release Michal to her joy at
the prospect of being reunited with David. When Ishbosheth asks
about her husband Paltiel it is Michal's turn to confess that they have
never lived together as husband and wife. She had agreed to enter
Paltiel's house on two conditions: that the children she had adopted
would come with her and that Paltiel would not approach her until she
was ready. The children proved to be a barrier against Paltiel and an
outlet for her pent-up love. But now Michal asks her sister Merab to
take the already grown children and she herself prepares to join
David. Her joy is nevertheless clouded by the tears that she and Paltiel
shed at their farewell. Both of them ride together, weeping until
Abner sends Paltiel home.

As for the meeting between Michal and David, in Malkiely's telling
of the story, David has been anxiously waiting. His heart overflows
when he finally sees her veiled figure. But when he rushes to embrace
her, Michal bursts into tears and then, embarrassed, withdraws. David
summons his other wife, Abigail, to ease and comfort Michal. He in-
troduces Michal as 'my queen' and promises her that Abigail will
prove a devoted friend, as indeed she does. Abigail looks after Michal
until Michal begins to feel at home in her new life. But remorse over-
takes her. She regrets leaving her sister, her husband and her brother.
She is no longer sure why she was brought to the palace. Her ambiva-
lence turns into horror when she learns that her brother Ishbosheth
has been murdered. Rumors that David may have been responsible
throw her into utter despair, but his genuine sorrow convinces Michal
that such allegations are false. Nevertheless, she does not completely
recover from the shock.

These losses frame Michal's reaction to David's dancing before the
ark. When the procession of the ark enters Jerusalem, all of David's
wives go out to join the festivities. Michal alone remains within.

She sees David dance and leap together with all the young ones and
she despises him. Her heart grows heavy. She thinks about her father
and brothers, all of whom have fallen by the sword. She sees David's
wives and children rejoice; she alone is barren, the sole remnant of
her family. She returns to her room and weeps. David, having entered

his house, notices Michal's absence and visits her room to ask about her welfare and invite her to the festive meal. She, however, rebukes him for his behavior in front of the people. David retorts with an attack, pouring salt on Michal's deep and bleeding wounds. He reminds her that he dances before the God who chose him over her father's house; he claims that it is an honor to dance with all the people who crown him king.

Michal remains silent. When David departs he hears her weeping and quickly returns to console her. Laying her despondent head on his shoulder, she consents to join the celebration but her sorrow never leaves (p. 302).

Malkiely does not end Michal's story here. The story continues, showing that Michal never really recovers from her losses. At the height of his courtship with Bathsheba (greatly altered by Malkiely from an afternoon affair into a long, yet unconsummated romance that began when David was still fugitive), David is summoned to Michal's deathbed where Abigail ministers to her needs. Michal begs David to forgive her father's persecutions and to promise that he will look after the remnant of Saul's house. Reassured, Michal dies in Abigail's arms and in David's company.

Malkiely's Michal is a steady, gentle, nurturing woman. From beginning to end she is propelled by compassionate concern for others: she helps young David feel at home in the palace, protects a stranger's children, secures a future for her only surviving kin. Although many of the women in *A King's Heart* are notably thoughtful and kind to one another, Michal is the most fully etched model of selfless devotion.

A shorter historical novel, *King David* by Yakob Goren,[1] pictures a very different Michal. The novel contrasts David's virtuous commitment to God with the worldly and self-serving Michal. While remaining largely true to the contours of the story in Samuel, this novel fills the gaps with dialogue in order to create an appreciative portrait of David. Michal does not fare well in this retelling. We first meet her as a wily and aggressive[2] seventeen-year-old, wise to the ways of the court (in contrast to her innocent and placid sister Merab). Once again (and not surprisingly) we learn that both sisters are in love with David

---

1. *Hammelek David* (Jerusalem: Keter, 1984).

2. These traits, in the Bible, in literature and in life, can be viewed both positively and negatively. Goren presents them clearly as flaws, not virtues.

who has just slain Goliath. In this version, however, David loves Merab. Michal, knowing this, nevertheless sabotages the marriage of David and Merab. She convinces her father Saul that she, Michal, will be the better instrument, as David's wife, for serving Saul's schemes against David: first, she is not the elder like Merab, and second, she will remain loyal to Saul's house (unlike Merab who is too enchanted with David).

Her plot succeeds although David continues to dream lovingly of Merab. David is still the naive country boy caught up in palace intrigue, a victim like Merab of Michal's manipulations. But he quickly grows up. When Michal learns that Saul plots to kill David she informs David. Interestingly, it is David and not Michal who plans the escape. Michal simply follows David's instructions. After he leaves, she stakes her hopes on the future, confident that he will someday be crowned Israel's king and claim her as his queen, both for her own sake and because she is King Saul's daughter (p. 48).

To punish her for her betrayal, Saul gives Michal against her will to Paltiel. This penalty proves benign because Paltiel is a kindly, agreeable man, eager to please Michal and easily manipulated by her. She ignores him altogether once Saul dies and as she begins to instigate her restoration to David. When the command to return comes, Michal enters David's camp in proper regal fashion. She arrives impatient, proud and elegant. Paltiel follows weeping, crushed by those royal powers that so lightly ignore the plight of ordinary people like him. Commanded to go home, he leaves. Michal herself never looks back.

True to the biblical tale, Goren mentions Michal again only when David brings the ark to Jerusalem. By then Michal has tasted disappointment. She is central neither in the palace nor in David's life and love. Her return had been unceremonious, meriting only two lines in the royal chronicles. Neglect alters her feelings towards David. On this fateful day Michal is ill. She drags herself to the window to watch the festivities only to catch David the king dancing like one of the commoners.

> 'I saw you from my window when the ark was returned', she commented in a dry voice, turning her back to him as he entered. . .
> 'Were you pleased with me?' David did not sense as yet that the wind had changed.
> 'Very!', she retorted (p. 134).

Facing him with eyes flashing with anger, Michal unleashes a barrage of accusations about his cheap behavior and misconduct. Stunned, David retorts in kind, reversing her accusations: it is precisely because he does not know the haughty ways of nobility but rather dances with all his might before God like a commoner that God has appointed him king of Israel. He tells her how he had hoped that their child would inherit the throne but how glad he is now that she has been prevented from having children. 'We are all equal before God', he snaps, leaving in anger. The episode closes. As in the Bible so in Goren's novel, Michal appears no more. David, not even the narrator, has had the last word.

Diverse perspectives on Michal recur in scholarly discussions. Whereas Gordon, Ashman and Malkiely all praise Michal's whole-hearted fidelity to David and to his welfare, the scholar A. Safrai, like the novelist Goren, contrasts her unfavorably with David. He accuses her of failing to distinguish genuine worth from mere appearance. In his essay, 'On Action and Intention (according to Chapters from the Book of Samuel)',[1] Safrai examines points of tension between action and intention in Samuel. He contends that, in these narratives, it is characters' focus on externals that lies at the root of their failure. He contrasts those who are able to probe beneath the surface to the heart of the matter (e.g. Hannah) with those misled by superficiality and mere appearances (e.g. Eli). Important turning points in the book as a whole, says Safrai, replay this tension and explain the consequences for Israel (i.e. the fate of the ark and kingship) and for its leading individuals (Samuel, Saul and David). Inappropriate emphasis on externals is exemplified in the initial introduction of Saul (1 Sam. 10.23-34) and in Saul's own insistence on keeping up appearances after the conflict with Samuel (1 Sam. 15.30). Saul's inability to grasp the right relation between intention and action leads inevitably to his downfall.

Safrai examines the story of David and Michal as one episode in this larger framework and overarching pattern. He concentrates on the final scene in the story, when David dances before the Ark and Michal rebukes him (2 Sam. 6), omitting any discussion of earlier incidents between Michal and David. According to Safrai, David's dance, and the simplicity of his garment, anger Michal because they are not in accord with her taste. His clothes and behavior are those of a com-

---

1. *Shma'aton* 18 (1981–82), pp. 34-42.

moner. She prefers him to appear unique because he is Israel's king. In this Michal represents Saul's way: a grasping of the external to the neglect of the internal (p. 39). David, however, objects and claims that before God there is no distinction between a commoner and king (2 Sam. 6.21-23). David does not intend to insult Michal by recalling her father at this juncture. His (or the narrator's) purpose is rather to underscore the difference between the two approaches. As for the conclusion of the episode, Safrai calls it strange. The statement that Michal had no child till the day of her death, says Safrai, may be yet another indirect commentary or hint about the text's position on this debate between Michal and David.

A different perspective is developed by Shula Abramsky, who notes the tragic dimensions of Michal's plight in an article on 'The Woman at the Window'.[1] Abramsky analyzes the thrice-told tale of a woman at the window and identifies common motifs in the fate of all three women: Sisera's mother, Michal the daughter of Saul, and Jezebel. She points out that all three women share a position (as queens) and a destiny: they are depicted as enemies of God and punished by a divinely appointed human who first appears as a friend but later betrays them. Their punishment is linked with death: they have no continuity; their house is doomed. All three are drawn to the window in anticipation. They enter, as a result, into a final and fatal dialogue. All three are queens and daughters of kings who, at the window, confront the inevitable end of their reign and who nevertheless face it regally (p. 114).

After a brief study of Sisera's mother, Abramsky focuses on Michal and her plight as a member of the household of two kings (Saul and David) each of whom seeks a dynasty. Although Michal at first appears to be different from the two other queens in that it is not God whom she challenges but a man, Abramsky traces the narrative to point out that the pattern nevertheless does conform to the other two. The emphasis in 2 Samuel 6 on David's dancing before God and on his appointment by God over God's people combine to present Michal's opposition to David as an opposition to God's elect. Her punishment (childlessness) at first appears to come from God but, like that of the other two women at the window, finally proves to come through a human instrument.

1. *Beth Mikra* (1980–81), pp. 114-24.

When David enters his house (as David, not King David), Michal, who had been at the window earlier, meets him as Saul's daughter. She carries the burden of Saul. Her fate is sealed by the action of the person who has been dear to her, who owes his life to her. David dooms her to a state of widowhood even though he, her husband, is still alive (much as he later dooms the concubines whom Absalom had violated, 2 Sam. 20.3). Abramsky asks, Why did David reclaim Michal only to have her live as a widow? Why was she childless even though God had not closed her womb? To answer these questions, Abramsky traces the relation between David and Michal from its inception. She argues that David's betrayal of Michal began long ago. She points out that David took other wives when he escaped Saul. It was only then (in retaliation?) that Saul gave Michal to another (1 Sam. 25). David obviously was not in a hurry to reclaim Michal when Saul died. Instead, the narrative reports that David had new wives and children (2 Sam. 3.1-5). He only asks for Michal in the context of political negotiations. Michal herself is not asked. After her husband Paltiel returns to his home, the reader eagerly anticipates a reunion between Michal and David. But the scene abruptly ends. A reunion between David and Michal is not even mentioned. Abramsky concludes that David does not wish to meet Michal, let alone stay with her. Her restoration is strictly a political calculation. All his dealings with Michal are political calculations, exploiting her love. David wants her back because he knows that only when Michal is under his surveillance can he be sure that she will not give birth to an heir and a competitor.

Abramsky notes that the story of the relationship between David and Michal is framed by a window. It is through a window that Michal rescues David because she is Saul's daughter and therefore knows Saul's designs; it is likewise through a window that David pronounces a death sentence, as it were, upon Michal, precisely because she is Saul's daughter (p. 121).

Either as a compassionate sister, a romantic heroine or a tragic victim, Michal in Hebrew literature is more often praised than blamed. In that process the audacity that marks her portrait in parts of the biblical text is sometimes tamed. Her fate continues to kindle the imagination of ancient and modern readers. Although she does not receive the kind of attention that biblical figures like Eve or Esther receive, voices are still raised to tell her side of the story. Heard, these voices help restore Michal to her rightful place as Israel's first true queen.

W. Ewing and J.E.H. Thomson

MICHAL
(in *The Temple Dictionary of the Bible*)*

[463] MICHAL, younger daughter of Saul (1 Sam. 14.49). She loved David, attracted no doubt by the heroism and chivalry of the young soldier (18.20), a love reciprocated, if we may judge from the liberal fashion in which the strange dowry was provided (vv. 25ff.). The demand of Saul betrayed his sentiments towards David. Very soon Michal had occasion, by feminine artifice, to save her husband's life (19.11ff.). After David's flight Saul gave Michal to Palti of Gallim (25.44). Her romantic affection of early days was probably undermined by David's marriages with Abigail and Ahinoam. When torn from Palti (2 Sam. 3.14ff.), probably in order that the presence of the king's daughter might in a way legitimate David's claim to the throne, she seems to have been quite estranged. This easily accounts for her contemptuous words on the day of David's joyful arrival with the ark (6.16, 20). Childlessness is indicated as the punishment of her contempt (vv. 22f.).

*   W. Ewing and J.E.H. Thomson (eds.), *The Temple Dictionary of the Bible* (London: J.M. Dent and Sons, 1910).

J. Cheryl Exum

MURDER THEY WROTE:
IDEOLOGY AND THE MANIPULATION OF FEMALE PRESENCE
IN BIBLICAL NARRATIVE*

> Nobody seems to go through the agony of the victim. . .
> Agatha Christie

[45] In this paper I want to investigate two literary murders. One is a
sacrifice, which has all the appearances of a murder, except that the
victim does not protest. In the other case, the victim does protest, but
the murder does not take place in the story, but rather by means of the
story. The story is the murder weapon, so to speak. The stories are
those of Jephthah's daughter, offered by her father as a sacrifice to the
deity, and of Michal, Saul's daughter and David's wife, denied offspring and voice in one fatal stroke, and thus killed off as a narrative
presence. One victim is nameless; the other, named, but both are
identified in terms of men: one, as a daughter; the other, as 'the
daughter of Saul' and 'the wife of David', but never without one or
both of these epithets. They thus illustrate the familiar position of
women in biblical times, as under the authority of their fathers before
marriage and of their husbands after marriage.[1] Neither functions as
an independent agent in the sense that, for example, Deborah, Rahab,
Delilah, and Jael do. Jephthah's daughter makes no real attempt to act
autonomously, whereas Michal unflinchingly asserts herself, with

 * Reprinted from Alice Bach (ed.), *The Pleasure of her Text. Feminist Readings
of Biblical and Historical Texts* (Philadelphia: Trinity Press International, 1990),
pp. 45-68. Used by permission. The article was previously published in *Union
Seminary Quarterly Review* 43 (1989), pp. 19-39.
 1. For a helpful discussion, see Phyllis Bird, 'Images of Women in the Old Testament', in *Religion and Sexism*, ed. R.R. Ruether (New York: Simon & Schuster,
1974), pp. 41-88.

deadly consequences.

The 'stories' of these two women are parts of men's stories, part of the 'larger story' that we take as *the* story. David Clines has argued [46] that there is no 'Michal story', that focusing upon a minor character in a story results in a distorted, or at least skewed reading of the whole.[1] He is right, of course, that there is no 'Michal story', nor is there a 'Jephthah's daughter's story', and for feminist criticism of biblical narrative that is precisely the problem. But one can nonetheless discern the submerged strains of Michal's voice and Jephthah's daughter's voice, and the challenge for feminist criticism is to reconstruct a version of their stories from that voice. This can be done at least partially, I think, by deconstructing the dominant (male) voice, or phallogocentric ideology of the narratives.

I do not speak of these women's stories in any absolute sense, as if by deconstructing the male voice, we will be closer to the 'truth' or 'the real story'. To suggest that there is one proper way to read the text results in an authoritarianism characteristic of phallocentric criticism—a position that feminist criticism rejects in its recognition (and celebration) of contradiction and multiplicity. A feminist reading will not be a neutral reading, 'neutral' or 'objective reading' usually being terms for what turn out to be androcentric readings. The relation of reading to truth involves the issue of interests, and our interests determine the questions we ask of a text.[2] In this quest after literary murderers, I am no more capable of telling the whole truth, and nothing but the truth, than the biblical narrators. Rather I shall use my interests to expose and undermine theirs, in the interest of possible truth.

For purposes of this study, I wish to set aside the question of who produced these stories, of whether or not, and to what degree, women might be considered responsible for these traditions. In my opinion, that question is secondary to the issue of gender ideology in biblical material. Feminists have long recognized that men control symbolic production. Theirs is the dominant world-view that also controls literary production, with the consequence that the female perspective will

1. 'The Story of Michal, Wife of David, in its Sequential Unfolding', pp. 129-40 above.
2. Mieke Bal, 'How Does an Author Become the Author of a Crime?', paper read at the 1988 Annual Meeting of the Society of Biblical Literature.

be muted, if not altogether excluded.[1] Since in patriarchal texts
women are frequently made to speak and act against their own interests, an important question faces us: what patriarchal function do these
narratives serve?[2] What is the motive for these murders? Pursuit of an
answer to this question is one option among other possibilities for
feminist analysis, and one that brings to light important facets of these
two women's stories. Finally, I hope to show how the female perspective, the female voice, cannot be silenced, even by literary murder.
The crime has been committed, the evidence is the text, and the female
perspective provides our clue for deconstructing it.

[47] Literary murder is, of course, different from the real thing,
and both of our cases can be construed as something else, which may
explain why the perpetrators have gotten away with murder for so
long. In the case of Jephthah's daughter, the ritual act of sacrifice
transforms murder into a socially acceptable act of execution.[3] We do
not witness Michal's actual death; there is no need for its description,
for by the end of 2 Samuel 6, she has ceased to play any role in the
Davidic house. As we shall see, poetics and ideology conspire to remove Michal as a narrative presence. There is no similar ideological
necessity to get rid of Jephthah's daughter. She is the innocent victim
of her father's vow. Since by accepting her death at the hands of the
father, she poses no threat to the patriarchal system, her memory is
allowed to live and to be celebrated within the story. This cannot, for
reasons we shall explore below, be the case with Michal.

1. See Gerda Lerner, *The Creation of Patriarchy* (New York: Oxford University
Press, 1986), pp. 5-6, 199-211, 231-33 *et passim*. The challenge for feminist analysis is to find women's (sub)texts within these phallocentric texts; cf. the important
work of Mieke Bal, *Death and Dissymmetry: The Politics of Coherence in the Book
of Judges* (Chicago: University of Chicago Press, 1988).

2. *Pace* Carol Meyers, *Discovering Eve: Ancient Israelite Women in Context*
(New York: Oxford University Press, 1988), pp. 24-26, I am not willing to forgo
the use of the term 'patriarchal' to describe the male gender bias of narrative; this
usage is widespread in feminist literature.

3. This is not to say that we are to condone Jephthah's sacrifice of his daughter,
but only that human sacrifice was practiced. No outright condemnation of Jepthah's
sacrifice appears in the text, but I think hints of disapproval appear in the disastrous
episode with the Ephraimites that follows the sacrifice; see my 'The Tragic Vision
and Biblical Narrative: The Case of Jephthah', in *Signs and Wonders: Biblical Texts
in Literary Focus,* ed. J.C. Exum (Decatur, GA: Scholars Press, 1989), pp. 71-72.

The Case of the Dutiful Daughter

The story of Jephthah and his daughter appears in Judges 11. In return for victory over the Ammonites, Jephthah vows to sacrifice to YHWH 'the one coming forth who comes forth from the doors of my house to meet me when I return in peace from the Ammonites' (11.31). His daughter is the one who meets him, and the alarming similarity in vocabulary brings out the dramatic impact: 'when Jephthah came to Mizpah to his house, behold, his daughter coming forth to meet him. . .' (11.34). Jephthah's response, rending his garments as a sign of mourning, and his awkwardly expressed agony and consternation, make it clear that he had not expected his daughter to be the object of his vow.

> When he saw her he rent his garments and said, 'Ah, my daughter, you have brought me very low and have become the source of my trouble. I have opened my mouth to YHWH and I cannot take it back' (11.35).

It has been frequently pointed out that rather than offering solace, the father accuses his daughter—a classic case of blaming the victim. But his words also, in my opinion, express his feeling of not being solely responsible for this awful turn of events.[1] Just as Oedipus did not intend to kill his father and marry his mother but does so only because he does not know their identity, so too Jephthah did not intend to sacrifice his daughter, but utters his vow without knowing who will be 'the one coming forth'. Both she and he are caught up in something beyond their control.

[48] The very act of making the vow occurs under ambiguous circumstances. Jephthah's success in battle against Ammon and his future as chief over Gilead rest upon divine favor. His attempt to settle hostilities diplomatically meets with failure and the battle lines are drawn. The spirit of YHWH comes upon Jephthah before he makes the vow, and it is not clear whether or not he utters his vow under its influence.

> The spirit of YHWH came upon Jephthah and he crossed over Gilead and Manasseh, and he crossed Mizpah of Gilead, and from Mizpah of Gilead he crossed over to the Ammonites. And Jephthah vowed a vow to YHWH. He said, 'If you will indeed give the Ammonites into my hand, then the one coming forth who comes forth from the doors of my house to meet me when I return in peace from the Ammonites shall be YHWH's and I

---

1. See Exum, pp. 67-69.

shall offer him [generic] up as a burnt offering' (11.29-31).

Is the spirit the driving force behind all of these events, or only some of them, and if so, which ones? To complicate matters even further the next verse tells us, 'Jephthah crossed over to the Ammonites to fight with them and YHWH gave them into his hand'. If not a tacit acceptance of Jephthah's terms, this statement at least implicates the deity. There is otherwise no divine action in the story and, disturbingly, no divine judgment upon Jephthah's act of human sacrifice. The imposition of the vow between the coming of the spirit of YHWH upon Jephthah and the victory renders it impossible to determine whether victory comes as the result of the spirit, or the vow, or both.

The problem lies not so much in the making of the vow as in its object. Had Jephthah vowed to build an altar to YHWH, as Jacob does in Gen. 28.20-22, or to dedicate to YHWH the spoils of battle, as Israel does in Num. 21.2, it is unlikely that his vow would have elicited much critical commentary. Even the vowing of a person to the deity is not unthinkable, as seen in Hannah's vow to give Samuel to YHWH all the days of his life (1 Sam. 1.11). But Jephthah vows the ultimate in order to ensure success, something from his household that will cost him dearly. What is sacrificed must be precious to be meaningful (cf. David's avowal, 'I will not offer burnt offerings to YHWH my God that cost me nothing', 2 Sam. 24.24). Not until the last two words in the Hebrew (*weha'alitihu 'olah*, 'I will offer him up as a burnt offering') do we discover that Jephthah intends a live sacrifice.[1] By holding us off until the last possible moment, the text alerts us to this unusual aspect of the vow and intimates its horror.

[49] Yet the vow alone does not determine the tragic outcome. Tragedy is assured when Jephthah's daughter, his only child, comes out to meet him. The conjuncture of these two events, the vow and the daughter's appearance, seals two fates: she to die and have no progeny; he to have no progeny and to die.[2] Jephthah takes her life 'according to his vow' (11.39). There is no last-minute intervention by the deity to save the child, no ram in the thicket. In the story Jephthah carries out the murder, and the deity is implicated.[3] And

1. On the debate whether Jephthah intended a human or animal sacrifice, see David Marcus, *Jephthah and his Vow* (Lubbock, TX: Texas Tech Press, 1986), pp. 13-18; cf. Exum, p. 67.
2. His death is reported in Judg. 12.7.
3. There are many parallels where a parent promises to a supernatural figure what

since this is a literary murder, we shall accuse the narrator of complicity in this crime.

How the young woman knows or surmises the terms of her father's vow is not stated. Her readiness to accept the inevitable is striking.

> She said to him, 'My father, you have opened your mouth to YHWH; do to me according to what has gone forth from your mouth now that YHWH has granted you vindication against your enemies, the Ammonites' (11.36).

The daughter submits to the authority of the father. His word is not to be countermanded but simply postponed: she asks only for a two-month respite before the vow is carried out. After a time of lamentation in the mountains with her companions, she returns to her father, and the text states, 'he did to her according to his vow which he had vowed' (11.39). We are spared the details, for we could hardly bear them (compare, for example, the piling up of details in the account of Abraham's near sacrifice of his son Isaac, where a *deus ex machina* assures a happy ending). A young woman's life is snuffed out in its prime. Yet it would be myopic to see what happens as any less Jephthah's tragedy than his daughter's, for his family line comes to an end when he is forced to take his daughter's life. To commemorate Jephthah's daughter, the women of Israel hold a yearly ritual four days each year.

The Case of the Nagging Wife

Michal's 'story' must be gleaned from scattered references in 1 and 2 Samuel, where she plays a significant but minor role in the events surrounding the demise of Saul's house and David's rise to the throne. For my purposes here, I will focus on Michal's fatal confrontation with David in 2 Samuel 6, though some summary of what happens earlier will be necessary.[1] Michal is King Saul's daughter, who loves David and becomes his wife. Saul and his house have been [50] rejected by YHWH (1 Sam. 13 and 15), and David has been secretly anointed king by Samuel (1 Sam. 16). David becomes a popular hero

turns out to be his or her own child; see Marcus, pp. 40-43; Exum, p. 68 n. 5.

1. For a detailed discussion of Michal's fate, see my forthcoming study, *Arrows of the Almighty: Tragedy and Biblical Narrative* (Cambridge: Cambridge University Press).

after his defeat of Goliath (1 Sam. 17 and 18) and Saul very early realizes the threat David poses to his kingship.

> 'They have ascribed to David ten thousands, and to me they have ascribed thousands; what more can he have but the kingdom?' And Saul eyed David from that day on (1 Sam. 18.8-9).

When he learns that his daughter Michal loves David, Saul is pleased and uses the opportunity to dangle a desirable prize before his rival, 'become the king's son-in-law'. He hopes that David will be killed trying to meet the bride price of a hundred Philistine foreskins. But why should it matter to Saul that Michal loves David? What do the woman's feelings have to do with it? Saul had already tempted David with his older daughter Merab—where love is not mentioned—but he gave her to another (1 Sam. 18.17-19). In fact, the reward for killing Goliath was rumored to be marriage to the king's daughter (1 Sam. 17.25). Thus for the charmed third time, David has a chance at what Saul seems unwilling to let him have. From Saul's perspective, Michal's love for David may be convenient but otherwise largely gratuitous. I think it is largely gratuitous from David's perspective as well. The situation is one in which the men's political considerations are paramount, while regarding the woman, we hear only that she loves. Already the text perpetuates a familiar stereotype: men are motivated by ambition, whereas women respond on a personal level. It would be much more to Saul's advantage if David loved Michal—but that is precisely what the text leaves unsaid, suggesting that David's motives are as purely political as Saul's. Note that the text tells us 'it pleased David well to be the king's son-in-law', not that it pleased him to have Michal as his wife. Saul even appears to recognize the threat Michal's love for David poses for him,

> When Saul saw and knew that YHWH was with David, and that Michal Saul's daughter loved him, Saul was still more afraid of David,[1]

and rightly so, for in the next chapter, Michal defies her father by helping David escape Saul's attempt on his life (1 Sam. 19.11-17).

In saving David from Saul, Michal loses him, for he leaves his house-within-Saul's-house, his advantageous position as the 'king's son-in-law', never to return. He does return to meet Jonathan and to

---

1. I prefer to follow the Hebrew here; instead of becoming a snare to David, Michal's love becomes a snare to Saul.

conspire with him to discover Saul's intentions (1 Sam. 20) and he hides for three days until Jonathan brings him news—but all this time, he apparently makes no effort to see Michal. David becomes a [51] fugitive and an outlaw, futilely pursued by Saul, and he manages to gain not one, but two wives while roaming about the countryside (1 Sam 25.42-43). At this point we learn that Saul had given Michal to Palti, the son of Laish (1 Sam. 25.44).[1] Saul's political motive seems clear enough, to deny David any claim to the throne through marriage. Time passes, Saul is killed in battle at Gilboa (1 Sam. 31), and David is anointed king over Judah. About Michal we hear nothing until David is offered the opportunity to become king over the northern tribes. (In the meantime David has acquired more wives and many children, 2 Sam. 3.2-5.) Then he does precisely what Saul had sought to prevent; he demands the return of his wife Michal as a symbol of his claim to Saul's throne. The description of her grief-stricken husband Paltiel, who follows in tears as Michal is being taken to David, draws attention to the absence of information regarding Michal's feelings. Michal's reunion with David is not reported, a highly significant textual silence that suggests a volatile subtext.

It is little wonder, then, that when Michal has her big scene in 2 Samuel 6, it is a veritable emotional explosion.[2] In the only dialogue that ever takes place between them, Michal accuses David of blatant sexual vulgarity, and he responds with a devastating rebuke. Immediately thereafter the narrator laconically informs us, 'Michal Saul's daughter had no child to the day of her death'.

A review of Michal's story reveals that only twice does she appear as an agent in her own right, here and in 1 Samuel 19, where she saves David's life. Elsewhere she neither speaks nor initiates action but is rather the object of the political machinations of the two men, her father and her husband, locked in bitter rivalry over the kingship. When used as a symbol to represent their conflicting interests, Michal is referred to as both Saul's daughter and David's wife (1 Sam. 18.20, 27, 28; 25.44; 2 Sam. 3.13, 14). The intense nature of the Saulide–Davidic rivalry, however, the exclusiveness of each's claim to the throne, makes it impossible for Michal to belong to both houses at once. She becomes a victim of their prolonged conflict, and her two

---

1. Reading the verb tense as past perfect.
2. See the perceptive analysis of Robert Alter, *The Art of Biblical Narrative* (New York: Basic Books, 1981), pp. 123-25 [reprinted in the present volume—Editors].

attempts to act autonomously by choosing her own allegiances result only in her own losses. In 1 Samuel 19, Michal is called 'David's wife', for she allies herself with her husband over against her father. She orchestrates David's escape into freedom by letting him down through the window when Saul seeks to kill him. But she thereby, in effect, loses her husband, who does not come back for her or seek her return to him until it is politically expedient. In 2 Samuel 6, she becomes once again 'Saul's daughter', for she speaks as the [52] representative of her father's house, and by doing so, forfeits her role in the house of King David.

In 2 Samuel 6, David and 'all the house of Israel' bring the ark of YHWH to Jerusalem amid great rejoicing. Michal, however, is inside, watching the fanfare through the window. From her perspective we see 'King David leaping and dancing before YHWH', and for the first time since telling us Michal loved David (1 Sam. 18.20), the narrator permits us access to her feelings: 'she despised him in her heart' (2 Sam. 6.16). That her love has turned to hatred serves as a pointed indication of her suffering at David's hands. It has been suggested that as a king's daughter, Michal finds the behavior of the present king beneath the dignity of that office. But her heated exchange with David when she goes out to confront him reveals much more. It doesn't take a psychologist to recognize that David's attire, or lack of it, is not the real issue.

> David returned to bless his house, and Michal the daughter of Saul went out meet David. She said, 'How the king of Israel has honored himself today, exposing himself today in the eyes of his subjects' maidservants as one of the worthless fellows flagrantly exposes himself' (2 Sam. 6.20).

That nothing less than the kingship is involved can be seen from Michal's reference to David as the 'king of Israel', and from David's reply, where he first takes up the subject of kingship and only then turns to the subject of his comportment.

> David said to Michal, 'Before YHWH who chose me over your father and over all his house to appoint me king-elect over the people of YHWH, over Israel—I will dance before YHWH. And I shall dishonor myself even more than this and be abased in my eyes, but by the maidservants of whom you have spoken—by them I shall be held in honor' (2 Sam. 6.21-22).

Notice the pointed references to Saul's rejection—'over your father', 'over all his house'—and to David's authority 'over the people of YHWH', and 'over Israel'. David's response to Michal touches on a critical issue that the narrative has repeatedly repressed but never really resolved: David's taking the kingship from the house of Saul.

With regard to what Michal considers his shameful behavior, David promises to go even further. How will he dishonor himself? I suggest the next verse hints at an answer: by ceasing to have sexual relations with Michal, by putting aside the woman who once risked her life to save his.[1] The juxtaposition of David's rebuke and the [53] narrator's statement that Michal had no children invites us to posit a causal connection. Significantly, however, the text carefully avoids this connection. Do we have here a case of male solidarity between the narrator and David? Or should we consider other possibilities? Since it is YHWH who opens and closes the womb (Gen. 20.18; 29.31; 30.2, 22; 1 Sam. 1.5, 6; Isa. 66.9), perhaps the deity bears responsibility (it has been suggested that Michal's childlessness is her punishment for speaking out against YHWH's anointed). No one to my knowledge has proposed that Michal refuses to have sexual relations with David, yet it would not be out of character for her. The very ambiguity hints at the text's unease about locating the responsibility.

The rift between David and Michal is not only inevitable, given the resentment Michal must surely feel toward David; from a narrative point of view it is essential, for any possibility that Michal and David have a child, who would symbolize the uniting of the two royal houses, must be precluded. The transfer of the monarchy from Saul to David is far from smooth and requires justification.[2] To be sure, Saul has been rejected as king by YHWH and David elected, but Saul has no intention of relinquishing his kingdom without a struggle, and after Saul's death, 'there was a long war between the house of Saul and the house of David' during which 'David grew stronger and stronger, while the house of Saul became weaker and weaker' (2 Sam. 3.1). One well-established political solution to the rift between the two houses would be their union through marriage and a child, who as a scion of both royal houses might someday reign. Theologically, however, that solution is unacceptable, for YHWH has declared that no descendant of Saul may sit upon Israel's throne (1 Sam. 13.13-14). Saul's house

1. That Michal's life might have been in danger had Saul discovered her role in David's escape (1 Sam. 19) is suggested by Saul's response of throwing a javelin at his son Jonathan, when Jonathan takes David's part (1 Sam. 20.33).

2. Jonathan plays a major role in effecting the transition; see David Jobling, *The Sense of Biblical Narrative* (Sheffield: JSOT Press, 1978), I, pp. 4-25.

threatens David politically and YHWH theologically. Accordingly, Saul's family is systematically eliminated. Jonathan and two of his brothers are killed in battle with their father (1 Sam. 31). Abner and Ishbosheth are treacherously murdered, and the narrator goes to great lengths to declare David's innocence (2 Sam. 3 and 4).[1] Shortly thereafter, we learn that Michal will remain childless, and the way is thus cleared for 2 Samuel 7, where YHWH promises David an eternal dynasty, a dynasty in which Saul's house will play no part.

Poetics and ideology work together to remove Michal from the narrative. The rejection of Saul's house requires that Michal have no children. But the narrative goes beyond simply reporting her childlessness; it chronicles in painful detail her humiliation and elimination. The woman provides an opportunity for narratively displacing a strategic and embarrassing problem at the political level onto the [54] domestic level, where it offers less of a threat. The animosity between the houses of Saul and David is then symbolically resolved as a marital conflict. In it David directs toward Michal the hostility one would have expected him to show toward Saul, who sought his life, and toward Jonathan and other members of Saul's family, who to varying degrees stood in his way. Michal, for her part, becomes the spokesperson for Saul's house (she speaks as 'Saul's daughter' not as 'David's wife') and her rebuke of David the king functions as a protest from Saul's house against David's usurpation of royal prerogative. As we proceed to reconstruct Michal's story, we shall seek in her protest another level, one that symbolizes the victim's outcry at being (literarily) murdered.

Words as Weapons

It is no criminal coincidence that in both our stories words make potent murder weapons. Not only are the words spoken by the male characters deadly instruments of power over women, but the storyteller also uses the women's own words against them. The central role words play in extinguishing the authentic female voice underscores the appropriateness of 'phallogocentric' to describe the narrative ideology. The seriousness of words and their power, especially in cases of

1. The so-called 'History of David's Rise' has been seen as an apology for David; see P. Kyle McCarter, Jr, 'The Apology of David', *JBL* 99 (1980), pp. 489-504; *1 Samuel* (AB 8; Garden City, NY: Doubleday, 1980), pp. 27-30.

blessings and curses, oaths, and vows, is well-documented in ancient
Near Eastern literature and assumed in Judges 11. Thus Jephthah
makes no attempt to modify the terms of his vow by which he is
bound to sacrifice to God his only child; nor does his daughter challenge its inviolability.[1] The word kills. The vow cannot be retracted
('I have opened my mouth to YHWH and I cannot take it back', Judg.
11.35), and both Jephthah and his daughter are caught up in its
immutable course toward fulfillment. But if words can kill, they can
also heal. The destructive power of language is counterbalanced in this
tale by its sustaining capacity.[2] Jephthah's daughter asks that one thing,
haddabar hazzeh, 'this word', be done for her, that she be given two
months during which to grieve in the company of her companions.
After her death, the women of Israel commemorate Jephthah's
daughter in a yearly ritual, understood as a linguistic act, not a silent
vigil. Jephthah's daughter finds life through communal recollection,
though different, to be sure, from the life she might have had through
family and children, the life her father took away.

[55] I shall return below to the subject of the women's commemoration of Jephthah's daughter and its complex effect on this story. For
now let us consider Jephthah's daughter's voice. How does she speak
against herself? By neither questioning the man who consigned her to
death nor holding him accountable. In encouraging her father to carry
out his vow, she subordinates her life to the communal good. The
seriousness of the vow is upheld, the need for sacrifice is satisfied,[3]
and paternal authority goes unchallenged. It might be argued that she
does not protest her fate because it would be useless. The futility of
protest, however, does not deter Michal, who thereby lays claim to
her own voice.

Michal and David engage in a battle of words in which David has
the last word because he holds the power. These are the only words he
ever speaks to her, words of rebuke, and they have the effect of criti-
cally wounding their victim. Unlike Jephthah's words, however,

---

1. The present story assumes the inviolability of Jephthah's vow, whereas Lev.
27.1-8 stipulates monetary payment by which a person vowed to God could be
released. In the midrashic literature, one finds various attempts to explain Jephthah's
ignorance of the law in this case; see Marcus, pp. 46-47.

2. For fuller discussion of this theme, see *Arrows of the Almighty,* ch. 3.

3. See René Girard, *Violence and the Sacred* (Baltimore: Johns Hopkins University Press, 1977).

David's do not kill. Here the narrative serves as the instrument of murder, accomplishing the deed in one blow. Depriving her of children is a symbolic way of killing Michal. Denying her a reply to David kills her off as a narrative presence. By representing her as challenging the king from a position of weakness, the narrator has Michal essentially commit verbal suicide. Notice how negative her portrayal seems at first glance. A king's daughter and a king's wife, Michal appears not as a regal figure, but rather as a jealous, bitter, and worst of all, nagging woman. She has overstepped her bounds, she dares publicly criticize the king's behavior, and we should not be surprised to see her put in her place by an angry and dismissive husband. On the surface her criticism sounds petulant and exaggerated—so what if the king makes a fool of himself? But we have seen that her words only barely cloak the real issue, the political problem that the narrator downplays by foregrounding the domestic dispute.

The Danger of Going Out

Jephthah came to Mizpah, to his house, and behold, his daughter coming out to meet him. . . (Judg. 11.34).

David returned to bless his house, and Michal Saul's daughter came out to meet David. . . (2 Sam. 6.20).

Both our victims meet untimely 'deaths' when they leave the security of the house to meet the man who will be instrumental in [56] their murder. The house is the woman's domain; here she is safe and can even exercise power, while outside in the larger world, men wield authority.[1] The men are the leaders, the heroes whose actions have far-reaching consequences affecting whole peoples. Jephthah has gone

---

1. Proverbs 31 offers a good example. The woman has considerable power over the household, while her husband 'sits among the elders of the land' (v. 23). The distinction between power and authority is helpful; authority is legitimate power, power recognized by society. See Michelle Zimbalist Rosaldo, 'Women, Culture, and Society: A Theoretical Overview', pp. 21-22; and Louise Lamphere, 'Strategies, Cooperation, and Conflict among Women in Domestic Groups', p. 99; both in M.Z. Rosaldo and L. Lamphere (eds.), *Women, Culture, and Society* (Stanford: Stanford University Press, 1974). See also Jo Ann Hackett, 'In the Days of Jael: Reclaiming the History of Women in Ancient Israel', in *Immaculate and Powerful: The Female in Sacred Image and Social Reality* (ed. C.W. Atkinson, C.H. Buchanan, M.R. Miles; Boston: Beacon Press, 1985), pp. 17-22; Meyers, pp. 40-44.

to battle, made a vow, and returned victorious; David has consolidated his kingdom and brought the ark to Jerusalem. The men have acted; the women respond and are caught up by forces beyond their control, though somehow apparently still under the control of the men. That is to say, both Jephthah and David could have reacted differently: Jephthah by seeking an alternative to the actual sacrifice; David by treating Michal with respect.

When Jephthah returns victorious from battle, his daughter goes out to meet him dancing and with timbrels. It may have been customary for women to celebrate military success in such a manner. In Exod. 15.20 the women acclaim the victory at the sea with timbrels and dancing. In 1 Sam. 18.6, after David's victory over Goliath, the women of Israel come out singing and dancing, with timbrels and musical instruments. Possibly Jephthah anticipated being met by a woman—more expendable than a man (?)—though, as his response indicates, he did not expect his daughter. The tragedy set in motion by Jephthah's vow is sealed when his daughter comes out to meet him. When David and all Israel bring the ark of YHWH to Jerusalem, Michal watches from the window. Earlier she had let David down through the window, out of her domain, where he was in danger,[1] to meet his destiny in the man's world of power. Having secured his position as king, David now has no need of Michal. In 2 Samuel 6, Michal occupies the private sphere of the home, safe, but excluded. References to 'all Israel', 'all the people, the whole multitude of Israel, both men and women', and 'all the people' underscore her isolation inside. When she goes outside to confront David in the public arena, she meets rebuke and greater exclusion—losing any role she might have had in the future of David's house.

The men return to their houses, to the domestic order preserved by women. Without the house, there is no 'outside'; the men need what the house represents and what it makes possible for them, the freedom from domestic responsibilities that allows them to concentrate on affairs of state. The house is both place and lineage, shelter and posterity. When the women go outside, houses are cut off. By sacrificing his daughter, Jephthah destroys his house (thus when the Ephraimites later threaten to burn Jephthah's house down over him, the remark is grimly ironic, since his house—his lineage—has already been de-

---

1. In *Arrows of the Almighty*, I explore the sexual symbolism in 1 Samuel 19, where Michal figuratively births David into freedom.

stroyed by fire). Michal's childlessness brings to an end [57] another
branch of Saul's house; in the end only the crippled Mephibosheth and
his son Mica will survive. Yet with Michal's removal, the future of
David's house is secured. With Saul's house out of the way, David receives from YHWH the promise of an eternal dynasty.[1]

Virginity and Childlessness:
The Politics of Female Sexuality

She had not known a man (Judg. 11.39).

Michal Saul's daughter had no child to the day of her death (2 Sam.
6.23).

What is particularly striking about these statements is that both occur
at the end of the story, as a kind of closure sealing the women's fates;
both are stated categorically, as if they were entirely neutral observations; and both are necessary. As sacrificial victim, Jephthah's daughter must be a virgin for reasons of sacrificial purity;[2] Michal, as we
have seen, cannot have children for ideological reasons. Since one
lived on through one's progeny, having offspring—many offspring,
especially sons—was important both to men and to women (witness,
for example, Abraham's concern over his childlessness). Understandably it mattered significantly to women, since women did not have
other opportunities, open to men, to leave their mark on the world.[3]
That the fates of both Michal and Jephthah's daughter involve childlessness indicates the extent to which patriarchal texts identify women

1. For very different, but fascinating analyses of the complexity of the symbolism
of the house in this material, see Bal, pp. 169-96; Joel Rosenberg, *King and Kin:*
Political Allegory in the Hebrew Bible (Bloomington: Indiana University Press,
1986), pp. 113-23.

2. The situation of the sacrificial victim is somewhat more complex, but need not
detain us. Married women are not good candidates for sacrifice because a married
woman has ties both to her parents' and her husband's families, either of which
might consider her sacrifice an act of murder and thus take vengeance; see Girard,
pp. 12-13. On the opposition between sacrificial purity and the pollution of
childbirth, see Nancy Jay, 'Sacrifice as Remedy for Having Been Born of Woman',
in *Immaculate and Powerful: The Female in Sacred Image and Social Reality*,
pp. 283-309. Girard argues that anyone who does not have a champion makes an
appropriate sacrifice.

3. Deborah is an important exception who proves the rule.

in terms of reproductive function. Without children, the women are somehow incomplete; they have not fulfilled their role as women. If to have no children means to die unfulfilled, it also means that the women have no one to stand up for them, no *go'el* to plead their cases. They can be eliminated without fear of reprisal.[1]

The categorical way in which Michal is denied offspring masks, as I indicated above, a narrative discomfort. Does David put Michal aside, so that she, like other of his wives later, will be shut up 'until the day of [her] death [the same phrase as 6.23], living as if in widowhood' (2 Sam. 20.3)? I suspect so. Regarding Jephthah's daughter, the text states, 'she had not known a man'. What is not an issue in patriarchal texts such as these is female sexual pleasure. Indeed, patriarchal literature, and thus the Bible in general, reflects the underlying attitude that woman's sexuality is to be feared and thus carefully regulated.[2] Patriarchy severs the relationship between eroticism and procreation. As Julia Kristeva observes, it affirms motherhood but denies the mother's *jouissance*.[3] Eroticism is not [58] associated with the mother but rather with the whore, the woman whose sexuality is commensurate with her availability. To intensify our critique we need only to acknowledge the importance of sexual fulfillment for women. In our examples, the women are denied not just motherhood, the patriarchal mark of female fulfillment, but also the pleasure of sex, the right of passage into autonomous adulthood that opens the eyes with knowledge (cf. Gen. 2–3). Jephthah's daughter will know no sexual fulfillment; Michal will have only memory of it.

As a related point of interest, it is ironic that a women's ritual (Judg. 11.39-40) serves to honor a virgin. It has been frequently suggested that the story of Jephthah's daughter is aetiological, aimed at explaining the women's ritual. There is, however, no evidence of such a ritual apart from this story. We shall explore below the androcentric

1. This is crucial according to Girard, p. 13.
2. In *The Creation of Patriarchy,* Lerner traces male control of female sexuality from its locus within the patriarchal family to regulation by the state. On woman's sexuality 'not so much as part of her feminine being but, rather, as an exclusive form of male experience', see Nehama Aschkenasy, *Eve's Journey* (Philadelphia: University of Pennsylvania Press, 1986), esp. pp. 123-24. Within the Bible, the Song of Songs is the great exception.
3. *About Chinese Women* (tr. Anita Barrows; New York: Marion Boyars, 1986), p. 26. On patriarchy's division of eroticism and procreativity, see Lerner, esp. ch. 7.

interest served by the women's commemoration of Jephthah's daughter. Is this really the kind of ritual women would hold, or simply a male version of a women's ritual? We do not know. We can only speculate about what form a genuinely female ritual might take were free expression of female sexuality possible. Might it be celebration of female eroticism, of uniquely female power, the power to give birth? (Already in Gen. 2–3, in a classic illustration of womb envy, the creative power of women is appropriated by the prototypical Man who, like Zeus birthing Athena from his head, symbolically gives birth to woman with the help of the creator god [no creator goddess is involved].) Is, then, the commemoration of the *death of a virgin* an androcentric inversion of female expression?

Opportunity and Motive,
Or Whose Interests Are Being Served?

The women occupy narratives that, like father or husband, seek to subordinate, and finally control, them. Jephthah's daughter accepts her fate with alarming composure. The vow is carried out, but the unnamed young woman who leaves behind no children as a legacy is not forgotten. Her memory is kept alive by the ritual remembrance of women. Because she does not protest her fate, she offers no threat to patriarchal authority. And because she voluntarily performs a daughter's duty, her memory may be preserved.

> It became a custom in Israel that the daughters of Israel went year by year
> to commemorate Jephthah the Gileadite's daughter, four days each year
> (Judg. 11.39-40).

[59] Patriarchal ideology here coopts a women's ceremony in order to glorify the victim. The phallocentric message of the story of Jephthah's daughter is, I suggest: submit to paternal authority. You may have to sacrifice your autonomy; you may lose your life, and even your name, but your sacrifice will be remembered, indeed celebrated, for generations to come. Herein lies, I believe, the reason Jephthah's daughter's name is not preserved: because she is commemorated not for herself but *as a daughter*. If we translate the difficult *wattehi ḥoq beyisra'el* at the end of v. 39 as 'she became an example in Israel'[1] rather than 'it became a custom in Israel', her value to the patriarchal

---

1. Marcus, p. 34.

system as a model is underscored.

Michal, in contrast, opposes the system that would have her remain inside, in her place, doubly subordinated as subject to her king and as woman to her husband. Here the message is: refusal to submit leads to rebuke and humiliation. Michal speaks out against the figure of authority—the husband/king—and is silenced. Unlike Jephthah's daughter, who participates in the patriarchal system, Michal cannot be honored because she speaks against male authority. I referred earlier to women's identification in terms of their relation to men, as daughters or wives or both. Jephthah's daughter performs her function as a daughter, and is rewarded with commemoration as a daughter by the 'daughters of Israel'. Michal, on the other hand, is punished by being denied her function as a mother. (She also loses her status as 'David's wife'; the narrator calls her 'Saul's daughter', and thus she, too, is reduced to being a daughter.) Submission is rewarded; opposition, punished. The women are sacrificed to patriarchal interests that the system remain intact and function properly.

The Speaking Subject: Deconstructing the Dominant Narrative Voice

To expose the phallogocentric interests served by these stories is not to accuse the biblical narrators of blatant misogyny but rather of reflecting a culturally inherited and deep-rooted gender bias. Thus the present inquiry seeks to read these stories without censoring them but without being confined to them.[1] The muted female voice provides the means for deconstructing the dominant, male narrative voice. What is repressed resurfaces in another form. In her speech, Jephthah's daughter submits to the authority of the father; in hers, [60] Michal opposes the authority of the husband. If speech confers autonomy, we shall need to look closely at how, and to what extent, these women (re)claim their stories through speech. But first, let us consider the other women in these stories, women who do not speak but who play a key role.

The women of Israel commemorate Jephthah's daughter for four days each year. Exactly what their ritual involves is not clear. The

1. I adopt this concept from Julia Kristeva, *Desire in Language: A Semiotic Approach to Literature and Art* (ed. L.S. Roudiez; tr. T. Gora, A. Jardine, and L.S. Roudiez; New York: Columbia University Press, 1980), p. xi.

Septuagint and the Vulgate understood the verb to mean 'to lament' or 'to mourn'; however, the only other occurrence of the word, in Judg. 5.11, refers to recounting the victories of YHWH. This usage suggests that the women recite Jephthah's daughter's story. These women, however, do not actually speak in the narrative. They remember, and their yearly ceremony is used by the narrator to keep alive the memory of the victim (only the narrative bears witness to their witness). Jephthah and the women of Israel represent two poles: he blames his daughter, 11.35; they praise her through memorializing her. Praising the victim can, however, be as dangerous as blaming the victim. The problem lies in the victim–victimizer dichotomy, a way of structuring experience that ignores the complicity of the victim in the crime.[1] If we make Jephthah the callous victimizer and his daughter the innocent victim, we fall into a patriarchal pattern of thinking. If we allow the women's ceremonial remembrance to encourage glorification of the victim, we perpetuate the crime.[2] How do we reject the concept of honoring the victim without also sacrificing the woman? We must recognize that guilt and innocence are not clear-cut. As I indicated above, Jephthah, like his daughter, is a victim of forces beyond his control; a vow made in ambiguous circumstances and in ignorance of its outcome forces his hand. Nor is the daughter innocent; she did not resist. She speaks on behalf of the sacrificial system and patriarchal authority, absolving it of responsibility. And the women of Israel cooperate in this elevation of the willing victim to honored status.

The role of other women in the account of Michal's rejection is not to immortalize, but to isolate through contrast. Who are the '(male) servants' women servants' (*'amhot 'abadav*), who, according to Michal, have relished David's sexual display, and by whom David avows he will be held in honor? These women are doubly subordinated—by sex, to all of David's male subjects or servants, and by class, to the royal couple, whose mutual rebukes derive their sting

1. Cf. Lerner's remarks on the complicity of women in patriarchy (pp. 5-6, 233-35).
2. Thus a reading such as Phyllis Trible's, that makes Jephthah all-bad, irredeemably guilty, and wholly responsible for the crime of murder, and his daughter helpless and totally innocent, simply reinforces the victim–victimizer dichotomy; see *Texts of Terror* (Philadelphia: Fortress Press, 1984), pp. 93-109. Bal, in contrast, completely reinterprets the daughter's death and the meaning of the women's remembrance; see pp. 45-68, 96-113, 119-22, 161-68 *et passim*.

from the imputation of inferior status to these women. Whether or not Michal means to include the '(primary) wives of the free [61] Israelites' in her reproach,[1] by implying that these women are below her dignity, she aims to disgrace the king, who turns her words around ultimately to shame the queen. A class issue intrudes to set the women over against each other and to obscure the gender issue. It has been argued that using class to divide women is one of the strategies of patriarchal ideology.

> The division of women into 'respectable women', who are protected by their men, and 'disreputable women', who are out in the street unprotected by men and free to sell their services, has been the basic class division for women. It has marked off the limited privileges of upper-class women against the economic and sexual oppression of lower-class women and has divided women one from the other. Historically, it has impeded cross-class alliances among women and obstructed the formation of feminist consciousness.[2]

Despite its possible anachronism, this citation is relevant to our text. Michal's privilege as a king's daughter and a king's wife isolates her from the other women in her story. By having her oppose herself to these women, the narrator leaves her to stand alone against the authority of her husband the king. Moreover, the sexually charged language Michal and David use in connection with these women and *David's* 'disreputable' behavior implies, perhaps, that Michal means to represent the '(male) servants' women servants' as not respectable. That is, the narrator has Michal introduce the distinction between women in a way that makes her appear haughty and elitist, thereby sharpening the unflattering picture of her. The '(male) servants' women servants' have been 'outside' and gotten an eyeful of the king. Yet the 'respectable' woman will not receive society's reward, motherhood.

Michal's going out to confront David is an act of self-assertion. Such boldness on her part cannot be tolerated; the narrator lets her protest but robs her of voice at the critical moment, allowing her no reply to David and no further speech. Whereas the narrator uses

1. The phrase, 'Hauptfrauen der freien Israeliten', is Frank Crüsemann's ('Zwei alttestamentliche Witze: I Sam 21.11-15 und II Sam 6.16, 20-23 als Beispiele einer biblischen Gattung', *ZAW* 92 [1980], p. 226), who thinks the remark refers only to lower class women. Cf. McCarter, *II Samuel*, p. 187, who believes Michal refers to 'all the young women of Israel, whether slave or free'.
2. Lerner, p. 139. See esp. ch. 6 for a fuller argument.

Michal's protest to eliminate her, her protest can be used against the narrator to bring to light the crime, to expose the gender bias of the story. By speaking out, Michal lays claim to her own story. She cannot avoid her fate, but she can protest it. She goes to her literary death screaming, as it were. Her protest thus serves as an indictment of the phallogocentric world view represented in and reflected by the narrative.

I have said that in 2 Samuel 6, Michal is eliminated from the narrative, but this is not quite the case. She reappears in an unexpected [62] context in 2 Sam. 21.8, to contradict the narrator's earlier claim that she had no child.

> The king took the two sons of Rizpah the daughter of Aiah, whom she bore to Saul, Armoni and Mephibosheth; and the hve sons of Michal, the daughter of Saul, whom she bore to Adriel the son of Barzillai the Meholathite; and he gave them into the hand of the Gibeonites, and they dismembered them on the mountain before YHWH (2 Sam. 21.8-9).

The usual solution is to read 'Merab' instead of 'Michal', with a number of ancient manuscripts, since Michal's sister Merab was the wife of Adriel the Meholathite. But this avoids pressing the embarrassing question of how Michal's name got here in the first place. Is this a simple case of confusion of women (who are notoriously hard to tell apart): Saul's descendants are killed off, so what difference does the mother's identity make? Or is it a Freudian slip that convicts the biblical narrator, an aporia we can read as Michal's refusal to be written out of the narrative? If so, the narrative still has the last, cruel word: it gives her children only to take them away again.

In contrast to Michal, Jephthah's daughter remains within the confines of the patriarchal word. Though she does not lay claim to her story, she makes some motions toward self-assertion. The two parts of her speech pull in different directions. In the first part, she surrenders volition. In the second, within the boundaries set by her father's vow, boundaries she accepts, she attempts to define herself, to lay some claim to her own voice: she asks for a period of two months in which to grieve, accompanied by her female companions.

> She said to him,
>> 'My father, you have opened your mouth to YHWH,
>> do to me according to what has gone forth from your mouth,
>> now that YHWH has vindicated you against your enemies the
>>> Ammonites'.

And she said to her father,
   'Let this thing be done for me,
   let me alone two months
   that I may go and wander upon the hills
   and bewail my virginity,
   I *and my companions*'.

Mieke Bal wants to posit a connection between the phrase which she translates, 'to lament in confrontation with my nubility', and a rite of passage, 'a phase of transition that prepared her for marriage'.[1] She finds here the woman's own point of view in contrast to the narrator's androcentric perspective, 'she had not known a [63] man', and she then proceeds to deconstruct the male concept of virginity via a detour into Freudian theory. Her resultant (re)reading of the entire story, a counter-reading, challenges the more traditional interpretations found within biblical scholarship and illustrates one way to reinscribe a female perspective. Another possibility of reading a different meaning into the phrase, 'bewail my virginity', presents itself if we suppose the young woman's familiarity with the sacrificial system (i.e., her better knowledge than ours about human sacrifice in the ancient Near East).[2] She laments not just unfulfillment but the clear and brutal fact of imminent death, recognizing that if she were not a virgin daughter, her father could not sacrifice her.[3] Such an argument, informed by anthropology and Girardian theory, involves the same kind of retrospective reasoning as the rabbinic objection—what if the 'one coming forth' had been a camel, a donkey, or a dog *(Bereshit Rabbah* 60.3; *Wayyiqra Rabbah* 37.4)—based on purity laws. I have already suggested that narrative necessity determines the outcome. The daughter's tragedy is that she—not another—is the one to come forth to meet Jephthah, and that she is an (I would even say, the) acceptable sacrificial victim. This takes us back to my earlier remarks about the

1. Bal, p. 49. Her argument appears mainly in chs. 2, 4, and 5.
2. For discussion of this topic, see Alberto R.W. Green, *The Role of Human Sacrifice in the Ancient Near East* (Missoula, MT: Scholars Press, 1975), p. 199. Green observes, 'During the formative period of the Federation of Israel, there is the strong implication that human sacrifice was practiced by the people as an acceptable aspect of their Yahwistic belief'.
3. I thank my colleague Ellen Ross for suggesting this idea. As my discussion above indicates, if Jephthah's daughter were married, her husband, not her father, would have power over her. If she had borne children, she would not be sacrificially pure; see Jay.

coincidence between the terms of the vow and the daughter's appearance, a conjunction of events apparently beyond human control.

The most interesting feature of the daughter's ceremonial lamentation is her inclusion of other women in the event. Only at the conclusion of her speech does she reveal that, unlike her father, she has companions with whom to share her distress. *Ra'yotay,* 'my companions', is her last spoken word in the narrative; *'abi,* 'my father', was her first. Symbolically, through speech, she journeys from the domain of the father who will quench her life to that of the female companions who will preserve her memory.

Ultimately the text denies autonomy to Jephthah's daughter and confines her voice within patriarchal limits, using it to affirm patriarchal authority. Yet her voice transports her to a point of solidarity with her female friends and with other daughters, the 'daughters of Israel', who refuse to forget (compare Michal's isolation). The resultant image is too powerful to be fully controlled by androcentric interests. The (androcentric) text segregates women: the daughter spends two months with female companions, away from her father and the company of men; the ritual of remembrance is conducted by women alone.[1] But as Gerda Lerner points out, when women are segregated ('which always has subordination as its purpose'), they transform such patriarchal restraint into complementarity and [64] redefine it.[2] We can choose to read this story differently, to expose its valorization of submission and glorification of the victim as serving phallocentric interests, and to redefine its images of female solidarity in an act of feminist symbol-making.

By exposing the phallogocentric bias in the stories of Jephthah's daughter and of Michal, I have sought to hear the women's voices differently, and by doing so to give the victims of literary murder a voice that identifies and protests the crimes against them and that claims for them a measure of that autonomy denied them by the larger story.

---

1. The Israelite women engage in ritual whereas the men are busy fighting, in the war with Ammon (10.17–11.33) and among themselves (12.1-6).
2. Lerner, p. 242.

Shoshanna Gershenzon

MICHAL BAT SHAUL

'And Michal, Saul's daughter, had no child till the day
of her death' (2 Sam. 6.23)

This was *his* city, taken from
The Jebusites, and opened to
Priests and short southern boys, sporting
Scarves ripped from Philistine corpses.

This was his home, rustling with younger
Women and their children, who bowed to her and
Scurried past towards laughter in the inner courtyards.

This was his god, silent now after the leaping and the
Carnival and the harsh street instruments and the cakes flung
To the crowd by the kitchen boys; breathing darkness
In the shut tent in the shut farm wagon.

She had loved the god that sang in the voices of the *nebiim*,
and blew through their sweet pipes, when they came down
from the high places, and her father always the tallest and the
best, his arms wide to catch her leaping body; she had loved
the hill country and the tall Benjamite warriors; they sang of
women taken in battle, but she sat safe on Saul's lap, gripping
his chief's fringes.

While his men roared and drank, she sat bathed
In the great grief that poured from his face, and forgave
All that he would do to her.

A warrior's daughter. A warrior's prize. An heiress whose
Patrimony was mumbled by scarred old men. A captive
　　　　woman
Of Benjamin dried by the southern sun, the desert always
Blowing in the corner of her eye. She followed it to heaped
　　　　stones
Under the last tamarisk. An odor stung; a hand accepted
Her coins and offered a rancid cup.

Louis Ginzberg

THE FAMILY OF DAVID
(from *The Legends of the Jews*)*

[116] David had six wives, including Michal, the daughter of Saul, who is called by the pet name Eglah, 'Calfkin', in the list given in the Bible narrative.[1] Michal was of entrancing beauty,[2] and at the same time the model of a loving wife. Not only did she save David out of the hands of her father, but also, when Saul, as her father and her king, commanded her to marry another man, she acquiesced only apparently. She entered into a mock marriage in order not to arouse the anger of Saul, who had annulled her union with David on grounds which he thought legal. Michal was good as well as beautiful; she showed such extraordinary kindness to the orphan children of her

* *The Legends of the Jews*. IV. *Bible Times and Characters from Joshua to Esther* (Philadelphia: Jewish Publication Society of America), pp. 116-17. Used by permission. Ginzberg's forms of reference to Jewish sources have been modified in this volume to accord with modern scholarly usage.

1. *Sanhedrin* 21a; *Genesis Rabbah* 82.7; *Numbers Rabbah* 4.8; *Midrash on Samuel* 11, 79, and 22, 111; *Midrash on Psalms* 59, 303; *Tosefta-Targum* and Ps.-Jerome on 2 Sam. 3.5. All these sources agree on the identity of Eglah and Michal, but they differ as to the reason why the designation 'little calf' was given to Michal; comp. Ginzberg, *Haggadah bei den Kirchenvätern*, pp. 41-42. According to an unknown Midrash quoted by Kimhi, 2 Sam. 21.10, David also married (took as concubine?) Rizpah, whom he greatly admired for the reverence and devotion she displayed for Saul's unlucky descendants; see *Midrash on Samuel*, *loc. cit.* Comp. also Jerusalem Talmud, *Yebamot* 3, 3d which reads: David married Rizpah. On Rizpah's noble deeds, see also Jerusalem Talmud, *Kiddushin* 4, 65c, and *Genesis Rabbah* 8.4.

2. *Megillah* 15a. This passage contains different views as to who were the most beautiful women. The unanimous opinion seems to be that there were only four women of perfect beauty, but there is no agreement on their identification. Sarah, Rachel, and Abigail are three of the undisputed beauties. As to the fourth, Esther, Vashti, Jael, and Michal are the competitors. Comp. also note 24 on vol. I, p. 60.

sister Merab that the Bible speaks of the five sons of Michal 'whom she bore to Adriel'. Adriel, however, was her brother-in-law and not her husband, but she had raised his children, treating them as though they were her own.[1] Michal was no less a model of piety. Although the law exempted her, as a woman, [117] from the duty, still she executed the commandment of using phylacteries.[2] In spite of all these

1. *Sanhedrin* 19b-20a. As to the legality of David's marriage with Michal, or rather Michal's second marriage to Palti, see note 80 on vol. IV, p. 72, and note 105 on vol. IV, p. 76. Palti, Michal's second husband, is highly praised for his control of his passions; see *Sanhedrin*, *loc. cit.*, and many other places; note 85 on vol. IV, p. 37. Obeying Saul's command, he went through the ceremony of marriage with Michal, and as far as the outside world was concerned, they lived as a married couple; but he never came near her, knowing that she was David's lawful wife. He placed a sword between her and himself, saying: 'The one who will dare to do it (i.e., have conjugal relations) will be slain with this sword'. On the expression נעץ חרב ... ידקר בחרב comp. also *Shabbat* 17a; *Yebamot* 77a. Accordingly there is not the slightest reason to assume, with Heller, *Revue des Études Juives* 49 (1904), 190, that this legend is dependent on Indian sources. Comp. also Gaster, *Exempla* 242, col. 2. On the view that God was the witness to Palti's continence (hence he is called Paltiel), see *Pirqe deRabbi Eliezer* 39; *Leviticus Rabbah* 23.10; Ps.-Jerome, 1 Sam. 25.44; note 85, on vol. IV, p. 37; Ginzberg, *Haggada bei den Kirchenvätern*, 33-35 and 64. On the children of Merab, see Josephus, *Ant.* 7.4.3, and Ps.-Jerome, 2 Sam. 21.8. The latter shares the views of the Rabbis that Michal brought up her sister's orphaned children, and this is why Scripture speaks of Michal as being their mother. As to the means employed by Michal to save David (1 Sam. 19, *seq.*), see *Midrash on Samuel* 22, 110-111; *Midrash on Psalms* 59, 303; Josephus, *Ant.* 6.11.4. According to *Midrash Haggadol, Sefer Bereshit* I, 337, Michal boldly declared to her father that she enabled David to escape because she was convinced of his innocence.

2. *Mekilta Bo* 17, 21; *'Erubin* 96a; Jerusalem Talmud, *Berakot* 2, 4c; *Pesiqta Rabbati* 22, 112b. With the exception of *'Erubin*, *loc. cit.*, Michal is described in these sources as 'the daughter of Cush', which is another name for Saul, who was called Cush, 'Ethiopian' (comp. Ps. 7.1), antiphrastically. Saul was distinguished for his beauty as the Ethiopian for his (dark) color; see *Sifre to Numbers*, 99; *Sifre Zuta to Numbers*, 204 (here it is said: Distinguished for his looks and his pious deeds); *Mo'ed Katan* 16b; *Midrash on Psalms* 7, 69, 70, 71-72 (this passage gives a different explanation of this designation of Cush); *Abot deRabbi Nathan* 43, 12; Targum and Ibn Ezra on Ps. 7.1. The legend about Michal using phylacteries is of midrashic origin. The last section of Prov. is said by the Haggadah to refer to the twenty-two pious women mentioned in the Bible (comp. *Midrash Haggadol* I, 344, *seq.*; *Midrash on Proverbs* 31; note 271 on vol. I, p. 291), each of the twenty-two verses of this section containing the praise of each of these pious women. It was therefore quite natural for the Haggadah to find in verse 25 an allusion to Michal, of

virtues, she was severely punished by God for her scorn of David, whom she reproached with lack of dignity, when he had in mind only to do honor to God. Long she remained childless, and at last, when she was blessed with a child, she lost her own life giving birth to it.[1]

whom one might have rightly said: 'And she rejoices at the last day' (this is the literal translation of the Hebrew), as it was in her very last day that she had the joy of motherhood (comp. vol. IV, p. 117). The first half of this verse reads: 'Strength and dignity are her clothing'. Now since in the Haggadah 'strength' עז is equivalent to 'phylacteries' (comp. *Berakot* 6a), it follows that the woman whose praise is sung in this verse (i.e., Michal) is lauded for having clothed herself with phylacteries. It should also be mentioned that לובש תפלין, which literally means 'clothing oneself with phylacteries', is the technical expression in Palestinian sources for putting on phylacteries; comp. Jerusalem Talmud, *Berakot* 2, 4c.

1. *Sanhedrin* 21a. The narrative given in 2 Sam. 4.20, *seq.*, was adorned with many legends by the Haggadah; comp. Jerusalem Talmud, *Sukkah* 5, 55c, and *Sanhedrin* 2, 20b; *Midrash on Samuel* 25, 124; *Numbers Rabbah* 4.20. The legend about Obed Edom in the last-named source is very old, see *Berakot* 63b-64a; Jerusalem Talmud, *Yebamot* 4, 6b; *Abot deRabbi Nathan* 11, 27; *Song of Songs Rabbah* 2.5; Ps.-Jerome, 2 Sam. 6.11. The reward of this pious Levite who lit the lamp twice a day before the ark which had been placed in his house, consisted in his having been blessed with many children. The women in his house gave birth after a pregnancy of two months only, and bore six children at one time. Israel became now convinced that the ark, far from bringing misfortune, as they thought, upon those who are near it, was a source of blessing and good fortune. It is true the people at Beth-Shemesh (see vol. IV, p. 63) and Uzza (see vol. IV, pp. 95-96) were punished when they came near to the ark, but this was on account of not having shown due reverence to the holy ark. See *Mekilta Wa-Yassa'* 6, 52a-52b. On Obed-Edom see also Josephus, *Ant.* 7.4.20.

D. Harvey

MICHAL
(in *The Interpreter's Dictionary of the Bible*)*

[373] MICHAL mī'kəl [מיכל, *probably shortened form of* מיכאל, *from* מי, כ *and* אל, who is like God? *cf.* MICAIAH]. The younger daughter of Saul (1 Sam. 14.49). Saul learned that she loved David and offered her to David, making the bride price a hundred dead Philistines, and hoping in this way to entice David to his death (18.20-25). David, however, was successful in the ordeal, won great popularity, married Michal, and aroused Saul's jealousy still more. Finally, when Saul sent messengers to kill David, Michal contrived his escape (19.11-17). Saul then gave Michal to Paltiel son of Laish (1 Sam. 25.44; 2 Sam. 3.15). Later, when David made his treaty with Abner, one of the terms of the agreement was that Michal should be returned to him. This was done, much to the grief of Paltiel (2 Sam. 3.13-16). When David brought the ark to Jerusalem, and performed the wild dancing associated with the Canaanite cult as part of the ceremony, Michal rebuked him. David apparently retaliated by giving her 'no child to the day of her death' (6.16-23).

The reference to Michal in most MSS of 2 Sam. 21.8 is probably an error for Merab (so RSV), Michal's older sister and wife of Adriel.

* Reprinted from *The Interpreter's Dictionary of the Bible* (ed. G.A. Buttrick; Nashville: Abingdon Press, 1962), III, p. 373. © 1962 by Abingdon Press. Used by permission.

G.P. Hugenberger

MICHAL
(in *International Standard Bible Encyclopedia*)*

[348] MICHAL mī'kel, mē'kal [Heb. *mîkal*, prob. a contraction of *mîkā'ēl*—'who is like God?'; cf. Phoen., Ugar., *mkl*; Gk. *Melchol*, as if from *mlkl* (?); cf. Syr. *mlky'l* < *malkî'ēl*—'God is my king']. The younger daughter of Saul; David's first wife (1 Sam. 14.49; 18.20ff.).

Saul saw in Michal's love for David an opportunity to have David killed: he set the brideprice for Michal at one hundred Philistine foreskins (1 Sam. 18.20-30; cf. David's similar design against Uriah, 2 Sam. 11). This plan failed, so Saul set an ambush, but Michal helped David to escape. When Saul confronted her she lied, saying that David had threatened her. This lie sharply contrasts Michal with her brother Jonathan, who defended David against Saul even at the risk of his own life (1 Sam. 20.32f.; cf. 19.4f.).

Apparently Michal's false testimony implied David's repudiation of the marriage, and so Saul gave her to Palti(el) (1 Sam. 25.44). However, because David and Michal had not been legally divorced, fourteen years later David demanded his wife back (2 Sam. 3.14ff.)—without violating Deut. 24.1-4. While one should not rule out a motive of love (1 Sam. 18.20ff.; 2 Sam. 6.20a), David's renewed marriage to Michal would legitimate his succession to the throne (cf. Tsevat and Levenson–Halpern).

Michal rebuked David for his unseemly self-degradation (at least in her eyes) when he danced before the Lord as the ark was brought up to Jerusalem (2 Sam. 6). The transfer and housing of the ark in Jerusalem, David's royal city, implied peace and the promise of dynastic succession (cf. Ulshoefer). David detected in Michal's rebuke an underlying bitterness that God had so established a dynasty for

* *International Standard Bible Encyclopedia* (ed. G.W. Bromiley; Grand Rapids: Eerdmans, 1986), III, p. 348. Used by permission.

David rather than her father (v. 21). For her rejection of God's purpose toward David, Michal was cursed with barrenness (2 Sam.
6.22f.; so Hertzberg, p. 281).

The mention of Michal's name in 2 Sam. 21.8 (AV following MT) is
based on a corrupt reading and ought to be corrected to Merab
(Michal's elder sister), with the LXX (so RSV, NEB).

BIBLIOGRAPHY

Z. Ben-Barak, 'The legal background to the restoration of Michal to David', in J.A.
Emerton, ed., *Studies in the Historical Books of the OT* (*SVT*, 30; 1979), pp. 15-29; H.W.
Hertzberg, *I & II Samuel* (Eng. tr., *OTL*, 1964); P.K. McCarter, Jr., *I Samuel* (*AB*, 1980);
J.D. Levenson and B. Halpern, *JBL*, 99 (1980), 507-518; M. Tsevat, *JSS*, 3 (1958), 237-
243; H. Ulshoefer, 'Nathan's Opposition to David's Intention to Build a Temple' (Diss.,
Boston University, 1977).

Abbey Poze Kapelovitz

MICHAL: A VESSEL FOR THE DESIRES OF OTHERS

From a few lines in the Bible, novelists and playwrights have fashioned images of Michal which suit their own literary and political
needs. The works examined here were all written in the twentieth
century and are all available in English. However their authors represent different eras and different cultures. This discussion will focus on
two plays, David Pinski's *King David and his Wives* (1919) and D.H.
Lawrence's *David* (1926), and three novels, Gladys Schmitt's *David
the King* (1946), Stefan Heym's *The King David Report* (1973) and
Joseph Heller's *God Knows* (1984). The writers vary widely in the
ways they interpret and distort the biblical material. Daughter of one
king, wife of another, the biblical Michal is a vehicle for the transfer
of power. Similarly, the literary Michal, in all her incarnations, is a
vehicle for the artistic ambitions of her chroniclers. Not one of them
can match the simple and haunting poignancy of the biblical image.

David Pinski wrote in Yiddish but he was known and admired by a
wide audience in the United States and abroad. In *King David and his
Wives*,[1] Pinski elaborates on the Biblical texts to show how David's
relationships with women determine and express the changes in his
character. The play is written in five sections which follow a straight-
forward chronology: 'Mikhal', 'Abigail', 'Bathsheba', 'In the Harem',
and 'Abishag'. (For this and subsequent works, I will follow the spell-
ing of characters' names as they appear in each text.)

   The Mikhal who appears in Pinski's drama is youthful, passionate,
and proud. Her moods shift quickly, and she expresses every one. The
scene is the garden of King Saul. David, having recently slain Goliath,
strums on his harp as he praises God. Mikhal enters, hides, and listens

---

1. David Pinski, *King David and his Wives*, in Joseph C. Landis, *The Great
Jewish Plays* (New York: Avon Books, 1966).

'with bated breath, eyes shut and hands clenched in ecstasy' (p. 165).
As soon as David speaks to her, she affects an attitude of pride and
disdain. Some verbal jousting ensues before they admit their passion
for one another. Mikhal tells David how insulted she had been when
no one seemed to be accepting the challenge to slay Goliath even
though she was a possible prize. When David appeared, she fell in
love with him at first sight. When he vanquished Goliath and then
refused the offer of Merab, Mikhal rejoiced. Now she interprets that
refusal as David's preference for her. David insists he slew Goliath
only for the glory of God and not for any personal gain. He is loath to
appear desirous of the king's riches or the king's daughter.

Jonathan appears and, in defiance of his father, encourages the
lovers to claim one another. For this he infuriates the already raging
king who comes to berate son, daughter and hero for their presumed
disloyalty to him. In Pinski's play, Jonathan's bond with David is
merely that of a potential brother-in-law.

David desires 'another Goliath' to earn his right to Mikhal. When
Mikhal insists she loves David for himself, not for his bravery, Saul is
amused by her feisty pride: 'Come to my arms', he tells her. 'You are
truly of my blood. No wonder Saul loves you best of all his children'
(p. 172).

Saul demands a new dowry—the heads [*sic*] of one hundred
Philistines. David insists he will bring back the heads of two hundred,
the better to prove his love for Mikhal. As David exits, Saul laughs,
certain that he has sent the young man to his death. Mikhal's triumphant last line, 'He-loves-me. He will conquer!', is accompanied by
Pinski's typically dramatic stage directions: 'a joyful expression on
her face, intense, exalted, breathing heavily' (p. 174).

Mikhal's fluctuating emotions are all in the service of one goal—to
marry the young man who fills her with overwhelming desire. When
one couples her passion for David with Saul's assertion that she is his
favorite child, one understands how doubly threatening David is to the
king. He is not only the courageous warrior, he is the successful rival
for Mikhal's affections. The process has begun by which sexual and
political power will be transferred from old to young. Saul still imagines he will triumph, but Mikhal sees the future: David will conquer.

Mikhal is referred to or appears in later scenes in Pinski's drama,
but she never again assumes center stage. In 'Abigail', Mikhal is mentioned once as David's wife, but the object of his passion is now

clearly Nabal's wife. The end of the scene sums up the new union:

> *Abigail* (bows her head, bends over slowly, and suddenly drops on her knees before him). Let your handmaid be a servant to wash the feet of the servants of my Lord.
>
> *David* (picks her up and takes her in his arms). My dove! My pious dove! (p. 188).

Even at her most adoring, Mikhal is no handmaid; she is, after all, the daughter of a king. And she is surely no pious dove!

The story of Bathsheba admits of no rivals. Although Nathan warns David that consummating his passion for Bathsheba may cause God to take the king's wives, these wives are, at this point, as unimportant to us as they clearly are for David. Bathsheba, in this version, is, at first, the loyal wife, outraged at the thought of a liaison with the king. She prays to God and beseeches her husband to save her from David's desire. She gets no response from God, but from Uriah the response is clear: David is the king and therefore is entitled to whatever he wants. Uriah goes off to battle, knowing that David's orders have ensured his death. The contemptuous Bathsheba now goes willingly to the king who, she asserts, 'shall cleanse me of my stain... shall make me chaste'. David 'meets her triumphantly with open arms' (p. 197).

The fourth scene of Pinski's play takes place 'In the Harem' and involves numerous wives and concubines. Mikhal's role in this group is defined by two incontrovertible facts—she is the first wife, and she is barren.

The Mikhal of this scene is more ambivalent and more interesting than the one we met at the beginning of the drama. As she observes the other wives arguing over which of their sons should succeed David, she laughs bitterly, 'Ha-ha, how they squabble over *my father's kingdom*' [emphasis mine]. This is a telling description from one who was once described as her father's favorite but who now describes her successors as 'all equally the king's wives' (p. 201). An unspoken hierarchy, however, clearly exists. When David enters the harem, all the concubines and all the wives except Mikhal and Bathsheba prostrate themselves. Although these two bow, they remain on their feet.

Seeking to find the cause of the commotion, David asks Mikhal to speak first. She speaks, as she often does, 'proudly'. But within moments, Mikhal is interrupted by Haggith and David turns to Abigail for her explanation. David then berates all the women for acting more like mothers than wives. The barren Mikhal is not only included in the criticism, she is singled out as being 'so old and frozen into ice' (p. 202).

In a poignant interchange, Mikhal not only reveals her current despair, but harkens back to the first scene of the play:

> *Mikhal.* I wish my death would come and free me from my degradation.
> *David.* Your degradation?
> *Mikhal.* To play a trifling part in David's life.
> *David.* And you wanted to be my everything?
> *Mikhal.* Mikhal, the daughter of King Saul, did not want to share her love even with God (pp. 202-203).

David rebukes her for going off with Phalti. She angrily reminds him that she had no choice—Saul gave her to a new husband and besides, David had already taken two new wives. David, who once announced he was unworthy to marry the king's daughter, now justifies his right, indeed his duty, to marry whichever beautiful women God brings to him. In fact, David asserts, he is still fired with passion. Although Pinski gives her no stage directions, we assume that it is with bitter irony that Mikhal responds, 'Rejoice! King David will take unto himself new wives' (p. 204). She speaks no more lines in the play. But as she and David's other women parade out, she 'shakes her head at David and, laughing derisively, leaves' (p. 205).

Perhaps mercifully, Pinski does not tell us her reactions to the events of the last scene—the ministrations of Abishag. But by now the audience knows Michal well enough to need no help from the playwright. Her image stays with us, proud, yearning, and ultimately unfulfilled. Once a necessary part of David's ascent to power, she is reduced at the end to being a cynical commentator on the life that swirls around her.

Michal has a similarly fluctuating role in *David*, D.H. Lawrence's 1926 play in sixteen scenes.[1] Reading this drama is like listening to a simple etude written by a great composer. The narrowness of the assignment necessarily limits the range of the genius. As a novelist, Lawrence is crucial to twentieth century English literature. His combination of psychological insight and linguistic daring brought the English novel to a new level of openness and intensity. Coming as it

---

1. D.H. Lawrence, *David*, in *The Complete Plays of D.H. Lawrence* (New York: The Viking Press, 1966).

does after some of Lawrence's greatest novels—*Sons and Lovers*, *The Rainbow* and *Women in Love*—*David* shares some of their power and passion, and much of their concern with the struggle of the 'special' individual to find his or her place in the world.

David himself is, of course, the special individual around whom the play revolves. The drama documents his life from shortly before the slaying of Goliath through his emotional parting from Jonathan. Michal is a feisty, rather charming supporting player in the personal and political intrigues.

At the opening of the play, Merab and Michal are lively to the point of 'brattiness' as they taunt the captive King Agag. Michal is the more outrageous of the two—spoiled, materialistic, and not above cruelly teasing her sister: '[Agag] looks like a crow the dogs have played with. Merab, here is a king for your hand' (p. 68). Jonathan rebukes Michal for being 'too much among the men', and Saul insists that both his daughters leave with their booty before Samuel arrives (p. 69).

When the girls next appear, in scene five, they are giggling and telling riddles with their maidens. Michal is being teased for her interest in David, and she reacts impatiently, clearly considering herself superior to the others. Saul enters, enraged by their lack of decorum. His fury centers on his younger daughter: 'Be still! Or I will run this spear through your body' (p. 84). Merab steals away, but Michal remains to argue with her father. For her efforts, she is called a witch and repeatedly threatened with death. Saul prefigures King Lear (a similarity later called to our attention by Joseph Heller's David) in his inability to trust those who truly love him. No docile Cordelia, Michal shrieks, but stands her ground: 'I will not be slain!' (p. 86).

Jonathan and David enter, and David rather gallantly defends Michal and tries to deflect the king's anger. Michal berates Saul for embarrassing her in front of David. A seductive byplay ensues between Michal and David, with her questioning the aptness of his complimentary metaphors. Michal leaves, Saul leaves, and the scene concludes with David and Jonathan confiding in each other, swearing eternal mutual devotion, and embracing.

Lawrence is not only a master at depicting intense bonds between men (cf. *Women in Love*), he is also unusually sensitive to the complexities of the female psyche. In scene six, he gives Michal a soliloquy in which she expresses the boredom, frustration, and despair which are the lot of women left behind when men go off to war. She also asserts a particular kind of determination:

> As for me, I don't know whether the Lord is with me, or whether He is not with me. How should I know? Why should I care? A woman looks with different eyes into her heart, and, Lord or no Lord, I want what I want (p. 92).

What she wants is David, and even the reader unfamiliar with the biblical text feels confident she will get him.

David kills Goliath, and Saul offers him Merab's hand. Jonathan and David re-affirm their covenant with each other, but Jonathan realizes the impossibility of his situation, 'split...between King and King-to-be,...torn asunder as between two wild horses straining opposite ways' (p. 108).

There is no doubt where Michal's heart lies. Lawrence underscores Saul's torment by having his daughters sing the famous verses:

> *Merab*. Saul in thousands slew their men!
> *Michal*. David slew his thousands ten!

As the songs continue, it is always Merab who mentions Saul or Jonathan, and always Michal who praises David. Although the bantering sisters still assume it is Merab who will be given to David, Michal aptly describes herself: '...I am Saul's very daughter, and a hawk that soars kinghigh' (p. 112).

When David hears that Merab has been given to another, and that Michal is to be his wife, he is delighted. In Lawrence's version, Michal and David share a mutual passion. In ecstatic, poetic language, they express their love for one another and their plans for the future. The king's men who come to announce the dowry, one hundred Philistine foreskins, reveal to Michal Saul's not-so-hidden agenda: 'dead men marry no king's daughters' (p. 130).

David, of course, is successful, but as Saul's son-in-law he is in constant danger because of the king's hatred of him. While David tries to devise plans to save his own life, Michal is obsessed by her love for her husband. One servant suggests to Jonathan that if Michal had a child to cherish, her love for David would be more diffuse and therefore more manageable. Michal herself sees her barrenness as determined by more than fate: 'Oh, how can I bring forth children to thee when the spear of this vexation each time pierces my womb?' (p. 137).

Hunted by Saul, David escapes thanks to Michal's energy and enterprise. She deceives her father to save her husband. Saul sees through her dissembling and warns her that David will bring them all down. Michal cries out, 'Ah, no! Ah, no!', and although her name is invoked by others, she never appears again (p. 143).

The last scene of the play depicts the farewell meeting of David and Jonathan. Jonathan sends David to safety and future glory. The drama ends with Jonathan alone on the stage, predicting David's triumph and his own death. Of David he says, 'Beyond thy passion lies prudence. . . [Thou] knowest no depth of yearning' (p. 153). Jonathan loves David, but sees him clearly. And how different David is from the passionate, imprudent Michal.

The vibrancy of any fictional character depends on the artistry of the writer. Thus a few scenes in Lawrence's 87-page play present a far more memorable image of Michal than that which emerges from the 630 pages of Gladys Schmitt's novel. Schmitt's *David the King* (1946) is the worst kind of historical novel—elaborating on a legend or an event without adding meaningfully to our understanding or pleasure.[1]

Schmitt makes odd condensations and interpretations of the biblical material. Thus Michal is 'the only daughter of the King of Israel' and Agag pays court to her before he is killed (p. 8). Schmitt is not alone in seeing the bond between David and Jonathan as carrying a strong erotic charge. However, she makes their unconsummated homosexual passion the central emotional force in David's life. All his relationships with women are attempts to escape from or to sublimate his feelings for Jonathan. Jonathan returns David's affections, but in addition he is infatuated with his sister Michal and blames himself for some of her romantic difficulties.

Michal, in Schmitt's version, is a sulky and oddly boyish seductress. She wants David, and knows it is her position as the king's daughter which makes her most desirable to him. The sexual tension between them is more perverse than romantic: 'He yearned after her with the stinging yearning of one who delights in what is evil as well as sweet' (p. 84). And from the start, the relationship seems doomed to be ultimately unfulfilling:

> She walked disconsolately before him. . . 'One is happier', she said, stepping onto the lawn, 'one is much happier dreaming of David than be-

---

1. Gladys Schmitt, *David the King* (New York: Dial Press, 1946).

ing at his side.'

This at least he could share with her. To sing in the King's tent at dawning, to be the King's armor-bearer, to eat the King's bread, to kiss the King's daughter on the lips—not one of these had been more than the muddied reflection of its dream. And what in all his life had risen to the stature that he had marked for it? The night beneath the dripping trees, the night with Jonathan (p. 85).

Perhaps influenced by 2 Sam. 21.19, Schmitt does not have David slay Goliath. He is mistakenly given credit for the bravery of another. Thus, he agonizes over the required dowry:

[Saul] has said he will ask no marriage portion, nothing save the foreskins of two hundred Philistines slain in battle. This he has said to mock me, because I have never slain a man, and my lord the King knows as much (p. 110).

Clearly, Schmitt is trying to de-mythologize David. Saul is reluctant to give Michal to David, not because he fears a valiant rival, but because he does not consider David worthy of his daughter:

He could have sworn before Jahveh that the boy did not love her, that he loved Saul more than her, loved Jonathan more than Saul, loved himself above Jonathan (p. 121).

Saul relents, worn down by the imprecations of his daughter and his wife. He accepts the two (not two hundred) Philistine foreskins David has managed to provide and allows the marriage.

The story resumes five years later with Michal confiding her despair to her friend Mara, Jonathan's wife. An unhappy marriage is made more painful by Michal's failure to conceive. Michal is tormented not only by the current situation but also by how little it resembles her earlier fantasies. Their life is a sordid domestic drama: the wife's attempts to enliven their dull existence by socializing with another couple are sabotaged by the fact that the husband is in love with the other man. A better writer could have fashioned an interesting novel from such a perspective, but Schmitt is a victim of her own verbosity and hyperbole:

The son of Jesse lay dreaming upon an island of peace, his spirit nourished by Jonathan's tenderness, his body lulled by love and the strengthening sun. When Michal called to him from the garden, breaking his sleep with the news that another morning was moving on towards noon and that fresh bread and cool curds lay ready in the shadow of the pomegranate tree, it seemed to him that there were no todays, no yesterdays, and no tomorrows (p. 159).

And on it goes, for nearly five hundred pages more.

Michal's whining self-pity intensifies as the political intrigue escalates:

> Either way, thought the Princess Michal, whether he is slain here or escapes into the wilderness, either way, whether he wins or loses, I will lose. It has always been so with me. When I am dead they will say of me that I was the one who always lost (p. 169).

David begins to see Michal as part of the doomed, cursed house of Saul. He moves on to to other wives and to children. His desire for Jonathan is replaced by mourning. No woman can truly satisfy David. When he is with Amnon's mother (here called Noi) he thinks, 'The King's daughter quarreled and ranted, and this one lies stiff as a corpse, and Abigail sighs and smiles. . .' (p. 293).

Michal is recovered from Paltiel for political reasons, but she never regains a place in David's heart. All warmth between them dies when she berates him for dancing wildly with the ark of covenant. Michal explodes with jealousy, with an accumulation of emotional slights, and with the snobbish fury of one who has married beneath herself. Snatching the earring she is about to put on, David responds in kind: 'If the daughter of Saul makes herself fair for my eyes. . . she labors in vain' (p. 421). He calls upon God to strike him dead if he ever touches her again.

Years later, when David considers his wives, he praises only two— Noi, 'the true wife who has looked to my house and nurtured my children, and the beloved [Bathsheba]' (p. 456). Michal has been sometimes useful to David but never really cherished by him. Schmitt describes David's selfishness and his coldness toward his wives, but the novel never comments upon his behavior. In a different book by a different writer, Michal might have emerged as a tragic figure. As it is, the sympathy we might have felt for her is undercut by our impatience with her character and the novel in which she resides. *David the King* has length but no depth.

Ironically, Schmitt's novel, which has no ostensible goal other than to elaborate on the Bible, deadens its source material. In contrast, Stefan Heym's *The King David Report* (1973) enlivens the ancient text while using it to comment on a modern political situation.[1] Heym's unspoken agenda is to explore the loss of innocence of European communists in the second half of the twentieth century. He does so by creating a first-person narrator, Ethan ben Hosaiah, who is akin to the tormented protagonists of Orwell's *Nineteen Eighty-Four* or Koestler's *Darkness at Noon*. Ethan, a poet and historian, is chosen by King Solomon's minions to write 'The One and Only True and Authoritative, Historically Correct and Officially Approved Report on the Amazing Rise, God-fearing Life, Heroic Deeds, and Wonderful Achievements of David the Son of Jesse, King of Judah for Seven Years and of Both Judah and Israel for Thirty-Three, Chosen of God, and Father of King Solomon'.

Ethan's mission, which he has no choice but to accept, is made clear: he is to shape the material in whatever way best legitimizes and supports Solomon's reign. To survive this challenge, Ethan must compromise his integrity as an historian, his purity as a poet, and his decency as a human being. He is thrust into an Orwellian world where words are as dangerous as actions, where the past is the servant of the present, and where the truth is a chimera. The often conflicting 'historical' accounts of David, that old revolutionary, must be shaped and combined to suit the needs of his political heirs. Out of depositions and pottery shards, Ethan must create a version of the past which will please his masters. To fail means the death of his body; to succeed means the death of his soul.

Ethan is both the consciousness and the conscience of the novel. He is also a version of Heym himself, carefully choosing the words which can safely convey his meaning. Just as the biblical characters become pawns in an intricate game of political chess, so, too, they are artistic pawns for Heym. Thus 'The Princess Michal' exists in the novel to serve as a particular kind of source for Ethan's research.

Michal summons the unsuspecting Ethan to her presence shortly after he begins his task. It is fitting that her go-between is Amenhoteph, the chief royal eunuch—a sexually ambiguous guide to a morally ambiguous world. Ethan meets the rejected wife of King David in a bower in the vineyards of King Solomon. The surrounding bowers are filled with the murmurs of heterosexual and homosexual encounters.

1. Stefan Heym, *The King David Report* (New York: G.P. Putnam's Sons, 1973).

On low cushions a woman half reclined, slender, the dark robe closed at her throat. . . The woman turned her face to me, an aged face, deeply lined, with a large painted mouth and large painted eyes.

I threw myself to the ground. 'Princess Michal!'

I had never seen her; but I had heard of her, as who had not: Saul's daughter, who lived to see all of her family slain but that cripple, Mephibosheth; twice David's wife, who laughed at him, and was left barren. . .

. . . her hands were skin and bone, and her teeth, or what was left of them, long and yellowish. . .

'You will write the story of David?'

Her voice had stayed young.

'At best, madam, I shall compile what other men will hand me; and even that is subject to the approval of the Wisest of Kings, Solomon.'

A peremptory move of her hand. 'What do you know about David?'

'But for the present incumbent of the throne, Solomon, David was the greatest man in Judah and Israel, the Chosen of the Lord God who made a covenant with David and beat down his foes and plagued those that hated him and swore that his seed should endure forever.'

'In other words', again the hand, 'you know nothing.'

I was silent.

'How, then, can you presume to write about him, or even compile that which is given you by others?'

'A man is his legend.'

She frowned.

'You wish to destroy the legend, madam?'

'I want that someone knows about him, after I am gone.'

I waited.

'He was of handsome build', she said, 'delicate when compared with my father's or Jonathan's. And there was the reddish hair above the tan of his face. And he came to us with his music and his poetry. . .' (pp. 31-32).

I quote at some length because Ethan's first interchange with Michal presents much of the richness of the novel as a whole. Michal is a combination of contradictions—looking old, sounding young; imperious but wistful; cynical about Ethan's abilities, but willing to confide in him. She and Ethan become partners in the task, so necessary to attempt, so impossible to accomplish, of discovering, preserving, and presenting the truth. The passage above also conveys some of the strength of Heym's writing. He presents characters powerfully and memorably through specific physical detail and idiosyncratic voices.

The deposition Ethan takes from Michal presents a startling but internally consistent account of passion and violence and intrigue. The young David conquers Saul's court with a mixture of charm and sexual magnetism. He makes love to Saul, to Jonathan, and to Michal. Sometimes able to soothe Saul with his music and his body, he cannot keep from inspiring a jealous rage in the half-mad king. Saul sends David off to battle, hoping he will die, but instead 'that pretty boy became as a man intoxicated by blood' (p. 37). Saul is infuriated by the chants of the women ('Saul has slain his thousands, and David his ten thousands') but cannot stop the inexorable movement of fate. Sent out again to obtain the bloody dowry, David doubles the portion. Michal graphically describes the result:

> He carried the basket unto my father, in the presence of the whole court. I still see him removing the cover and tumbling a pile of blood-encrusted penises on the table, and I can hear him counting up to the full two hundred.
>   And that night he came to me holding a whip, and I lay before him and he punished me, and I suffered it (p. 38).

Michal's account may or may not be accurate. As Ethan later tells Amenhoteph, 'Let us say the Princess dreamed, and I was privileged to listen to her dreams' (p. 60).

In her second deposition, Michal tells Ethan how her bravery and cunning make it possible for her 'helpless' husband to escape Saul's murderous wrath. In retaliation, the mercurial Saul gives her to Phalti, a terrified, misshapen pageboy who happens to catch his eye. Phalti, she says, not only waited on her; he also comforted her when she longed for David.

Michal does not summon Ethan again, and although he has other sources, he wants information only she can provide. When he meets with Amenhoteph to ask for another interview with Michal, the eunuch warns him that his conversations with Michal have angered Solomon and may prove dangerous. Amenhoteph sees to it that Ethan is truly endangered. Drugging him with wine, he tells the historian, 'I will lead you to a place from where you will view history in the making' (p. 123). What the dazed Ethan sees is Abishag ('the stupidest woman in Israel', p. 61) making love with Adonijah. As witness to this treasonous coupling, Ethan is in peril whether he conceals the truth or reports it.

Soon after, Amenhoteph arranges a third meeting between Michal and Ethan. This time, however, the eunuch will be present so that he can report anything 'noteworthy' back to Solomon.

Ethan knows, as everyone does, that David has Michal returned to him when it is politically expedient. Of all the contemporary writers considered here, Heym is the most interested in imagining the complicated emotions of a woman in that situation:

Question: Had you no longer any feelings for him?
Answer: The feelings of a woman are not considered important.
Question: But you felt happy when your brother Ish-bosheth informed you that David had sent to him, saying, Deliver me my wife Michal. . .
Answer: I felt exultant!. . . [ellipses Heym's] And bitter. And full of fears. And there was poor Phalti (p. 127).

Michal reports what went through her mind as she journeyed back to David: that he wanted her because he had paid for her, or that he wanted the woman he had once loved. But why the long silence? Because of his other women, or because of his young men. And finally she decides that he wanted her because all he really cares about is his status as the one chosen by God to rule. As the daughter of Saul, she legitimizes his claim to Saul's throne. Amenhoteph interrupts Michal's musings to warn her she is talking about the father of the present king. Michal replies, 'I am speaking of my husband' (p. 128).

To the husband who would be king, Michal insists that her brother Ish-bosheth is the true king of Israel. Soon after, David summons her to see the bloody head of her brother, and commands the assassins to repeat their 'heroic' tale to the sister of their victim. Michal ends her third and last deposition, certain about the accuracy of her memory, but finally puzzled by some of David's actions. She is the chronicler, the victim, and the survivor of David's cruelty.

Michal never speaks directly to Ethan again. But he learns more about her from other sources. Fearful of Amenhoteph, Ethan tries to arrange a meeting with Michal through Jehoshaphat ben Ahilud, the recorder. Jehoshaphat refuses, but does provide Ethan with a surprisingly frank memorandum David himself has written about the quarrel with Michal after he dances with the ark of God.

The memorandum presents Michal through the eyes of someone who fears and despises her. Michal never lets David forget that she is the king's daughter. Her contempt for David is compounded by sexual jealousy and her bitter awareness that he has rejected her. Their interchange reveals their strongest bond: they know better than anyone else how to hurt one another. David begins:

. . . as for the maidservants. . . I am not ashamed for what they might see,

> for it has served many a maid; but you shall be passed by and shall be childless to the day of your death.
>
> As though you had approached me in love even once, she says hoarsely, after you took me from Phalti. . .
>
> Whereupon I say, Why should I add by my own seed to the blood of Saul which is my enemy?
>
> Oh David! she exclaims. And then, The Lord God knows that your heart is but a clump of ice which freezes those who love you and is deadly to your soul; the day will come when you will feel its cold spreading through you, and all the ministering to you of all the daughters of Israel will not infuse you with warmth. . . (p. 148).

Ethan wants to ask Michal about the quarrel, but his request is denied. Solomon no longer trusts him, and we suspect that the proud Michal refuses to speak directly of her humiliation. Jehoshaphat and Ethan must try, without her help, to separate out the personal from the political. Michal, who legitimizes David's right to Saul's throne, also serves as a constant reminder of the House of Saul. Is there, then, a causal relationship between David's memorandum and the subsequent hangings of the seven male descendants of Saul? In Heym's account, two of the seven are Saul's sons by Rizpah; the other five are the sons of Merab raised by her sister. Jehoshaphat reports that in contrast to Rizpah's dramatic (and perhaps cunning) mourning, Michal bore the deaths with 'dignity'. We are left to speculate whether that dignity bespeaks her royal bearing, her lack of feeling for her foster sons, or her profound despair of ever getting through to David's heart.

The richness of Heym's book lies in how many questions it raises without presuming to provide any final answers. Michal emerges as an intriguing enigma. So do the other characters, particularly the women. Heym presents a poignant portrait of tragic, mad Tamar. Ethan's three women—his wife, his concubine, and the mother of his sons—are all distinct individuals. And Ethan himself raises the essential question about Bathsheba as he goes to interview her:

> [H]ad she been just the helpless soldier's wife coerced to quench the fire in the bowels of the King, or was she the moving spirit of the crimes which followed upon the original sin, using her body and the fruit of her womb to beguile the King until it was her son that sat on the throne. . . (p. 170).

Ethan never knows for sure, and neither do we. He completes his assignment—more in accord with the demands of reality than of truth.

He and his sons and their mother are allowed to return to the safety of obscurity. But his companionable wife is now dead, and his beloved concubine has been appropriated by Solomon for his harem.

Heym's first-person narrator is a self-effacing chronicler of the lives of others considered far more important than himself. A very different narrator regales us in Joseph Heller's *God Knows*.[1] Here it is King David himself, and 'warts and all' would be far too kind a cliche. Heller's David is lusty, petulant, self-justifying, self-aggrandizing, and yet oddly appealing. *God Knows* is a contemporary attempt to both replicate and demystify the power of the legendary character. Like the king himself, Heller's novel exhibits will without restraint, wit without wisdom, and an acute awareness of human foibles without the underlying sympathy which informs comedy at its best.

Heller is a clever, facile writer, and his experiment almost works. One suspects he is trying to recapture the mixture of *joie de vivre* and cynicism which characterizes his comic masterpiece, *Catch-22*. However, what seems generous there seems repetitious here. The 'looniness' of *Catch-22* always seems to be shaped by the centered vision of its creator. However, in *God Knows*, the reader has no sense of an artistic intelligence which decides what to include and what to omit. In this novel, Heller is to words as David is to women. One can never, it seems, have enough of either. This promiscuity, this lack of taste, reveals not love but contempt.

Michal is the most notable victim of David's (and Heller's?) essential misogyny. Ordinarily, it is a mistake to identify the protagonist with the author, but how is one to respond to a book which calls Michal the first Jewish American princess?

> 'Well, thank God that's over with', said the first of my brides on our wedding night. 'I certainly hope we have a son so I'll never have to go through *that* again!'
> . . . 'I had married a JAP! I am the first in the Old Testament to be stuck with one' (pp. 141-42).

One can only be grateful that Heller doesn't enumerate the others.

The zest of David's vulgar narration cannot be denied. In the following passage David not only re-creates some of the important events of his life, he also places himself in a panorama which starts long be-

---

1. Joseph Heller, *God Knows* (New York: Alfred A. Knopf, 1984).

fore his birth and ends long after his death:

> Abraham dumbfounds me still for having performed with apparent ease
> a feat of incredible difficulty. He circumcised himself. . . . I speak with ex-
> tensive, irrefutable knowledge of some of the mechanics of circumcision,
> acquired in the days of my betrothal to Michal, when I went merrily saun-
> tering down from the hills with my nephew Joab and a band of stout-
> hearted singing volunteers to collect those hundred Philistine foreskins to
> pay Saul in exchange for her. It takes six strong Israelites, we figured, to
> circumcise one live Philistine. The job turned easier after I finally got used
> to the idea of killing the Philistines first. It did not cross my uncompli-
> cated mind that Saul was setting a snare for me. It did not occur to him I
> might survive. Each of us had underrated the other. . . and he had the big
> advantage: he knew he wanted to kill me, and I did not.
>
> Even with the passage of so many years, and even with the knowledge
> that she helped me escape the blades of Saul's assassins, I am unable to
> retrieve a single fond recollection from my long marriage to Michal. In-
> stead, welling up within me. . . is the same vindictive resentment I experi-
> enced for her the day she marred my triumph after I had finally brought
> the ark. . . into Jerusalem. . . [S]he was a baneful person who spoiled
> my good days and rejoiced in my bad and who would never allow herself
> to extol or admire me or to view me as most others did in the mythic
> dimensions of a hero king, or as a huge, monumental figure immortalized
> on a great pedestal of white marble, and that's another thing that pisses me
> off about that Michelangelo statue of me in Florence. He's got me stand-
> ing there uncircumcised! Who the fuck did he think I was? (pp. 42-43).

Hundreds of pages later, David is still singing the same song of
resentment and narcissism. Heym must have Michal outlive David so
that she can be a source of information for Ethan. Heller has Michal
die first so that David can tell us over and over again how he rejoiced
at the news of her suffering and death.

Heller's David is an entertaining raconteur. It is difficult to re-read
the biblical text without having his version of the material intrude.
This David vigorously denies the scurrilous rumours about him and
Jonathan. Abigail is the only wife who ever loved him. Bathsheba is
the great passion of his life—a materialistic, manipulative vamp whose
main goal in life is to become Queen Mother. (As David would say,
What does she think this is, England?) Solomon is a humorless, literal-
minded dolt who is serious when he suggests that the two women
divide the baby in half.

Philip Roth's Portnoy says that his life is one long Jewish joke. Perhaps Heller is trying to say the same thing about King David. David is

such a fascinating subject because he is such a paradoxical figure—poet, warrior, shepherd, ruler, lover, brute. When confronted with the spare biblical text, the reader somehow holds all these contradictions in suspension and melds them into a meaningful whole. Heller is too heavy-handed in his juxtapositions of the familiar words from Bible with mean-spirited anachronisms. Thus one of many accounts in the book of Michal's death:

> They went through the usual—the bone marrow and the biopsy. My dreams came true: the biopsy was positive, and we had no chemotherapy. 'My cup runneth over!' I cried in my joy (p. 226).

Towards the end of the novel, David reminds us of his claim that he has the best story in the Bible. (Earlier, he has protested how outrageous it is that, with such a story, he doesn't have even one book named for him.) It is telling, though, that in the same passage he asserts the dark philosophy which undercuts all the exuberance of his life: 'God is a murderer... Sooner or later He murders us all...' (p. 241). Heller never reconciles the contradictory impulses of his novel. And Michal, like the other characters in the book, cannot escape from the essential pettiness of Heller's vision.

Like all literary characters, Michal is a medium through which the writer communicates with the reader. She is necessarily defined and limited by the imaginations of those who transmit and those who receive her story. The added sadness in her case comes from our sense that she was similarly defined and limited by the king who gave her and the king who accepted her for however long she served his ends. The contemporary reader, like Heym's Ethan, can only hope to fashion out of the many contradictory tales a coherent image which does justice to a proud and poignant woman.

Abraham Kuyper

MICHAL
(from *Women of the Old Testament*)*

[109] Michal was the younger of the two daughters who were born to Saul by Ahinoam. Her older sister's name was Merab. Saul hoped that each of these daughters would assist him in causing David's death at the hands of the Philistines. David was to give Saul a hundred fore-skins of the Philistines as his dowry for both Merab and Michal. Natu-rally, Saul supposed that David would be killed before the hundredth Philistine had yielded his life.

Princess Michal was a woman who gave expression to her feelings. She was by no means impervious to the fervor of infatuation. But her most characteristic trait was her desire for prestige. She was always busily plotting for it, and for that she dared to do things. Michal had been deeply impressed by the young man who had killed the giant Goliath. She grew passionately fond of him and made no attempt to conceal her love. When Saul sent his assassins to [110] kill David, she quickly devised a means to deceive her father's emissaries. She placed an idol in David's bed. Soon after that incident, however, her ardor for David waned. Phalti, she thought, was making a better bid for royalty than he, and she would do anything to secure and hold the glamor of royalty. She knew how to charm men. She succeeded so well in Phalti's case that when she later left him in favor of greater glamor, he followed on behind, weeping all the way. But Michal did not weep. Personal pride and the love of prestige leaves no room for these emotions. David had in the meantime been crowned a king and had expressed a willingness to have her again as his wife. Why should not such a woman as Michal was, leave Phalti in the lurch, then, and go to reign as a queen in Hebron?

* *Women of the Old Testament* (Grand Rapids: Zondervan, 1933, r.p. 1961), pp. 109-12. Used by permission.

Naturally, she could never have become David's ideal love. The things that motivated and inspired each were simply too different. It is true that David had pronounced weaknesses and that he occasionally fell into terrible sins. In spite of these occasional overt actions, however, David was a man who lived for more than himself. The service of God was essentially the highest ideal of his life. He did not become proud of himself when he was made a king. Listen, for instance, to his petition in the nineteenth Psalm: 'Keep back thy servant also from presumptuous sins; let them not have dominion over me: then shall I be upright, and I shall be innocent from the great transgression'. David knew that pride was the devil's own peculiar vice, and he sensed profoundly the fatal consequences of it.

Michal did not. As a Jewess, she had, perhaps, [111] prayed to the Covenant God. But we know that she persevered in idolatrous practices from the fact that she kept an image in her house. Hence she was not in the least affected by the fact that the ark of God was returning to Moriah. David certainly was elated by that event. He was so exhilarated by it that he joined the others as they sacredly danced before it. He was happy, not because it involved personal profit, but because God's honor was restored. Michal's reaction was quite different. She stayed at home and watched the excitement of the throng from her window. She felt that it would hurt her queenly dignity to mingle with the common people. When she noticed that King David participated in the ovation as hilariously as any, and that he joined the daughters of Jerusalem's rabble as they danced their glee before the ark, she felt that she had been poignantly insulted. Why, it was a flagrant breach of etiquette, and, just as it would be to any woman who had no appreciation of essential virtues, a breach of etiquette was as terrible a violation as any Michal could conceive of. In response to her reprimand, David firmly told her the truth. He voiced a judgment of the Lord. God never blessed her with the gift of a child.

Merab bore five sons. David was given many sons and daughters. But Michal was selfish and self-centered; she was proud and fanatically eager for pseudo-prestige. And Michal bore no children until the day of her death.

Because of her indifference to the holiness and perfection of love, Michal was singularly fitted to play the role that she did. She could charm David and Phalti in turn. She caused the simple to stare as she moved [112] about in glistening splendor. But she never achieved the greater attainment of being a mother appropriately.

David's life was devoted to the service of God and to that of his subjects. Saul used a helpless Israel as the means to glorify his own person. Michal embodied that same spirit. She supposed that David should have made it his whole duty to increase her queenly splendor.

Herbert H. Lockyer

MICHAL
(from *All the Kings and Queens of the Bible*)*

[224] Let us begin with Michal, the younger of two daughters born to Saul by Ahinoam. Actually, Michal was Saul's substitute wife for David, who should have had Merab, the elder daughter, as the result of his prowess as a fighter. But Merab was given to Adriel.

Michal's name is a contraction of the archangel Michael, which means 'Who Is Like God'. Deeply impressed with the poet-warrior who killed the giant Goliath, Michal made no attempt to conceal her love for this handsome young man. She must have been a woman of unusual strength of mind to declare her love in that age.

When Saul learned of Michal's love for David, there was murder in his heart. He offered to give Michal to David and deceitfully had the message conveyed to him through his servants, 'The king hath delight in thee and all his servants love thee, now therefore be the king's son-in-law'. Saul then made a despicable demand. He required no dowry of David. All he asked David to do was to strip 100 Philistines of their foreskins. David, realizing the honor of being the king's [225] son-in-law, slew 200 Philistines and gave Saul a double supply of what he requested. Saul never thought David would come out of that encounter alive. But God preserved David, and Saul had to fulfill his part of the bargain and give him Michal to wife.

In spite of the evident divine preservation of David, Saul was bent on his death, and so we come to that episode when Michal risked her own life to save the husband she loved. Her love was put to the test, and quick to discern her husband's danger, she outwitted the messengers sent to slay David, whose escape she aided. When the messengers

* *All the Kings and Queens of the Bible* (Glasgow: Pickering & Inglis, 1965), pp. 224-25. Reprinted by permission of William Collins Sons & Co. Ltd, Publishers.

came they found they had been tricked by the image in the bed. Pretending that David had threatened to kill her if she did not aid him in his escape, Michal soothed her father's jealous mood. Although a Jewess, professing faith in the covenant God of Israel, Michal must have had some association with idols as the 'image' she provided proves.

The next glimpse we have of Michal is when David ascended the throne of Israel. Forced to be a fugitive because of Saul's jealousy, Saul took Michal from David and gave her to Phaltiel. Saul and Jonathan were killed at Mount Gilboa, and David's first act as king was to make Jerusalem his capital and place there the sacred ark of the covenant, symbol of God's presence. As king, David demanded the return of his wife, Michal, which Abner arranged. Such a demand seems to indicate that David still had a deep regard for his first wife.

We are told that Phaltiel wept when Michal was forced to leave him, but she shed no tears. She was returning as a queen. Quickly, however, any love that may have lingered in her heart for David through the years of separation, turned to scorn. Taking off his royal robes of gold and purple, and left with only simple under-garments, David danced before the Lord in joy over the Ark's return, and the haughty queen, misinterpreting David's enthusiastic display, 'despised him in her heart'.

Unfortunately, she could not keep her scorn to herself but that night cut David deep with the lash of her biting sarcasm, 'How shamelessly did the king uncover himself to-day!' Perhaps Michal resented being thrown from one husband to another. Back as David's wife she wanted a position as queen. But David did not yield to her whim to increase her queenly splendor. In no uncertain terms, he rebuked Michal for interpreting his humility as vileness and for her failure to recognize the essential significance of his religious acts. That all close relationship between them was severed is implied in the statement that Michal 'had no child unto the day of her death'.

Personal pride and love of prestige, so foreign to tears, appear to have been Michal's faults.

MICHAL
THE WOMAN WHO TRICKED HER FATHER
(from *The Women of the Bible*)*

[109] *Scripture References*—1 Sam. 14.49; 18.20-28; 19.11-17; 25.44;
2 Sam. 3.13, 14; 6.16-23; 21.8; 1 Chron. 15.29.

Name Meaning—This name is allied to the previous name Michaiah,
and also to Michael, and mean[s] the same—'Who is like
Jehovah?' Michal, along with its cognates, illustrates the
comparatively small class of proper names composed of
more than two words. It is a name describing an admir-
ing acknowledgment of the transcendent unapproachable
majesty of the divine nature.

Family Connections—Michal was the younger daughter of Saul,
Israel's first king. Her mother was Ahinoam. She became
David's first wife, was given to Phalti the son of Laish,
of Gallim, for a while, but was recovered by David. As
the aunt of her sister Merab's five sons, Michal cared for
them after the somewhat premature death of her sister.

Michal, although a princess, does not appear to have had a very
commendable character. Desire for prestige, fervor of infatuation,
indifference to holiness, and idolatry mark out this Jewess who knew
the covenant God yet persevered in idolatrous practices. Closely associated with David, her career can be broken up thus—

She Loved David

What young woman would not be attracted by such a strong, athletic
young man, who was 'ruddy, and withal of a beautiful countenance,
and goodly to look to'? Further, David was the young shepherd who
defied and killed the giant Goliath who had terrified Michal's father
and his people. Thus Michal grew passionately fond of David, and
made no effort to conceal her love for this much-lauded champion of
Israel. While there may not be very much to admire in Michal, we
cannot but express sympathy for her experiences in an age when
women were treated as chattels, being thrown from one husband to
another. But while 'Michal, Saul's daughter, loved David', she did not

* *The Women of the Bible* (London: Pickering & Inglis, 1967), pp. 109-11.
Reprinted by permission of William Collins Sons & Co. Ltd, Publishers.

love the Lord as David did. What a different story might have been written of her if she had been a woman after God's own heart!

She Married David

Saul had vowed that the man who killed Goliath would become his son-in-law, and Merab, Saul's first daughter should have been given to David, but Saul, regretting his promise, gave her to another man. David was now a veritable hero among the people, and Saul's jealousy prompted him to devise means whereby David would be slain by the Philistines. Learning of Michal's love for David, Saul asked as a dowry, usually paid to a father according to Eastern custom, the fore-skins of 100 Philistines. David slew 200 Philistines, and Saul was forced to give his daughter to wife to the man whose death he had planned. As David had been victorious, Saul dared not go back upon his word. How Saul illustrates the adage that 'Jealousy is as cruel as the grave'!

She Delivered David

Still bent on destroying David, Saul had David's house surrounded. In a frenzy of envy Saul had messengers 'watch David to slay him in the morning'. But Michal's love smelled danger, and, discovering her father's intention, 'let David down through a window; and he fled and escaped'. Then, as a truehearted wife she tricked her father and his emissaries. With her husband safely out of the way, Michal put a hair-covered image in David's bed, and when the men burst into the sup-posedly sickroom, they found that they had been cleverly tricked. When Saul heard he had been outwitted, he accused his daughter of disloyalty to her father, and was most bitter in his reproach. Michal, however, pretended that David had threatened to kill her if she did not help him to escape.

She Forsook David

After this incident, Michal's love for David waned. Where was the pleasure in being [110] the wife of a man forced to spend his days a fugitive, hunted like a wild animal in the wilderness? Phalti of Gallem was a better catch, she thought, seeing he was on his way to royalty which she was eager to secure and hold. So Michal became the wife of Phalti. This was an illegitimate union seeing David was alive and was in no way lawfully separated from Michal as her husband. That Phalti cared for Michal is proven by the way he followed her, weeping, when she decided to leave him for her former husband.

She Was Restored to David

With Saul's death, circumstances changed for David whom God had already chosen to be king over His people. Michal and her husband Phalti were living in the east of Jordan during the short rule of Ish-bosheth. Abner made an arrangement to assist David to take over the kingship of the nation, and David made the restoration of Michal the one condition of the league. So despite Phalti's sorrowful protest, Michal was forcibly restored to David as he returned from his wanderings as king. Evidently his ardor for Michal was the same as at the first, and his desire to claim her proves how he wanted her as queen in Hebron.

How pathetic it is to read of Phalti with whom Michal had lived for some considerable time. We see his sorrow as he went with her in tears, only to be rudely sent back by Abner! We do not read of Michal weeping as she left the man who had showered so much affection upon her. It did not require much force to make her leave Phalti. Her pride and love for prestige left little room for weeping and although she knew she could never become David's ideal love, seeing she had been the possession of another man, yet as his first wife Michal thought of the position that would be hers at court.

She Despised David

The closing scene between Michal and David is most moving, for what love Michal might have had for David turned to scorn and disdain. After making Jerusalem his capital, David brought the sacred Ark of the covenant, the ancient symbol of Jehovah's presence, to Moriah. On the day of the Ark's return David was so joyful that, stripping himself of his royal robes, he 'danced before the Lord with all his might'. Michal watched from a window and seeing David—the king—leaping and dancing before the Lord, she 'despised him in her heart'. Although she had loved him, risked her life for his safety, she now abhors him for his loss of royal dignity. Her haughtiness was shocked by David's participation in such an excitable demonstration.

Nursing her contempt Michal waited until David returned to his household. When they met, she with a biting sarcasm, revealing 'her self-pride, and lack of sensitiveness to her husband's magnificent simplicity', sneeringly said, 'How glorious was the king of Israel today, who uncovered himself today in the eyes of the handmaids of his servants, as one of the vain fellows shamelessly uncovereth himself!' For her there were no pious and affectionate feelings at the return of the Ark to Zion. Like her father, Saul, she had no regard for the Ark of God (1 Chron. 13.3). But David, mortified by Michal's pride as a king's daughter, was curt in his reply. Resenting her reproach, he made it clear in no uncertain terms that he was not ashamed of what he had done 'before the Lord' who had chosen him rather than any of Saul's family to reign as king. Michal had missed the essential significance of David's career, that in spite of his failures he was a man after God's own heart. As Alexander Whyte put it, 'What was David's meat was Michal's poison. What was sweeter than honey to David was gall and wormwood to Michal...At the despicable sight [of David dancing] she spat at him, and sank back in her seat with all hell in her heart...Michal is a divine looking-glass for all angry and outspoken wives.'

She Lost David
After such an outburst of reproach we read that 'Michal the daughter of Saul had no child unto the day of her death', and such a final flat statement practically means that she lived apart from David, more or less divorced (2 Sam. 6.16). The estrangement between them likely became more acute because of the other wives now sharing David's prosperity. Childless till her death was a punishment appropriate to her transgression. David was given many sons and daughters, and her sister Merab bore five sons, but Michal never achieved the great attainment of being a mother. She ended her days without the love and companionship of a husband, caring for her dead sister's five children, all of whom were ultimately beheaded.

What can we learn from this story of Michal and David? Misunderstanding arose in their relationship because of a clash of temperament, outlook and purpose. Had Michal shared David's faith in God how different life would have been for both of them. But Michal made no effort to understand her husband's Godward desires and so passed a wrong judgment upon him. How certain we should be of a person's motive for his acts or attitudes before we condemn him. Further, had Michal loved David enough, she should have sought his forgiveness after he had explained his demeanor before the Lord. 'She worshipped him when he was poor and unknown and now that he is King "she despised him in her heart"...David realized they could never love the same God. Therefore he cut her from his heart.' But being eaten up with pride there was no tolerance in her heart and so harmony was impossible. Love brings harmony and understanding into every human relationship. A fellow-minister confided in Alexander Whyte that he preached and prayed best when his wife stayed at home. This was something of the gulf between David and Michal. How different it is when husbands truly love their wives and wives sincerely reverence their husbands!

Norah Lofts

MICHAL
(from *Women in the Old Testament*)*

[107] The story of Michal and David opens in the land of faery and ends in the dry dust of psychology. It is a familiar pattern. There are many books in which, as the story advances, a certain light seems to fail and die, and at the end one is left thinking how sad it is that a thing which started so well should have ended so badly; and one cannot bear to look back again at the bright beginning, and is sad for an hour. To such stories this one belongs.

It opens in the palace of the king of Israel where a neurotic man finds solace in the harp music of a shepherd boy, and a young princess hovers in the background, feasting her eyes and her ears and falling in love. It ends with a hard-mouthed woman saying bitter words to another king made dizzy by a music not his own.

Michal was the daughter of Saul, the first king of Israel. The twelve tribes, slowly soldering themselves into a nation, had abandoned the rule of the Judges. Samuel, the last of the line, unwillingly and with dire warnings, had anointed Saul, who was not only Jehovah's choice but also the natural choice of a primitive people, in that he was physically the [108] pick of all the tribesmen, a likely warrior and a man of certain spiritual perceptiveness.

Saul, in his early days of kingship, seemed likely to fulfil his promise, for he planned and conducted successful campaigns against several indigenous Canaanite tribes who resisted the establishment of the Jews as a nation. But in the flush of success he disobeyed Jehovah's direct command and over the matter of the Amalekites' property proved himself to be greedy and materialistic. The divine favour was withdrawn from him and he became conscious of his loss and was

* *Women in the Old Testament: Twenty Psychological Portraits* (London: The Religious Book Club, r.p. 1950), pp. 107-21. Used by permission.

troubled by what the Bible calls 'an evil spirit from the Lord'—a vastly significant statement. And if one chooses to understand that as middle age encroached Saul lost his vigour and his ambition and his courage and drifted into a form of melancholia not far removed from madness, that is only putting the same situation into another mould of words.

A new champion of Jewish nationalism was needed—and found. Saul's son was passed over, and before he died old Samuel was sent to perform another anointing, this one a secret. The sacred oil was smeared upon the smooth boyish brow of David, the youngest son of a substantial sheep farmer of Bethlehem. Saul was still king, but his house was doomed and his successor already chosen.

Some premonition of disaster may have visited him, for his melancholy, his evil spirit, increased, and his desperate servants, searching for some palliative, suggested harp music as a means of exorcism. Who could provide it? Was there not a shepherd boy of Bethlehem with a reputation as a maker of sweet music and as a singer of songs? So they mentioned his name to Saul, and Saul sent to Jesse, David's father, and the proud farmer sent his son with his harp and a present of bread and meat and wine down to Gibeah where the king had his palace. And perhaps to Jesse and to David, who knew about that secret anointing, this movement from sheep farm to palace seemed just like a step on the predestined [109] road; but to Saul David's arrival would be without ulterior significance. The new harpist had come; let there be music.

The first meetings between the king and the king-to-be were pleasant ones, marred by no shadow of jealousy. Even Jesse's offering of food and wine was acceptable to the king of a poor, pastoral people; and David's music delighted him. Probably Saul, tormented, hag-ridden man, saw in the handsome young shepherd the ghost of his own youth, for he, too, had been a handsome young man, full of vigour and confidence; and their upbringings had been almost identical. When Samuel had met Saul and anointed him he had been searching for his father's asses, David had tended his father's sheep. So simple and direct was the step from the farm to the throne in those days. And the harp music proved to be effective. Saul was cheered and comforted and so pleased with his new musician that he sent a message to Jesse saying that he found David indispensable and intended to give him a proper appointment as his armour-bearer.

It is likely that during this happy period Michal saw David for the first time. Elaborate palace procedure and court etiquette had not yet been evolved by the Jews and there would be nothing to prevent the young princesses, Merab and Michal, from listening to the wonderful music made by the young man from Bethlehem. And the beautiful young man who could accompany his music with songs of his own making, who had easy good manners and an air of confidence and high destiny, proved as attractive to Saul's daughters and son as to the king himself. It is part of the tragedy of this story that three of the members of this doomed family should love the man who was to supplant them. Saul's later hatred and ferocity had its roots in a love that had rotted; Jonathan's affection for him has become a byword; Michal married him and risked her life to save his. And as the shepherd boy's brown fingers plucked at the strings, and his voice lifted in song, he must sometimes have [110] remembered the old prophet and the oil and the anointing and known that one day he would sit in Saul's place. So towards the listening princesses his eyes would turn with an unabashed appreciation, which they, in their innocence of the secret, would find all the more entrancing in a shepherd boy.

But this first happy visit to court was not prolonged, and so far as David and Michal were concerned nothing more than an exchange of glances, bold and languishing, had happened. The Philistines, against whom the Israelites had waged intermittent warfare for many years, gathered a fresh army, and with a new champion ready to challenge any Israelite who dared venture into the field against him, opened a new campaign. Three of Jesse's older sons joined the army and the democratic rule of the day empowered him to call David, the king's armour-bearer, back to the farm to help with the sheep. And if, during the quiet rural interval the shepherd boy dreamed of marrying a king's daughter his dreams would have centred about Merab. For Merab was the king's elder daughter, that traditional, fairy prize held out to enterprising young men since the beginning of all legends. It may be that it was with an eye on Merab that David accepted the challenge of the Philistine champion, Goliath of Gath.

He was with the army on that particular morning upon a peaceful and humble errand. Jesse had sent down some supplies for his soldier sons and had entrusted David to deliver them into the fighting line. Every child knows the story of the next hour of that day, and how the over-grown creature who had kept all the Hebrews paralysed with terror appeared to the shepherd boy to be merely an excellent target for his sling, the weapon with which he had practised during the long monotonous hours of sheep-tending back in Bethlehem.

But that slung stone slew more than the Philistine champion; it killed the happy relationship between Saul [111] and his young musician. For as soon as they saw Goliath defeated the Philistines fled in panic and the Jews, strong in their confidence in Jehovah now that He had sent them a deliverer, pursued their enemies and indulged in one of those ruthless, wholesale slaughters which, though logical and perhaps necessary to their own survival, make unhappy reading. Thirty thousand Philistines, we are told, died that day and the pursuit drove on as far as the two chief cities, Gath and Ekron, which were thoroughly sacked.

The credit for that triumphant day went to David, and Michal was far from being alone in her adoration for him. Half the women in Israel were in love with him then; and it was their enthusiasm which enlightened Saul. They came out to meet the young hero, chanting, 'Saul has slain his thousands and David his tens of thousands', and for Saul everything was changed. He might be, as he showed himself to be, genuinely grateful to the young man who had slain the terror and ended, with one stroke, a long war of nerves; he might reward him and praise him; but he could never like him again. For how could he listen to those singing women and not remember the time, not so long past, when he had been a hero, too; when his conquests had been lauded in the streets and the power of confident leadership had reposed in him. And could he avoid the thought that it should have been himself, the crowned, chosen leader of Israel, to offer, at least, to confront Goliath?

There was at first no open enmity. The war was over, Jesse's older sons returned to Bethlehem and David stayed on at Gibeah, still trying to please and soothe Saul with his music. But Saul 'eyed David from that day and forward', and now that he hated the maker of the music the harp lost its curative quality. Even as David plucked melody from its strings Saul's evil spirit triumphed and on two separate occasions moved him to throw his javelin across the music-filled room, intending to pin David against the wall. [112] Twice David escaped, and probably there escaped with him a rumour of the king's malady, a rumour that would widen and darken as time went on.

When the mad moment had passed Saul promoted David and made

him captain over a thousand men. This action was dictated by a neurotic mixture of motives. Partly he would wish to compensate for his lapse into frenzy; partly he would wish for an excuse to get the young hero out of his palace, his city and his sight; partly he hoped that a young, inexperienced soldier suddenly raised to authority would make a fool of himself in the eyes of all Israel. But David 'behaved himself very wisely', and his popularity grew.

So Saul cast about for a means of making this cautious young man reckless, and his eyes rested upon his two daughters. Merab was the elder, the more glittering prize; so when David, summoned into the dangerous presence again, came, Saul promised him that if he were valiant and active in warfare he would give him Merab for his wife. So one of the dreams dreamed on the sunny pastures of Bethlehem had almost come true. But the promise was never kept.

No conclusive reason for Saul's change of mind is given us, and it is possible to accept sheer spite as a reason for Saul's breaking of the promise, and marrying Merab to Adriel the Meholathite. But is it safe to overlook the possibility that Michal had a hand in the business? She was in love with David. She was, as the later events in the story prove, a crafty and resourceful young woman. She could play, successfully, a very double game. Even after her marriage to David she retained to a surprising extent her father's confidence. Is it too much to expect that during this period, while she endured the torture of knowing that David was risking his life many times over in order to qualify for marriage with Merab, Michal applied some of her cunning to the business of getting David for herself? Was it she who suggested to Saul, who was neurotically suggestible, that [113] marriage to Merab would strengthen his rival, marriage to herself would weaken him? They must at least have talked the matter over and she must have acted and spoke with deceptive falsity, for when Saul was told that his second daughter loved David he was delighted and said, 'I will give him her that she may be a snare to him'. What sort of snare, and for whom, the king was to discover at his cost.

So Michal married David.

He was to have so many wives, this second king of Israel; and to so many of them a story was to adhere for all time. There was Abigail, whose shortsighted, drunken husband, Nabal, refused sustenance to the exiled David in a moment of extremity. She was to ride out with the offering her husband withheld and was to be Nabal's widow and

David's wife within a space of a few days. There was Bathsheba, who was to take her innocent bath, be the death of her husband, Uriah, and go up to the palace to bear Solomon. Women were important in David's life; in his last days, with the chill of death upon him, they were to bring the beautiful young Shunamite, Abishag, to his couch in the hope that the old fire would kindle. But Michal was his first wife: and in marrying her he received honour. Afterwards he bestowed it. He was Michal's lover in a very special sense, for she had his untried youth. And he respected her. At a critical moment he obeyed her implicitly; there is no other record of his putting himself into human hands, a passive taker of orders. She may have stood to him as a symbol of an ambition attained, as a pledge of the validity of that secret anointing. She was certainly his superior in sophistication, a thing which matters to a young man. Saul may have kept his father's asses as David his father's sheep, but Michal was a princess, reared in a palace, skilled in intrigue. Did they laugh together in the evenings, when, his military duties done, he came back to their house, over Saul's credulity, Saul's madness, Saul's animosity? Did he [114] tell her about Samuel's visit to the sheep farm, and did she realise that she would in time be queen of Israel while Merab was merely the wife of Adriel? They were, after all, a young couple, married, with all the shared secrets and jokes and intimacies that marriage implies.

But their happy days together were very few. Jonathan, Michal's brother, had managed to patch up a precarious truce between Saul and David and once again David played his harp in the king's presence. And once again Saul's hand strayed to his javelin and once again David escaped from the presence of his would-be murderer. But this time the simple removal of his presence was not enough, and when he reached his own house—with a fine tale to tell his wife about her father's behaviour—Michal told him that the house was already being watched, that he had entered it as a rat enters a trap and that unless he managed to escape in the night, by the morning he would be killed.

It was not, for her, an easy situation. She was still in her father's confidence and though that may have seemed amusing and interesting while the truce between Saul and David held, the moment had come when she must face reality and choose between her father and her husband. And as she betrayed Saul she may have remembered the days of her youth when Saul had been cheerful and confident and kind, a hero to his children as to the whole nation. But she loved David. So now that the double game had ended and she was obliged to decide upon a course of action, she put her long-practised craft and subtlety at his service.

She could not flee with him, for she must stay behind to gain time; and there would be no place for her in the life which he must hitherto lead as a hunted outlaw in the hills and the caves and the waste places. So she let him down through a window, her heart fluttering with nervousness and apprehension, her eyes full of tears, her delicate palms seared by the rope. And David must have wept too; he was a man [115] of easy emotions. As his feet touched the ground he would look up, she down, and their eyes would meet and each would wonder when, if ever, they would look upon one another again. 'This was the parting that they had...'

Michal turned back into the bedroom and took an image and some goat's hair and arranged it in David's bed. And when the men who had watched the house for his homecoming and been back to report to Saul that David was now safe in the trap, returned and asked for him, she said, 'He is sick'. So they went back to the palace for further instructions, and Michal counted the moments, reckoning the fugitive's progress through the night. And presently the assassins returned and this time she led them into the bedroom. Another moment gained, and then the inevitable exposure.

She kept her head. David had gone, it was essential for her own well-being to remain on good terms with her father. So she said that David had threatened to kill her unless she aided his escape. And Saul believed her. Anything pointing to David's villainy would be credible to him; besides, he trusted Michal. It is a tribute to this woman's skill in the gentle art of sail-trimming that both David, making his way to the mountains and outlawry, and Saul, gnawing his fingers with frustrated fury in Gibeah, should equally have faith in her partisanship.

Some years elapsed before Michal and David met again, and in all that time nothing seemed less likely than that they would ever be united. Michal went back to her father's court, and there news of her fugitive husband would reach her from time to time, for Saul was careful to keep track of his enemy's movements and made many plans for his arrest or murder. The stories that came in were wild and varied. Sometimes David, with his little band of guerrillas, culled from malcontents, runaway servants and escaped debtors, was living in caves and hiding-places in the hills; sometimes [116] he took service as a mercenary with alien kings who offered him sanctuary and pay.

One can imagine Michal's feelings and the invidiousness of her position in the court of Israel when it became known that David had sold his sword and the swords of the six hundred who followed him to Achisch, king of Gath, Israel's hereditary enemy.

Other stories came in too, less shocking to the general public in that age of polygamy, but no more welcome to Michal's ear. David had married again. Presently there were two women with him: Ahinoam, a woman of Jezreel, and Abigail, the Carmelite. It seemed that David had renounced his nationality and his wife and that Michal would be left to live out her days, years and years of days, as a lonely woman who was neither maid, wife nor widow.

From such a fate her realistic, mundane, ordinary human nature saved her. She may have known her romantic moments when, leaning against a pillar in the background of the throne room she had listened to a young man singing and playing his harp. But she was not a romantic; and her story is not a fairy tale. She neither pined away from sorrow nor remained steadfastly faithful to her lost love, defying her father when he attempted to make a second marriage for her. Instead she married Phalti; and if she retained any mournful memories, any yearnings for her vanished young harpist, young hero, young husband, she hid them well, for Phalti was very happy with her, as indeed almost any man might have been. For although Michal was ordinary enough, she was intelligent and pliable of mind, a worldly creature at home in the world and happy in it, capable of setting her sail according to the prevailing wind. Such women are responsible for much of the happiness in the life of men.

Even David, through all these tumultuous and eventful years, had remembered her. He had acquired what for a man in his circumstances was a large harem of women; there [117] were six of them by the time he was acknowledged king of Israel, and each had borne him a son. Yet after the battle of Mount Gilboa and the death of Saul and his son Jonathan, when the adherents of Saul sent Abner to tender their capitulation and pledge their allegiance and ask his mercy, the first thing David said to them was, 'Well, I will make a league with thee; but one thing I require of thee, that is—thou shalt not see my face except thou first bring Michal, Saul's daughter'.

It was a wonderful compliment. A woman or two may have started a war in the history of the world. Helen, we know, 'launched a thousand ships and sacked the topless towers of Ilium', but I can think, off-hand, of no other woman whose possession has formed the operative clause in a peace treaty.

Abner and Ishbosheth, Michal's brother, accepted David's terms, and they tore her away from Phalti, who followed her, weeping unashamedly along the road until Abner ordered him back. And then the pair who had last looked upon each other through the gathering night with a rope dangling and a wall looming between them came face to face again.

The meeting, after many years, of erstwhile lovers is never an emotionally simple thing. Romantic stories which pretend that it is so ignore the work of time and affect to believe that during the interval the minds and bodies of the lovers have been in a kind of cold storage from which at the moment of reunion they are able to emerge unchanged. But the fact is otherwise. Experience develops, and living changes people, and those who come together after years of absence are not identical with those who had parted. So it was with David and Michal. They had both developed along lines which were already laid down for them when they whispered their tearful farewells through the darkness.

[118] Materially their positions had reversed, too. When they parted he had been a favourite out of favour, fleeing for his life, with no inch of land to call his own, no house to be his home. And she had been the daughter of the ruling monarch. When they met again David was already king of the greater part of Israel and on the eve of being king of the whole, and she was the daughter of a dead and defeated and dis-graced king, and the wife of a nonentity.

But that could have been adjusted. David had remembered Michal even if she had forgotten him; and he owed her his life; and whatever his faults, a conventional materialism was not one of them. He had remembered her with love, and now he was prepared to take her back and give her her rightful place as his first wife.

Unfortunately, during those intervening years, they had developed upon divergent lines. Michal, never a very spiritually minded woman, had grown hard and conventional. Saul's affection for David was—if we except his superstitious visit to the woman of En-dor—the last evi-dence of his consciousness of the world behind the world and it is not likely that for Michal's husband he would have chosen a very godly man. Michal had become accustomed to the single-minded devotion of an ordinary human being; and now—no longer in her first youth—she was called upon to adjust herself to the very unordinary man into whom her talented shepherd boy had grown.

David, on the other hand, although during his exile he had done many things to modern eyes unbecoming in a godly man, had never lost his awareness of the spiritual world or his faith in, and his consciousness of, Jehovah as the moulder of his destiny. The conception of God as a Being invisible and intangible, yet existent and vital and immanent, was still in its infancy, and one sees over and over again in the Old Testament story that a man's conscious acknowledgement of this invisible force is of vastly greater importance than his [119] actual behaviour. (Morally judged, Esau was preferable to Jacob, just as, by all standards of hospitality, centuries later, Martha was preferable to Mary; but in the eyes of Heaven what mattered was the attitude of *mind*.) In this respect David had never failed. He might be bloody and lustful and tricky, but he was these things in the sight of his God. He might take the holy shewbread from the altar and share it with his hungry hoarde of mercenaries, but when he did so it was not because he believed that there was nothing behind the altar, but because he was certain, from the moving of the spirit within himself, that what was behind the altar would understand and condone.

For years he had lived in close touch, often in direct communication with, the unseen; and these same years had hardened Michal, who had loved him, into her mould—the ordinary, conventional, worldlyminded woman who could make happy almost any man except one of David's type.

Upon the minor, nerve-fraying, destructive differences that were inevitable between them, a pair of lovers too late reunited, history sheds no light. The historian is busy with David's further triumphs and has no time to spare for Michal's bewilderment and muddled memories of a young lover and fitful regrets for Phalti. But their story ends in a noisy clash of personalities. That was inevitable, for Michal, though ordinary enough, was no cipher and David was God's troubadour.

Soon after their reunion he scored another victory against the Philistines and then went on to turn the Jebusites out of Jerusalem, that strongly fortified, rock-founded city which had defied all former attempts of the Israelites to capture it. It was the obvious future capital of the country, and when it fell David visualised in it the Great

Temple and the Great Palace which were to be for Bathsheba's son to rear. But as a first step he must bring up the Ark of the Covenant and place it with solemn ceremonial upon the spot where he [120] himself intended to build the Temple, and the day when the Ark moved into Jerusalem was incomparably the greatest day that Israel had ever known. Dancing, shouting crowds, hysterical with religious and patriotic fervour, followed the Ark into the captured city and David, the religious, as well as the civil and military head of the nation, threw himself into the dancing and singing without restraint. He would have done so if he had still been the shepherd boy of Bethlehem, for he was a musician, a poet, immensely susceptible to the significance of a situation. For years Saul had hunted him down as men hunt wild animals, yet when Saul was dead David had taken his harp and composed a song, immortal and haunting in its beauty. 'Ye daughters of Israel, weep over Saul, who clothed you in scarlet with other delights.' If he could feel thus about Saul, who was his enemy, how violent must have been his emotion at this coming into the new capital of the Ark of Jehovah, who had through all these years guided and favoured and supported him?

Michal, from her privileged place along the line of procession, looked down and saw the man she had loved, the king of Israel, behaving like a drunken man, his clothing disarrayed, his face distorted, dancing and shouting, oblivious to everything in the world save that the Ark, the only earthly manifestation of Israel's God, was coming in triumph into the city which God had given His people. Subject to no such spiritual afflatus herself, she looked at him dispassionately and thought that he looked like a drunken clown. Any observer of another person's complete abandon feels the same, especially if the abandon arises from an intoxication which the observer has never known. And Michal had never been religiously drunk. To her earth-bound eyes the Ark was just a little wooden structure being borne on two poles; and David's transport of emotion an hysterical, shocking lapse from dignity.

[121] There may have been eyes as blind, hearts as unmoved, as hers in Jerusalem that day; but their possessors refrained from speech. Michal, however, as soon as the ceremony was ended and David had returned home in a state of happy exhaustion, spoke her mind. The words were few, but they had venom, and pungency, and were full of the wish to hurt. 'How glorious', she said, 'was the king of Israel

today, who uncovered himself in the eyes of the handmaidens of his servants as one of the vain fellows uncovereth himself.' It was all there—her shame for him, her utter lack of understanding, the blow which her respect for him had sustained. One can even see the hint that she, daughter of a king, had a better notion than he, the upstart, of how a king should behave. But the barbed speech proves, too, that she was not, even now, indifferent to him. No woman feels shame for, or wishes to hurt, the man in whom she is no longer interested.

Other men have suffered bitter criticism from their wives and either borne it with fortitude or ignored it. But for David Michal had trodden on holy ground. His answer to her was simple. 'It was before the Lord which chose me before thy father and before his house to appoint me ruler over Israel.' And he added, with truth (for we remember Uriah), that he would do worse things, vile things, things that would make him base in his own sight.

That was the end of things between them. David never looked upon her as his wife again. The Old Testament says that the worst fate for a Jewish woman befell her—she bore no children to the day of her death. Josephus says she returned to Phalti and bore him five children.

Looking back to the story's beginning, when a young princess fell in love with a handsome young shepherd to the strains of the music of a harp, who shall say which is the sadder ending?

Peter D. Miscall

MICHAL AND HER SISTERS[*]

Introduction

I will present brief scenes or glimpses of Michal and of the other women (and men) that I discuss. I will not develop a full and consistent portrait of any of them. The narrative of the books of Samuel (and of Kings) does not present such portraits, especially of women. On the one hand, this partialness and brokenness of characterization is an integral part of the biblical perception of human character; this applies even to Moses and David who occupy such large blocks of material. On the other hand, given the length and fullness of the depiction of male characters such as Samuel, Saul and David, the partialness and the limitedness of the portrayals, that is, the glimpses, of the women involved with the men are striking. The contrast in the treatment of Michal and Jonathan, both children of Saul, is an excellent example.

In my readings I pay attention to textual details, including punning. Part of this reading process involves comparing and contrasting the biblical passages analyzed and the different women portrayed in them, as well as asking how the reading of one passage or portrayal can affect that of another passage. Much of my reading is based on implication rather than on explicit statement.

I will be concerned mainly with Michal, Merab, Rizpah and Bathsheba, with brief comments on Abigail, Ahinoam and Abishag. I focus on them as women in themselves and in their relations, or lack of relations, with others. The latter necessitates considering them as important members of the royal families of Saul and David; therefore a portion of this essay has to consider the men since it is their domi-

---

[*] Reworking of a paper presented as a response to other papers to the Narrative Research on the Hebrew Bible Group, Chicago, November 1988.

nance of story and text that highlights the glimpses of the women.

For general background, I consider that a major theme of Samuel–Kings is the negative and critical presentation of kings and kingship (see Polzin; Miscall, 1983, 1986). The narrative wants to show what kings, including David, actually do and what dynastic kingship, with its drive for continuity and succession, entails for the royal family and for their subjects. I focus on these women who belong to a royal family.

One of Samuel's main warnings about 'the way of the king' is that he will take many of the Israelites for his military, building and personal projects (1 Sam. 8.11-18):

> He will take your daughters to be perfumers, butchers and cooks. . . He will take your men servants and women servants. . . for his own work (8.13, 16).

We will see that this warning is mild in comparison to how kings actually treat women. In short, women, whether mothers, daughters or wives, are chewed up and spit out in royal politics and power plays.

Merab

Saul's daughters are first mentioned in the family note at the close of 1 Samuel 14: 'the name of the first-born was Merab and the name of the younger was Michal' (v. 49). They are next alluded to in the Goliath story. The army asserts that if someone kills the Philistine braggart, the king will reward him with wealth and 'will give him his daughter' (1 Sam. 17.25). Nothing more is explicitly said of this reward, especially the giving of the hand of the king's daughter, in the aftermath of David's killing Goliath (18.6-16). Instead, Saul reacts to David's success with anger and jealousy and the feelings are so intense that he twice tries to kill David. His reaction to David's success then turns to fear. One part of this may be a fear that he will kill David in one of his insane fits; he sends David away from him to the battle front to avoid this possibility (18.13).

Perhaps as a reward for killing Goliath or for his overall success against the Philistines, Saul offers his daughter to David:

> 'Here is my eldest daughter Merab; I give her to you as a wife. Only be my warrior and fight the battles of the Lord.' And Saul said [to himself], 'Let not my hand be upon him; let the hand of the Philistines be upon him' (18.17).

Saul's inner statement does not explicitly connect David's marriage
and death as cause and effect. It may be his intention to continue to
keep David away from him so that he won't kill him or attempt to kill
him. This is expressed in NIV, 'I will not raise a hand against him. Let
the Philistines do that!' (also see NRSV).

After David's (sincere or insincere) objection that he is unworthy to
be the king's son-in-law (*ḥtn*),

> at the time of the giving of Merab, Saul's daughter, to David, she was
> given to Adriel the Meholathite as a wife (18.19).

This may or may not be a result of David's objection. What is noteworthy is that Merab, the king's oldest daughter, is merely an object,
whether reward or not, to be handed back and forth. We know
nothing of her feelings and reactions to the plans and to the change in
plans. David doesn't even mention her by name. 'Son-in-law' is a
phrase that relates two men and leaves the daughter and wife, who is
essential to the relationship, out of the equation. Merab's marriage to
Adriel is narrated with passive and impersonal constructions, 'the
giving of' and 'was given to'. We cannot even be sure that Saul is the
agent of this change in the destiny of his daughter.

Michal and the In-Laws

There is an initial point of contrast with the appearance of Michal[1]
since, for the only time in biblical narrative, we are told of a woman's
love for a man (Alter: 118), and her father's reaction is striking.

> Michal, Saul's daughter, loved David. When Saul was told, he was
> pleased. Saul said [to himself], 'I will give her to him, and let her be a
> snare to him, and let the hand of the Philistines be against him' (18.20-
> 21).

If Michal's love for David pleases Saul, are we to understand that
Merab did not love David and that this had something to do with her
marriage to another? In any case, Saul's concern is not with his

---

1. My reading of Michal is particularly indebted to the work of Alter and Exum
and is, in most ways, a reading that complements, rather than disputes, their
interpretations. Further, without Exum's attempt 'to hear the women's voices
differently' (1989: 36), I would not have been concerned with Michal and her sisters
as women in the royal houses.

daughter's love and what that may mean for her but with the fact that the love is for David whom he so greatly fears.

The story, in fact, is about the maneuvering between these two in-laws. Michal is mentioned by name only at the very beginning and end of the episode. Saul speaks of three things to himself—giving her to David; she should be a snare; the Philistines can fell David—and the relation, causal or not, between them is not explicit at first.

Saul proceeds with giving her but leaves 'her', Michal, out of the proceedings. David is offered a second chance 'to be the king's son-in-law'. (The verb *hithattēn*, to be a son-in-law, occurs five times in vv. 21-27; from the end of v. 21 to that of v. 27, Michal is never mentioned by name, by the appellation 'Saul's daughter', or even by pronoun.[1]) Saul follows the offer up with a 'secret' message to David that he is delighted with David and that all his servants 'love' David. The latter assertion may be true (see vv. 5 and 16), but it blatantly omits mention of Michal's love for David which should be the basis for the proposal.

David protests his unworthiness, as with the proposal that he marry Merab, to be the king's son-in-law and again says nothing explicit about Michal. Saul focuses on the claim of poverty in David's protest and counters it with a unique bride price, a hundred Philistine fore-skins. This time, to himself, he thinks a clear causal relation. 'Saul was counting on David falling at the hand of the Philistines' (v. 25). Now it is David's turn to be pleased, not by a woman's love, but by a grotesque offer that provides an opportunity to prove his military power. In fact, he doubles the number of foreskins so that 'he could be the king's son-in-law'.[2] Finally Michal re-enters the story by name but only to be handed from father to husband: 'And Saul gave to him Michal his daughter as a wife' (v. 27).

Saul fulfills his opening proposal even though the hand of the Philistines has not been against David. Now, at the close of the

---

1. Moses also has a father-in-law, Jethro, and his daughter Zipporah, Moses's wife, is frequently left out of the relational equation. Moses and David, who are different on so many counts, are similar in their relation to and in their treatment of women, even if their wives. In an earlier work I noted a connection between David, who becomes a bridegroom through the blood of Philistine foreskins, and the 'bridegroom of blood' in Exod. 4.24-26 (1983: 91-92).

2. Fokkelman (pp. 227-42) develops the motif of doubling and its many manifestations. I have noted parallels with Jacob and Samson (1983: 87-88).

episode, he reacts quite differently to Michal's love for David, perhaps realizing that her love cannot be exploited, that she is not to be a
snare for David, that she is not to lead him into trouble or disaster.[1]
Exum, in fact, regards Michal's love as a snare for Saul (1989: 24,
note 12).

> Saul realized that the Lord was with David and that Michal, the daughter
> of Saul, loved him. He grew ever more afraid of him and was his enemy
> the rest of his days (18.28-29).[2]

The Escape
Jonathan, Saul's son, may love David (18.1) and greatly delight in him
(19.1), but he does inadvertently serve as a snare. He reconciles the
two in-laws and the reconciliation results in Saul's third attempt 'to
pin David to the wall with the spear'. David eludes the throw a third
time and 'flees and escapes' (19.9-10). Saul gives up his indirect
approach and 'seeks to kill David' with a direct attack (19.1-2, 10). He
sends messengers to kill David. Michal, who was supposed to be the
snare, is now David's wife (v. 11). Explicitly and on her own initiative she urges him to escape and save himself.

Because of her love for him, she chooses her husband over her father; this is an ironic anticipation of David's later rebuke to her that it
was 'the Lord who chose me rather than your father' (2 Sam. 6.21).
She, now and only now Michal in her own right and without relational
epithet, not only helps David escape but also covers up for it to give
him added time.

Saul's sole intent is to kill David (vv. 11-15). Michal accomplishes
his escape and is questioned about the deception by Saul. It is Michal
and Saul, not father and daughter, who play this scene, and her
response is chilling.

> Saul said to Michal, 'Why did you let my enemy go and escape?' And
> Michal said to Saul, 'He said to me, "Let me go! Why should I kill
> you?"' (19.17).

Is Michal's response part of her deception or is it an accurate report

---

1. Worship of foreign gods is the main snare, *môqēsh*, in the narrative in
Genesis–2 Kings; see Exod. 23.33, Deut. 7.16 and Judg. 2.3. A covenant with the
inhabitants of the land and Gideon's ephod are snares (Exod. 34.12 and Judg. 8.27).
Moses is a snare for the Egyptians (Exod. 10.17).
   2. I note the pun between Michal's love, *'ōhēb*, and Saul's enmity, *'ōyēb*.

of what actually happened? Is David's flight a temporary absence from Michal or is this the beginning of the alienation that reaches its climax in 2 Samuel 6?

2 Samuel 22

The incidents in 1 Samuel 19 are punctuated by reports of David's flight and escape. The verb 'to escape' is the niphal waw-imperfect, *wayyimmālēṭ* (vv. 10, 12, 17, 18), or the piel participle, *memallēṭ* (v. 11), 'to save'. David escapes Saul's attempts to kill him; the verb 'to kill', *mût* in various forms, occurs eight times in 19.1-17.

Perhaps at this time, perhaps later,[1] David sings a song to the Lord which celebrates his deliverance from the power of Saul. He sings of the incredible threats to him and of his appeal to the Lord. In mighty and terrible fashion, and because of David's plight and righteousness (2 Sam. 22.21-25), the Lord comes down and saves David. David gives no credit to Michal's indispensable role in the rescue despite his verbal allusions to the narrative in 1 Samuel.

> Encompassed me, the cords of Death, and the torrents of Belial over-whelmed me.
> The cords of Sheol surrounded me; confronted me, the snares of Death
> (2 Sam. 22.5-6).

David puns on the threat of Saul (*shā'ûl*) and the cords of Sheol (*she'ôl*). This alerts us to other wordplay. David is confronted by 'the snares of Death (*mōqeshê-māwet*)', a clear allusion to the snare (*môqēsh*) that Michal is supposed to pose and to Saul's blatant attempts to kill (*mût*) David in 1 Samuel 19. It also alludes to David's reported threat to kill Michal (1 Sam. 19.17).

Michal rescues (*memallēṭ;* 1 Sam. 19.11) David, but David praises the Lord, his rescuer (*mepallēṭ;* 2 Sam. 22.2, 44),[2] David employs a near-homophone to describe the rescue; he can come no closer than this to admitting Michal's role. However, there is an insidious allusion to Michal's continuing story.

---

1. The contents of 2 Sam. 21–24 stand in an uncertain temporal relation to the preceding narrative of David's life. Brueggemann discusses some of the issues in his article; however, à propos of my essay, he says nothing of Michal (Merab) and Rizpah in 2 Sam. 21.1-14. I don't address the time issue further since the exact time when David recites the song is not the significant point.

2. I transcribe the Hebrew words from 2 Sam. 22 in slightly changed form to highlight the wordplay with 1 Sam. 19.

David adds wives to his house. He takes Abigail after she saves him from slaughtering her husband and his men and bringing future bloodguilt on himself. Despite this act, she plays no significant role in David's house or life. She, along with Ahinoam, accompanies David on his flight from Saul (see 1 Sam. 27.3, 30.5 and 2 Sam. 2.2); she is listed with her son Chileab (2 Sam. 3.3) and then is not mentioned again. In her very perceptive reading of the story of Abigail in 1 Samuel 25, Alice Bach observes that

> After Nabal's death, Abigail becomes a widow, *'almanah*. The word is derived from the root *'lm*, meaning dumb, without speech. From the same root comes the noun *'elem*, meaning silence. . . In spite of her marriage to David, Abigail remains a widow, that is, she survives without speech in the text. Her name is mentioned twice to remind the reader that she lives. Although she has a son, he is Chileab, like (his) father, and thus not connected with his mother. We do not hear her voice again (p. 53).

When David takes Abigail, he also takes Ahinoam of Jezreel (1 Sam. 25.43).[1] I emphasize the 'taking' since we are immediately told of a 'giving': 'Saul gave Michal his daughter, David's wife, to Palti son of Laish who was from Gallim' (25.44). In royal families, women do not marry; they are taken and given by others.

Palti is heard of one more time. In his negotiations with Abner, David demands the return of Michal, Saul's daughter. We can only assume that Abner's reply was positive. David sends directly to Ishbosheth, Saul's son, 'Give me my wife Michal whom I betrothed with a hundred Philistine foreskins' (2 Sam. 3.14). The latter is a not-so-veiled reference both to David's penchant for bloody violence and to the threat to Ishbosheth if he should not act in accord with David's demand.

> And Ishbosheth sent and took her from her husband, Paltiel of Laish. And her husband followed her weeping to Bahurim. Abner said to him, 'Return!' and he returned (2 Sam. 3.15-16).

Even in this powerfully emotional scene we see and hear 'her husband' and not 'her'. Does she also weep and mourn? Does she love

---

1. Ahinoam appears here and in 1 Sam. 27.3; 30.5; 2 Sam. 2.2; 3.2. She is the mother of Amnon, David's firstborn in Hebron (2 Sam. 3.2). Because he rapes Tamar, Amnon is killed by Absalom. Nothing is said of Ahinoam after 2 Sam. 3, and the fate of her son is the first sign that the sword will never depart the house of David.

Paltiel as she did David? We do not know, for she is again taken and given.

Palti is a name based on the verbal root that underlies *mepallēṭ* and would probably mean 'My Rescue' if it were a noun.[1] Paltiel would mean something like 'God is my Rescue'. This is ironic. Saul takes Michal from David and gives her to Palti, 'My Rescue', but it is David, not Saul, who is rescued. It is also perverse. Michal rescues David; God rescues David. But no one, human or divine, rescues Michal, not even Paltiel, 'God is my Rescue'.

The Explosion

We have glimpses of Michal, of what she does and of what happens to her. We have one glimpse of her feelings: she loves David. In 2 Samuel 6 we get another. But in between we hear nothing of what she feels about David's departure or about her being handed back and forth. However we understand the total complex of her emotions, they explode when

> Michal, the daughter of Saul, saw King David leaping and dancing before
> the Lord, and she despised him in her heart (2 Sam. 6.16).[2]

Michal knows the violence and blood that have allowed David to reach this point, and we can easily imagine the contempt when she sees the 'king' dancing 'before the Lord'. David returns and is met by 'Michal the daughter of Saul'. A brutal and angry exchange occurs and is followed by the announcement, 'and to Michal the daughter of Saul there was not a child to the day of her death' (2 Sam. 6.23).

Sometime after this there was a three-year famine and David consulted the Lord about it (2 Sam. 21). The Lord told him that 'there is bloodguilt upon Saul and his house because he put the Gibeonites to death'. Saul had apparently, at some earlier time, attacked the Gibeonites 'in his zeal for the Israelites and the Judahites'. David, perhaps fearing that a mere sacrifice or other ritual might suffice to atone for this wrong, and having a good idea of what the offended party will demand, consults the Gibeonites and not the Lord. Is this evidence of David's zeal for the Israelites and the Judahites or of his zeal to put

---

1. I assume a noun, *peleṭ*, with the first singular pronominal suffix.
2. Alter's discussion (pp. 122-26) of the scene is a fundamental starting point for contemporary readings of 2 Sam. 6; Clines, Exum, Polzin and I build on it. Exum refers to the scene as 'a veritable emotional explosion' (1989: 24).

more Saulides to death so that Saul 'will have no place anywhere in the territory of Israel'? Seven of Saul's sons are to be handed over to be hanged. In these exercises of royal power in clashes between rival houses, it is not just daughters who are given to another.

> The king took the two sons of Rizpah, the daughter of Aiah, whom she bore to Saul, Armoni and Mephibosheth, and the five sons of Michal, the daughter of Saul, whom she bore to Adriel, the daughter of Barzillai, the Meholathite (2 Sam. 21.8).

They are put to death in the spring and Rizpah protects the corpses and then the bones until late fall:

> Rizpah, the daughter of Aiah, took sackcloth and spread it for herself upon the rock from the beginning of the harvest until water from heaven fell on them. She did not allow the birds of the heavens to light upon them by day or the beasts of the field by night (2 Sam 21.10).

According to Deut. 28.26, the latter are covenant curses. Rizpah keeps the effect of the covenant curses from those whose only sin is to be in Saul's family. Her silence and her vigilance speak of the failure of words to express the grief and the horror of the atrocity much as Paltiel's tears and David's weeping for Absalom voice their unspeakable grief (Josipovici: 191-209).

Her compassionate vigil does not go unnoticed. David is told of it and responds by gathering the bones of the seven, along with those of Saul and Jonathan which are still at Jabesh-gilead, and burying them in the tomb of Kish, Saul's father. Is David inspired or shamed by Rizpah's care? Does he want to show a similar respect for the bones of Jonathan and Saul? Or is he worried by it? Does it draw too much attention to the family of Saul? He wants to bury all the bones and seal the memories of Saul and of his house in a tomb.

In any case it is only men, and not women, who are entombed. We are told nothing of the ultimate fate, of the death and burial, of Merab, Michal or Rizpah. We know of the fate of fathers, sons and even of a grandfather (Kish), but not of that of women, whether mothers, daughters or wives.

On the other hand, the women figure the end of the house of David. The covenant curses fall on Judah, Jerusalem and the final kings of the Davidic dynasty. Zedekiah's sons are killed in his sight (2 Kgs 25.7), but this time there is no Rizpah to watch over their corpses and their bones. Zedekiah and Jehoiachin both die in Babylon. And there is no

David to gather, for whatever purpose, all the bones and place them in the ancestral tomb. The bones are scattered abroad from Jerusalem to Riblah to Babylon.

Rizpah

Rizpah is Saul's concubine (2 Sam. 3.7) and she bears him two sons (21.8). We are not given the two pieces of information in the same context. In the first, Ishbosheth angrily upbraids Abner for 'going in to my father's concubine'. On a first reading this appears to be a claim to Saul's status and authority on the basis of parallels with Reuben's lying with his father's concubine (Gen. 35.22) and Adonijah's request for Abishag (1 Kgs 2.13-25). This reading is given greater strength and seriousness when we learn that Rizpah has two of Saul's sons; Abner is laying claim not just to Saul's concubine but also to two of Saul's sons. Abner is attempting to replace Ishbosheth as Saul's heir. However, the attempt is not to make himself king but to put himself in the position to transfer the kingdom to David. David accepts Abner's offer on condition that Michal, Saul's daughter and his wife, be returned to him; he wants no Abner going in to her.

David doesn't have to worry about Michal's children, whether his or Palti's, since 'to Michal the daughter of Saul there was not a child to the day of her death' (2 Sam. 6.23). However, in 2 Sam. 21.8 we are told that David took 'the five sons of Michal, daughter of Saul, whom she bore to Adriel, the son of Barzillai, the Meholathite'. Apparently this was Merab's husband (1 Sam. 18.19).[1] Did she die in the interim or was she also a victim of the brutality of royal politics? Husbands and wives have again been separated and the wives given to others. The final outcome is total humiliation for Michal since these five sons are handed over for execution. With a slight adjustment of the preposition, David arranges it so that the previous assertion is accurate: 'to Michal the daughter of Saul there was not a child at the day of her death'. The women in the royal families might wish that

---

1. We could argue that this Adriel, the son of Barzillai the Meholathite, is different than the Adriel the Meholathite whom Merab married. This, however, strikes me as special pleading of the type reflected in the translations which replace MT 'Michal' with 'Merab' which is attested in some Septuagint manuscripts. Even if we go with either of these readings, we still have the situation in which women are being handed back and forth between husbands.

they had only been taken to be perfumers, butchers and cooks and to do the king's work.

In summary, I comment on Michal and Rizpah since we get at least a glimpse of their feelings. Michal is a woman who loves and who, because of that love, saves her husband from her father. In time this love turns to hatred and fury. Michal ends childless and without comment on her emotions and reactions to the brutal turn of events. Because of her children, Rizpah is also a pawn in royal politics with no hint of her views of or feelings about Abner and Ishbosheth. Like Michal, she ends childless but her silent and compassionate vigil speaks volumes for her emotion and for her stamina.

Bathsheba

Bathsheba is another woman who is taken, indeed, raped, if we read the narrative with Mieke Bal (1990). Sternberg's lengthy tortuous reading (pp. 186-222) of the story in 2 Samuel 11 with all its alternatives and gaps, still manages to 'gap' Bathsheba; her feelings, other than her being a willing participant in adultery and infidelity, aren't subjected to alternative understandings.[1] What, indeed, does she make of all this: rape or adultery, pregnancy, her husband's death or murder and her marriage to the king?

At the close of the episode we are informed that 'The wife [*'ēshet*] of Uriah heard that Uriah her husband [*'îshāh*] was dead and she mourned her husband [*ba'lāh*]' (2 Sam. 11.26). The dead man is named twice, but not the grieving wife. The threefold mention of wife or husband emphasizes the lost marital relationship; mourning (*sāpad*) recalls Israel's mourning for Samuel (1 Sam. 25.1; 28.3). We can only guess at her, Bathsheba's, emotions at this news and at David's next move. 'When the time of mourning [*hā'ēbel*] was over, David sent and gathered her to his house; she became his wife and bore him a son' (2 Sam. 11.27). Still no name for her and no comment on her feelings.

The mourning period (*'ēbel*) anticipates the feigned mourning of the wise woman of Tekoa that leads to Absalom's return (2 Sam. 14) and David's mourning at the tragic outcome of Absalom's revolt (2

---

1. In *Lethal Love* (1987: 10-36), Mieke Bal discusses interpretations of 2 Sam. 11 by Sternberg and others. I am indebted to it for my overall interpretation of Bathsheba here and in 1 Kgs 1–2.

Sam. 19.1-9). This evil for the house of David is forecast in the Lord's reaction: 'The thing which David had done was evil in the sight of the Lord' (2 Sam. 11.27). Apparently the Lord doesn't consider Bathsheba a participant in the crime.

Because David took 'the wife of Uriah the Hittite' to be his own wife, violence will always beset his house and the first sign is that the son to be born will die: 'The Lord struck the child that the wife of Uriah bore to David' (2 Sam. 12.10-15). No one, God, prophet or narrator, seems to know that this woman is named Bathsheba. David grieves greatly before the child's death and resumes normal life afterwards. What of Bathsheba? Does she mourn before or after?

David does comfort her and it is now 'Bathsheba his wife', but this may be more a sign of his desire for another son than of affection for his wife. The passage brims with names:

> David comforted Bathsheba his wife. He went to her and lay with her and she bore a son and he named him Solomon. And the Lord loved him. He sent word through Nathan the prophet and he named him Jedidiah because of the Lord (2 Sam. 12.25).

With the exception of David and the Lord, this cast of characters drops from the narrative; when they resurface much later, they will have changed.

In his closing years David is ministered to by a beautiful young woman named Abishag who lies in his bed beside him to keep him warm. In the meantime, Adonijah plots to become king and excludes from his party, among others, Nathan the prophet (1 Kgs 1.7, 10). Nathan retains his title but he is no longer called and sent by the Lord to ensure that the Lord's beloved Solomon, Jedidiah, succeeds David as king; instead Nathan calls and sends Bathsheba to bring this about by subterfuge. Nathan is now court conspirator, not great prophet of the Lord.

Bathsheba is still Solomon's mother (1 Kgs 1.11-13), but she seems to be no longer considered David's wife. Throughout the two episodes in 1 Kings 1–2 that she appears in—1.1-31 and 2.13-25—she is referred to as Solomon's mother and she calls Solomon her son. She also calls him David's son (see 1.17) but not 'our son'. David likewise says 'your son' and 'my son' but not 'our son' (2 Kgs 2.30, 32).

What must Bathsheba feel and think of all this? What has gone on in the preceding years to bring about this state of affairs? Or was this the original state of affairs? Was Bathsheba always the mother of David's son rather than his own wife? In the intervening years Bathsheba was only one of David's wives at court, perhaps left in Jerusalem to her own devices while he fled from Absalom.

When she goes to the king's chamber to carry out Nathan's instructions, she sees 'the very old king and Abishag the Shunammite ministering to him' (1.15). He is 'the king', not 'David' or 'her husband'. What does she feel? Let me propose a reading that parallels her with Michal, though she is not the powerless pawn that Michal was. She knows power politics and does not stand by idly to watch her son, and herself, die (1.12, 21). She will not be left to keep a silent vigil over her son's corpse.

When she sees the king and Abishag, she is infuriated and despises the old fool in her heart. There is nothing to be done about David, but she will not end up childless. Nathan offers her the perfect opportunity to act on behalf of Solomon, and act she does. Alter notes how she adapts Nathan's instructions when she actually speaks to David; she is not just a tool in this court intrigue (pp. 97-100). The plan succeeds. David agrees or is gulled. 'Solomon your son will succeed me as king, and he will sit on my throne in my place' (1.30). To his servants, however, he says, 'Solomon my son' (1.33). David dies and Solomon's rule is established.

> And Adonijah, the son of Haggith, came to Bathsheba, the mother of Solomon. She said, 'Do you come in peace?' And he said, 'In peace' (1 Kgs 2.13).

The following scene between Adonijah and Bathsheba alludes to earlier scenes. His introduction to his request refers back to the passages that speak of the transfer of the kingdom from Saul, whom all Israel looked to as king, to David. And the transfer was the work of the Lord. (See 1 Sam. 13.13-14; 15.27; 28.15-19; 2 Sam. 6.20-23.)

> You know that the kingdom was mine and that all Israel looked to me as king. And the kingdom has turned and gone to my brother for it is his because of the Lord. Now I have one request to ask of you; don't refuse me (1 Kgs 2.15-16).

Adonijah wants Abishag to be his wife. Previously Abner had gone in to Rizpah, Saul's concubine, and Ishbosheth had challenged him about it. Abner reacted in anger and promised 'to transfer the kingdom from the house of Saul and to establish David's throne' (2 Sam. 3.7-11). Involvement with a woman who in some way belonged to a previous king can involve transfer of a kingdom. To transfer the power Abner has first to transfer Michal from Paltiel back to David. We have seen these passages before; handing women back and forth is a major exercise of royal power.

When Michal angrily rebukes David, he responds that he danced before the Lord 'who chose me rather than your father' (2 Sam. 6.21). The last two contradictory references about her having and not having children refer to Michal as 'the daughter of Saul' (2 Sam. 6.23; 21.8). Now that the kingdom has been given to David, Michal, at least in name, can be given back to Saul.

But Bathsheba will not be silenced and pushed aside as Michal was nor will she keep a silent compassionate vigil over her son's body as Rizpah did. She knows well how kings, whether husband or son, act, and she knows well what Solomon will do when presented with Adonijah's request for Abishag. Taking a woman means taking a kingdom: 'you might as well ask for the kingdom for him' (1 Kgs 2.22). The countermeasure is death. 'King Solomon sent Benaiah, son of Jehoiada, and he struck him [Adonijah] and he died' (2.25).

Ultimately, however, Bathsheba shares the fate of the other royal women who have come before her. Solomon answers his mother (2.22) and shifts to speak of the Lord and of his father David. He takes an oath to the Lord before Bathsheba; he does not speak directly to her. What he swears to is similar to what David once said to Michal. It is the Lord who has set him 'on the throne of my father David' and has given him a dynasty, a house; it is the same Lord who chose David and not Saul and his dynasty, his house (2 Sam. 6.21). Adonijah, his brother, dies and Bathsheba, his mother, drops from the story. The kingdom is established in his hands, but his mother, who helped establish it, is forgotten as was Michal who saved David and helped establish his kingdom.

BIBLIOGRAPHY

Alter, Robert
    1981   *The Art of Biblical Narrative*. New York: Basic Books [selections from pp. 114-25 reprinted in this volume].
Bach, Alice
    1989   'The Pleasure of her Text.' *USQR* 43: 41-58.

Bal, Mieke
    1987   *Lethal Love: Feminist Literary Readings of Biblical Love Stories.* Bloom-
                ington: Indiana University Press.
    1990   'De-disciplining the Eye.' *Critical Inquiry* 16: 506-31.
Berlin, Adele
    1983   *Poetics and Interpretation of Biblical Narrative.* Sheffield: Almond Press.
Brueggemann, Walter
    1988   '2 Samuel 21–24: An Appendix of Deconstruction?' *CBQ* 50: 383-97.
Clines, David J.A.
    1988   'The Story of Michal, Wife of David, in its Sequential Unfolding.' Paper
                read to the Narrative Research on the Hebrew Bible Group at the Annual
                Meeting of the Society of Biblical Literature, and published in the present
                volume (pp. 129-40).
Exum, J. Cheryl
    1988   'Michal and Jonathan.' Paper read to the Narrative Research on the
                Hebrew Bible Group at the Annual Meeting of the Society of Biblical
                Literature.
    1989   'Murder They Wrote: Ideology and the Manipulation of Female Presence in
                Biblical Narrative.' *USQR* 43: 19-39 [reprinted in this volume as pp. 176-
                98].
Fokkelman, J.P.
    1986   *Narrative Art and Poetry in the Books of Samuel. II. The Crossing Fates (I
                Sam. 13–31 & II Sam. 1).* Assen: Van Gorcum.
Jobling, David
    1978   *The Sense of Biblical Narrative.* Vol. 1. Sheffield: JSOT Press.
Josipovici, Gabriel
    1988   *The Book of God: A Response to the Bible.* New Haven: Yale University
                Press.
Miscall, Peter D.
    1983   *The Workings of Old Testament Narrative.* Philadelphia/Chico: Fortress
                Press/Scholars Press.
    1986   *1 Samuel: A Literary Reading.* Bloomington: Indiana University Press.
Polzin, Robert
    1989   *Samuel and the Deuteronomist: A Literary Study of the Deuteronomic His-
                tory, Part Two: 1 Samuel.* San Francisco: Harper & Row.
Sternberg, Meir
    1985   *The Poetics of Biblical Narrative: Ideological Literature and the Drama of
                Reading.* Bloomington: Indiana University Press.

Robert Polzin

A MULTIVOICED LOOK AT THE MICHAL NARRATIVES[*]

In recent years, scholars have written many words about the ark narratives.[1] Much of the energy expended on these texts—as on most others in the Bible—has been in the area of excavative scholarship, especially compositional history.[2] What is not generally apparent in the secondary literature is a dedicated effort to work out how the stories about the loss and eventual return of the ark fit into the overall story-line of the Books of Samuel. What factors—ideological, esthetic, or historiographic—may be supposed to account for the selection and combination of these stories about the ark and the specific details subsequently worked into them? What are the compositional relationships ('compositional' in the poetic not genetic sense) between these stories of the ark and their immediate and remote context in the Deuteronomic history? Do the earlier ark narratives really interrupt material about Samuel's life and career, or vice versa? Or do they fit in with their immediate context in ways that make plausible suggestions of literary artistry and careful attention to detail? Questions of this type will fuel my discussion.

Scholars especially since the time of L. Rost have been intrigued by

[*] Presented to the Narrative Research on the Hebrew Bible Group, Society of Biblical Literature, Chicago, November 1988.

1. See the bibliographies in P.D. Miller and J.J.M. Roberts, *The Hand of the Lord* (Baltimore and London: Johns Hopkins University Press, 1977) and A.F. Campbell, *The Ark Narrative (1 Sam. 4–6; 2 Sam. 6). A Form-Critical and Traditio-Historical Study* (Missoula, MT: Scholars Press, 1975).

2. A welcome exception to this pattern is the work of J.T. Willis, whose two articles, 'An Anti-Elide Narrative Tradition from a Prophetic Circle at the Ramah Sanctuary', *Journal of Biblical Literature* 90 (1971), pp. 288-308, and 'Samuel versus Eli', *Theologische Zeitschrift* 35 (1979), pp. 201-12, while concerned additionally with source-orientated questions, are still the best discussions I know of concerning the compositional unity of 1 Sam. 1–7.

the interconnections between the ark story at the beginning of 1 Samuel and the one found in 2 Samuel 6.[1] One of the most obvious dissimilarities between the two stories is the utterly joyful and triumphant tone of 2 Samuel 6 in marked contrast to the many instances of divine wrath exercised against Philistine and Israelite alike in 1 Samuel 4–6. Only two incidents becloud the triumphalism of 2 Samuel 6: God's killing of Uzzah who put out his hand to touch the ark—an event delaying for three months David's bringing of the ark to Jerusalem—and Michal's despising of David in her heart (v. 16) for 'uncovering himself before the eyes of his servants' maidens' (v. 20). Each incident is resolved apparently in David's favour; the ark's sojourn of three months in the house of Obed-edom, the Gittite, brings the LORD's blessing upon him and courage to David to complete the ark's transference to Jerusalem, and Michal's contemptuous attitude toward David results in her remaining childless to the day of her death (v. 22). The narrator's voice seems utterly intent upon emphasizing the glory of David's kingship here at its beginning by removing any obstacle to David's glorious rule, be it the LORD's temporary anger against an impulsive priestly action or Michal's fruitless despising of David. Michal's negative attitude toward David appears to be an impotent non-issue, and her subsequent lack of offspring a narrative comment on this fact.

The Davidic Voice in the Two Ark Stories

When we step back and look at the two ark stories in their literary context, however, the royal voice proclaiming the glories of David's rule sounds even stronger. For the earlier ark narrative is imbedded within a larger story-line about the rise of Samuel and the fall of the house of Eli that functions very much like an opening parable about the rise of David and the fall of the house of Saul, itself a story that occupies us until the second ark narrative supplies an appropriate, if temporary, climax. The interconnections and symmetries between the first ark story as parabolic introduction and the second ark story as historiographic conclusion reveal an artistry that fully justifies David Damrosch's recent claim that '1–2 Samuel has become the masterpiece

---

1. For a useful discussion of Rost's position, together with a review of the literature, see Campbell, *The Ark Narrative*.

of biblical narrative.'[1] It seems likely that the journey of the ark from Shiloh in 1 Sam. 4.4 to Kiriath-jearim in 1 Sam. 7.1 (signifying that the Glory once lost to Israel under the Elides returned to Israel under the leadership of Samuel) foreshadows and reinterprets the triumphant journey of the ark from Baale-judah to Jerusalem in 2 Samuel 6 (signifying here the victory of David over all his enemies.) The itinerary of the ark in 1 Samuel 4–6 is from Shiloh to the house of Abinadab on the hill, with a few months' stopover amongst the Philistines; its itinerary in 2 Samuel 6 is from the house of Abinadab on the hill to Jerusalem, with a few months' stopover amongst the Philistines.[2] Whatever one is to do with the urban discrepancy between the 'Kiriath-jearim' of 1 Sam. 7.2 and the 'Baale-judah' of 2 Sam. 6.1, and whatever one imagines the specific literary history behind these two ark narratives to be,[3] it is clear that each account in its present narrative shape and location is patterned to reflect the other in striking correlations—all orchestrated in a manner that serves the Deuteronomist's larger ideological purposes. Let me describe how such an interconnection is forged in the text.

The similarities between 1 Samuel 4–6 and 2 Samuel 6 are suggestive in terms of structure, thematic detail, and language. We have al-

1. D. Damrosch, *The Narrative Covenant: Transformations of Genre in the Growth of Biblical Literature* (San Francisco, 1987), p. 260.

2. The stopover is 7 months in 1 Sam. and 3 months in 2 Sam.

3. For a source-oriented treatment of some basic questions here, see J. Blenkinsopp, 'Kiriath-Jearim and the Ark', *Journal of Biblical Literature* 88 (1969), pp. 143-56. Blenkinsopp, as is usual, develops proposals for reconstructing the historical situation, basing himself in part upon assumptions of the literary history of the ark narrative. Thus the present text is assumed to be historiographically unreliable, but certain source-oriented theories help this scholar sort out and propose a plausible historiographic reconstruction. But what does serious doubt about its literary historical assumptions mean for the plausibility of Blenkinsopp's historical reconstructions?

G.W. Ahlström, 'The Travels of the Ark: A Religio-Political Composition', *Journal of Near Eastern Studies* 43 (1984), pp. 141-49, sees the ark narrative as a 'literary fiction with a tendentious, religio-political thread' (p. 142). Ahlström, in referring to H. Timm ('Die Ladeerzahlung [1 Samuel 4–6; 2 Samuel 6]', *Evangelische Theologie* 29, pp. 520ff.) assumes its author to be exilic, so that 'Psychologically the ark narrative would have been encouraging for the people of the exile' (p. 143). For Ahlström, 'the ark narrative should be seen as a literary composition which has intentionally conflated Shiloh with Kiriath-Jearim–Jerusalem up through the story of the imprisonment and travels of the ark' (p. 149).

ready mentioned the similarly structured itinerary: the ark travels from one Israelite town to the other with a few months' stopover within Palestinian territory. The ark makes its journey accompanied by the two sons of the priest in whose care it was placed: Eli in 1 Samuel 4 and Abinadab in 2 Samuel 6. Death accompanies the ark's chaperones in each story: both of Eli's sons are killed in 1 Samuel 4; Uzzah, one of Abinadab's sons is killed in 2 Samuel 6. The ark is carried upon a 'new cart' in both stories. Each cart is appropriately described as going toward its destination with rejoicing on the part of the Israelites.

References to sacrifices before the LORD also accompany both journeys: at Beth-shemesh in 1 Sam. 6.14-15, and every six paces from Obed-edom's house to Jerusalem in 2 Samuel 6.

All these similarities might be seen as details one would normally expect in the kind of ark story found throughout the history, whatever the literary or ideological purpose for which it is used in each particular location within the final shape of the text. Could we not view these similarities simply as evidence of an original 'ark narrative', as scholars since Rost have tended to emphasize? No matter what genetic considerations one may advance in this regard, it is significant that specific linguistic or thematic details appear in each story *in dialogic contrast* to apparent counterparts in the other, so that something more deliberately poetic may be presumed to be operative.

30,000 Israelites are singled out to die at the beginning of the first story (1 Sam. 4.10); 30,000 chosen men of Israel accompany the ark in glory at the beginning of the second story (2 Sam. 6.1). Panic, death and destruction follow the first ark everywhere, even turning the brief rejoicing of the men of Beth-shemesh (1 Sam. 6.13) into mourning when the LORD makes a great slaughter amongst them (1 Sam. 6.19); there is hardly anything but rejoicing in 2 Samuel 6. We find mostly the language of curse in 1 Samuel 4–6, the language of blessing in 2 Samuel 6; the sound of Israel crying (*qol hehamon*) in 1 Sam. 4.14 typically becomes the blessed Israelite multitude (*hamon*) of 2 Sam. 6.19. This language of curse affects Israel and Philistia alike in 1 Samuel 4–6 just as its blessed counterpart affects Israelite and Philistine alike in 2 Samuel 6: 'And the LORD blessed Obed-edom [the Gittite] and all his household' (6.11); 'And David blessed the people in the name of the LORD of hosts' (6.18).

2 Samuel 6 even incorporates a thematic play on the *kbd/qll* dicho-

tomy in the dialogue between David and Michal (vv. 20-23) just as 1 Samuel 4–6 continues to do in the sorcerers' counsel to the Philistines (vv. 5-6). What unites these contrasts between honouring and cursing is the Deuteronomist's introductory meditation on kingship as honouring or cursing God:

> I promised that your house. . . shall go in and out before me forever. . . those who honour me I will honour, and those who despise me shall be lightly esteemed (*yeqallu*) (1 Sam. 2.30).

> And I tell him that I am about to punish his house forever. . . because his sons were cursing (*mᵉqalᵉlim*) God (1 Sam. 3.13). Give glory to the God of Israel. . . Perhaps he will lighten (*yaqel*) his hand from upon you (1 Sam. 6.5).

> I will make myself yet more contemptible (*unqalloti*) than this [says David to Michal]. . . but by them [the maidens] I shall be held in honour (*'ikkabedah*) (2 Sam. 6.22).

Only the final statement is obviously spoken by a king in defence of his actions as a king; the other statements never directly refer to royal performance, yet this is their main subject matter.

We see a final connection between the two pericopes in the first question that concludes 1 Samuel 4–6: Who is able *to stand before the LORD*, this holy God? (6.20). It is true, as McCarter remarks, that 'standing before the LORD' is used here specifically of priestly attendance upon the ark,[1] and that texts such as Deut. 10.8 and Judg. 20.27-28 indicate the priestly connotations of this phraseology in connection with the ark. At this level the question looks to the solution narrated in 7.1 where a suitable priestly attendant for the ark is finally found. Nevertheless, more is at stake here than priestly concerns.

First, the question at the end of ch. 6 about who could *stand* before the LORD has an intrinsic connection with the beginning of the ark's sojourn in Philistia and the statement twice given there: 'and behold, Dagon fallen (*nopel*) before the ark of the LORD' (5.3, 4). Who can stand before the LORD's ark? Certainly not a rival god.

Much more important than the intrinsic narrative contrast between 'stand' and 'fall' with its emphasis on divine power, are the details tying this account to monarchic themes. For one thing, reference to *cherubim* in connection with the ark such as we find in 4.4 is never

---

1. P.K. McCarter, Jr, *1 Samuel* (AB, 8; Garden City, NY: Doubleday, 1980), p. 137.

found in the Deuteronomic History outside of a royal context.[1] More
to the point, 'standing before the ark' is a right not just of priests, but
of kings also, as 1 Kgs 3.15 shows concerning Solomon: 'Then he
came to Jerusalem and stood before the ark of the covenant of the
LORD and offered up burnt offerings and peace offerings and made a
feast for all his servants'. Throughout the entire Bible, no one except
priest or king 'stands before the ark'.

When we examine the ark story in 2 Samuel 6, we find that the ark
is the one which is called by the name of *'the LORD of hosts who sits
enthroned on the cherubim'* (v. 2) just as the ark is described in 1
Sam. 4.4. Who stands before this particular ark? Although 2 Samuel 6
never refers to David as *standing* before the LORD, his typical position
throughout is 'before the LORD': before the ark he makes merry
(vv. 5, 21), dances (v. 14), leaps and dances (v. 16), and offers sacrifices (v. 17). And in response to the question, 'To whom will it go
away from us?' (1 Sam. 6.20), David, who is Israel's king *par excel-
lence*, is made to respond with another question: 'How can the ark of
the LORD come to me?' (2 Sam 6.9). 1 Samuel 4–6 looks to the triumphant David of 2 Samuel 6.

The Deuteronomist's Voice within and between the Two Ark Stories

In a recent book on 1 Samuel,[2] I have suggested that 1 Samuel 1–7
forms a parabolic introduction to Israel's tragic romance with kingship that fills the rest of the Deuteronomist's magnificent history. In
this overture to Israel's royal history, the Deuteronomist compares
'the having of sons' to Israel's 'request for kings'. More than a story
about the rise of Samuel and the fall of Eli, 1 Samuel 1–7 is about the
glorious rise of kingship in Israel and its tragic fall, epitomized in the
royal figure of Eli, grown old and heavy (*kabed*), falling backward
off his throne to his death (1 Sam. 4.18). The central place of the loss
and recovery of the ark in 1 Samuel 4–6 consists of Israel's exile in
Babylon. When the ark returns leaderless to Israel, the Deuteronomist
provides an ideological recipe for Israel's eventual return to the land:
as the ark was returned leaderless by two milch-cows whose calves
(*banim*, 'sons') had been taken away from them, so Israel will one day

1. See 2 Sam. 6; 1 Kgs 6; 8; 19.
2. R. Polzin, *Samuel and the Deuteronomist* (San Francisco: Harper & Row,
1989).

return to their homeland without the kings on account of whom Israel had had to go into exile in the first place.

If we are to understand the ideological place of Michal in the story of David's glorious beginning in 2 Samuel 6, we have only to see how the theme of women and the having of sons functions in the narrative up to this point. In the opening chapters of 1 Samuel, notice that kingship and the cause of the exile are tied together through two women's having of sons. First, Hannah asks God for a son in ch. 1 just as Israel asked God for a king in ch. 8; that is to say, the birth of Samuel prefigures the birth of kingship. Then the loss of the ark, symbolizing the exile of Israel, is epitomized in the birth of Ichabod to the wife of Phinehas: 'And she named the child Ichabod saying, "The Glory has gone into exile from Israel... for the ark of God has been captured"' (4.22). That the eventual victor, Samuel, prefigures the eventual victor, David, is nicely seen in the narrator's description of Samuel as a boy, 'girded with a linen ephod' (1 Sam. 2.18) and of David as a victorious king 'girded with a linen ephod' (2 Sam. 6.14).

Notice also that the interweaving of the themes of king and of exile in 1 Samuel is best seen in the narrative similarities between the fate of the ark at the beginning of the book and the exploits of David at its end. In both cases war with the Philistines provides the occasion for a prophecy in which the death of an Israelite leader's sons is foretold (chs. 2 and 28). The death of Saul and his sons, prophesied by Samuel in ch. 28, is an uncanny re-enactment of the parable that introduced the history of kingship in Israel at the beginning of the book. One may even suggest that Saul's reign itself acts like a kind of shadow-parable by which the reader is meant to look forward to David's day and beyond—even to the exile—and see the same false start and providential delay that embodied Saul's rule. As the rise of Samuel prefigures the fall of kingship at the beginning of the book, so the resurrection of Samuel functions in a similar way at its end. God's vision to Samuel happened at night in 1 Samuel 3; so does Samuel's vision to Saul in 1 Samuel 28.

Not only do Eli's and Saul's sons die at the beginning and end of the book—the first pair are symbolic kings and the second trio potential ones—but Israel also falls into 'the hands of the Philistines' in 7.3, 14 and 28.19. As I have been suggesting, the double defeat of Israel in 1 Samuel 4, together with the capture of the LORD's *ark* and its sojourn in Philistine country, carried exilic overtones that complemented the downfall of kingship prefigured in the collapse of Saul's house. In much the same way at the end of 1 Samuel, the prophesied defeat of Israel and the collapse of Saul's house are accompanied by the enforced sojourn of the LORD's *anointed*, David, in Philistine country. There are both ideological significance and narrative symmetry in the Philistine interludes of chs. 5–6 on the one hand, and chs. 27–30 on the other. It can hardly be accidental that both the ark of the LORD and the anointed of the LORD remain in Philistine country a sufficient number of months to cause serious harm within it: 'The ark of the LORD was in the country of the Philistines seven months' (6.1); 'and the number of the days that David dwelt in the country of the Philistines was a year and four months' (27.7). During these sojourns, when the LORD's ark and the LORD's anointed were lost to Israel, their presence in Philistine country caused havoc: the plagues within the Philistine pentapolis on one hand, and David's raids upon the inhabitants of the land on the other.

In short, the rise of Samuel and the fall of Saul form a kind of parabolic *inclusio* in 1 Samuel concerning the role of kingship in the exilic fate of Israel, so that by the time we get to our second account of the ark in exile in 2 Samuel 6, we ought to be able to see that here, as in 1 Samuel, the voice extolling the glories of Davidic kingship is easily overwhelmed by the Deuteronomist's voice emphasizing the intimate connection between the birth of kingship and Israel in exile. But whereas Hannah's asking for a son whom she would give to the LORD all the days of his life (1 Sam. 1.11) placed her in the role of a sinful Israel about to ask for a king, here in 2 Samuel 6 Michal's despising of David and her subsequent *childlessness* to the day of her death (2 Sam. 6.23) may represent a kingless Israel-that-might-have-been-but-never-was. For Michal opposed David's uncovering himself and thereby making himself contemptible. It may be no accident that 'to uncover oneself' and 'to go into exile' are the niphal and qal of the same root *galah*. The royal glory (*kabod*) about which David speaks to Michal in 2 Sam. 6.22 specifically, and the narrator to the reader in 2 Samuel 6 generally, also involves the abasement of Israel signified by the naming of Ichabod, that is to say, 'No-Glory'. In Israelite kingship, David's glorious reign included, the glory has departed from Israel, for the ark of God has been captured (1 Sam. 4.22). Michal and her childlessness, then, may represent the Deuteronomist's hope that the Glory would one day return to Israel, and that Israel, like

Michal, would remain kingless before the LORD to the day of her death.

In the light of all we have seen so far, to view the history as originally hopeful about kingship before a second edition put all the blame on Manasseh's shoulders, as many scholars following Cross have sought to do, is to ignore complex compositional relationships that tie together the introduction in 1 Samuel 1–7 with the succeeding monarchic history. Such neglect sees the final form of the history as much less coherent than it may be in its thorough-going identification of kingship in general—not just Manasseh's in particular—as a fundamental cause of Israel's captivity. Even if we were to grant Cross's genetic assumption that explicit references to Manasseh's role in causing the exile (in 2 Kings 21 and elsewhere) read easily as editorial additions, this, in my opinion, does not dissolve the clear picture, throughout the entire history and before such supposed revisions, of an Israel disastrously bent on monarchic aspirations. If Noth's solution to the genetic composition of the History is now more than ever suspect, his depiction of its strongly anti-monarchic ideology turns out to be poetically accurate.

Maurice Samuel

THREE WIVES
(from *Certain People of the Book*)*

[191] My feelings about Michal's love for David rise in part from the setting of those early days and in part from what happened later: I must remember how she defied her father and saved David's life; how David abandoned her, and in what manner he sent for her after many years; how she became embittered, and her tongue poisonous. The end throws its light back on the beginning.

David had come to the palace out of nowhere, a bewilderingly beautiful boy with a magical gift for the harp. By occupation he was a shepherd. The family, though descended from the wealthy Boaz, was obscure, and its flock was small. It must have looked like a great thing at first, that this unknown lad from the countryside should have the power to calm the nerves of the distraught king, and to win his love, and be given the title of armor-bearer. But we have seen how the unpredictable Saul used him at the beginning. David came [192] and went, a hireling by the hour, one might say, sent for when needed, and alternating as shepherd and court harpist. It is not surprising that his brothers were unimpressed. And what was the effect on Michal, who had fallen in love with David?

Here was the young and radiant genius, a stranger to the ways of courts, apparently indifferent to advancement or divinely ignorant of its techniques; here was the princess who loved him. When we discover later that she was capable of drastic action, and could face danger like a man for the man she loved, when we discover also that she had a mind and tongue of her own, we can go back to reconstruct with confidence the opening scenes. She saw David slighted by her father, whose fitful affections she mistrusted; she saw him needing the protec-

* *Certain People of the Book* (New York: Union of American Hebrew Congregations, 1955), pp. 191-206. Used by permission.

tion and guidance of one whose affections were as steady as they were deep. The more successful David showed himself by pure ability, un-backed by cunning, the greater the risks he ran, and therefore the more his need of her.

The wonder-boy of a musician turned out to be a wonder-boy of a warrior. He justified the additional recommendations of his unnamed friend: 'Prudent in affairs... and the Lord is with him'. His star was rising with everyone. 'Jonathan loved him as his own soul', and 'David had great success in all his ways'. His star rose with Saul, too, but the higher it rose with him, the fiercer became his impulse to bring it down. Prudent David might be, and Michal might acknow-ledge it, but prudence was not enough against the unpredictability of a madman. She might even feel that the Lord was with [193] David; in that case she was the instrument of the Lord, planted by Him in the palace.

I have described Michal as 'romantic'. The word is modern, the state of mind old. The Oedipus complex was not invented by Freud, and not even, it is well to note, by Oedipus. If 'romantic' means unrealistic, and if David was quite capable of looking after himself, then we could hardly find a better word for Michal's conception of her role in David's life.

Part of our wisdom comes from hindsight. We know the whole of David's career. Michal loved him in its early phase, when her father made repeated attempts on his life, openly in fits of madness, and only half covertly in plots that actually involved his daughters. There had been a promise that the man who slew Goliath would be given the hand of one of them, and 'great riches' besides. For a time nothing more was heard of this. Had the slayer of Goliath been another than David, we should have reason for surprise—though not too much, in view of the man we are dealing with. On the other hand it would have surprised us greatly if Saul had kept the promise without further ado when the slayer was David. But he came round to it at last, with a mind clouded by pitiful criminal calculations.

'And Saul said to David: "Behold my elder daughter Merab, her will I give to thee to wife; only be thou valiant for me, and fight the Lord's battles". For Saul said: "Let not my hand be upon him, but let the hand of the Philistines be upon him".' I am a little sick at these words. What Saul planned so feebly against David, David will one day carry out with savage efficiency [194] against Uriah the Hittite. Saul's calculations were transparent, and the Text does not bother to indicate their secretiveness. They were also pitiful and pointless because David needed no incentive to fight the Philistines, and as Saul's son-in-law he would not be more the marked man than as the slayer of Goliath. These homicidal meanderings of Saul's disappeared and reappeared. For David did not marry Merab. We read: 'And David said unto Saul: "Who am I, and what is my life, or my father's family in Israel, that I should be son-in-law to the king?" But it came to pass at the time when Merab Saul's daughter should have been given to David, that she was given unto Adriel the Meholathite to wife.'

We have a clear indication of a last-minute change. We are free to think that Saul shrank from having to pray for his daughter's widow-hood; or that David's reluctance was genuine and sustained, though not at all because of the childish trap, which to him did not look like one; or that Michal worked against the marriage. The last surmise has the best warrant because the next sentenc reads: 'And Michal Saul's daughter loved David'. We are also free to infer that Merab was not in love with David; we are perhaps invited to do so. What happened next is explicit. Michal must have spoken of her love, for her father learned of it; and he fell back once more on the dream of sending David to his death. This time he even concocted the semblance of a plan.

'And Michal Saul's daughter loved David; and they told Saul, and the thing pleased him. And Saul said: "I will give him her, that she may be a snare to him, and [195] that the hand of the Philistines may be against him."' Again David expressed great reluctance. Saul had the men of the court speak to him, and David's answer to them was: 'Seemeth it to you a light thing to be the king's son-in-law, seeing that I am a poor man, and lightly esteemed?'

On the whole, allowing for our hindsight and some inside informa-tion, Michal's attitude was distinctly romantic. David's guilelessness or helplessness, which made her tremble so for him, is hard to find even in the early record. He was loved by Michal, by her brother Jonathan, and by the court; he was the slayer of Goliath and the hammer of the Philistines; and if that was not enough he had the art of winning popu-larity: 'All Israel and Judah loved David; for he went out and came in before them.' Also he knew what no one else but Samuel knew, that he was in truth the anointed one, the next king. And yet he said to Saul's men that he was poor, and therefore held in slight esteem. In his case the sequitur was false, while the premise itself was dubious. Saul never gave him the 'great riches' due him; nevertheless David after his marriage to Michal carried on successfully, did greatly in battle, and was foremost among 'all the servants of Saul'. He was not fishing for riches. He had to talk as he did because this had been his excuse for refusing Merab. But now Saul, with the delusion of a genuine plan at work in him, insisted. The messengers went back and forth, negotiating, and there was never a mention of the monetary reward. 'And the servants of Saul told him: "On this manner spoke David". And Saul said: "Thus shall ye say to [196] David: 'The king desireth not any dowry, but a hundred foreskins of the Philistines, to be avenged of the king's enemies". For Saul thought to make David fall by the hand of the Philistines. And when his servants told David these words, it pleased David well to be the king's son-in-law.'

It pleased him well; so well that he went out at once with his men and killed not one hundred but two hundred Philistines and brought their foreskins and 'gave them in full number to the king'. And how did the prompt collection of this gruesome and disgusting dowry please the princess? Was she thrilled by David's extravagance, or horrified by his recklessness? I must use the stencil again: we are not told. We are not told what anybody thought about it. And strangely enough I do not remember it as figuring prominently in the popular denunciations of the Bible. To me it is one of the most horrible of the horrible deeds ascribed to its heroes or its villains: this exuberant killing of an extra hundred Philistines, this exuberant mutilation of an extra hundred corpses, as though the first hundred, the condition of the bargain, were unworthy of the esteem in which David held himself, or of his regard for Princess Michal.

For we are speaking here of the lovely shepherd boy, the bewitching harp-player, who advanced on Goliath with a simple sling, exclaiming: 'Thou comest to me with a sword, and with a spear, and with a javelin, but I come to thee in the name of the Lord of hosts. . .' The Tradition, which like the Bible itself rightly makes a tremendous to-do about David's murder of Uriah, is not greatly concerned with the repulsive exploit of the [197] two hundred foreskins. I, who see David as the most passionate of the God-seekers, have never ceased to recoil from it. Almost as much as the murder of Uriah I juxtapose it with the words so often spoken of David: 'For the Lord was with him'.

What do these words mean? Used by the unnamed friend of David, or by Saul, or by any other contemporary of David's early days, they could mean success and worldly happiness. But how is it when they occur in the Text as the verdict of the chronicler? Much depends on when the chronicler lived. David's career was brilliant in the light of the after ages; to one who wrote shortly after his death it was a mixed thing; and whatever successes he scored were more than offset by failures and by personal wretchedness: the death of Jonathan, the death of Bathsheba's child, sinfully begotten, the rape of his daughter Tamar by his son Amnon, the murder of Amnon by Absalom's command, the rebellion and death of Absalom, and so on to the very end: the thwarting of David's dearest ambition, to build the Temple, and the rebellion of his son Adonijah. It was God Himself who forbade him to build the Temple, on the grounds that he, the anointed, had shed much blood. So he had—but nearly all of it that of the enemies of Israel. In what sense, then, was God with him? In a literal sense that perhaps even the chronicler did not always mean; for the chronicler himself is an evolving figure, and we who interpret him are also chroniclers. God was with David in a terrifically literal sense; for David was possessed, haunted, inhabited, and harassed by God-consciousness. His earthly passions were demonic; [198] equally demonic, if one may so put it, was his anguish over them, and his longing to find himself in God. The heart that could riot in blood-lust, and swell with self-righteousness, could tremble like a child's before the denunciation of the prophet Nathan, accepting punishment without protest; and it could beat to the strains of unearthly music, to give it forth again for our everlasting consolation.

We are going to see how much of this was understood by Michal, whose hand he won with the two hundred Philistine foreskins.

They were married. 'And Saul saw and knew that the Lord was with David; and Michal Saul's daughter loved him. And Saul was yet the more afraid of David; and Saul was David's enemy continually.'

The recurrent impulse to put David out of the way became more urgent. Saul was mad enough to call on Jonathan and the men of the court to murder David; it was no longer a flash or outburst; it was settling into that sustained obsession which was to overshadow the rest of his life. But for the moment Jonathan pleaded successfully for his soul's friend. 'And Saul hearkened unto the voice of Jonathan; and Saul swore: "As the Lord liveth, he shall not be put to death". And

Jonathan brought David to Saul, and he was in his presence as before-time.'

David's self-confidence is astounding. He returns again and again to the center of danger. It may be that side by side with his faith in the anointing there was a deep and troubling concern for Saul. But the limit was reached at last: 'And there was war again; and David [199] went out, and fought with the Philistines, and slew them with a great slaughter; and they fled before him. And an evil spirit from the Lord was upon Saul, and he sat in his house with his spear in his hand; and David was playing with his hand. And Saul sought to smite David even to the wall with the spear; but he slipped away out of Saul's presence, and he smote the spear into the wall; and David fled and escaped that night. And Saul sent messengers unto David's house, to watch him, and to slay him in the morning.'

This is Michal's hour, and here she is established. Here her romanticism fuses with realism. She was not alone in defying her father's madness against David; Jonathan had done it before and would do it again; but she was a woman, and on that occasion Saul's fury seems to have surpassed all bounds.

'Michal David's wife told him, saying: "If thou save not thy life tonight, tomorrow thou shalt be slain". So Michal let David down through the window; and he went, and fled, and escaped. And Michal took the teraphim, and laid it in the bed, and put a quilt of goat's hair at the head thereof, and covered it with a cloth.'

I do not like that picture of David escaping into the night and leaving Michal to face the music. He must have been convinced that the situation was desperate; and he was at last beginning to find the king's explosions intolerable—two reasons why he should have hesitated to leave Michal behind, and two grim reflections on his failure to send for her at the first opportunity. Something of a strain between him and Michal is revealed here, almost accidentally. She kept teraphim in her room—[200] idols; she had neither David's devotion to God, nor the tact to conceal her lack of it. But it is not an excuse.

It is horrifying to learn of the frenzy in which Saul was now raving. 'And when Saul sent messengers to take David, Michal said: "He is sick". And Saul sent messengers to see David, saying: "Bring him up to me in the bed, that I may slay him".' We have never seen him in such a condition before. We must take it that Jonathan was away at the time, and this is another count against David.

'And when the messengers came in, behold, the teraphim was in the bed, with the quilt of goat's hair at the head thereof.' What happened, apparently, was this: the first time the messengers came she let them peep in at the door, and that was enough for them. The second time they brushed her aside.

At what exact moment Michal had to face her father, and where and whether she was brought before him, or whether he came to her house, is not recorded. Her answer to his reproaches was both impudent and courageous. 'And Saul said unto Michal: "Why hast thou deceived me thus, and let mine enemy go, that he is escaped?" And Michal answered Saul: "He said unto me: 'Let me go; why should I kill thee?'"' It did not explain why she had not raised the alarm at once; it did not explain why she had delayed discovery by her ruse, and given David as much time as possible to make good his escape. It explained nothing. It was the equivalent of a defiant: 'I did it'.

And here, in the most astounding way, Michal drops out of the picture. Always when I follow David through [201] the years of his outlawry, there is a nagging at the back of my mind: 'Where's Michal? What happened to Michal? She loves him. She saved his life.' David is on the run from Saul, but he is not alone. He takes his parents to him; his brothers join him. We read: 'And every one that was in distress, and every one that was in debt, and every one that was discontented, gathered themselves unto him'. Then why not Michal? For if anyone was in distress and discontented, it was she.

She was of course not in debt—not to David: he was the debtor. That had much to do with his unforgivable silence. He was managing alone. He fled first to Samuel, and then to Ahimelech the priest; he picked up the sword with which he had cut off Goliath's head, and he became the outlaw. He made his headquarters in the famous cave of Adullam. He deposited his aged parents with the king of Moab. He ranged throughout the country. He smote the Philistines and he smote the Amalekites. 'He abode in the wilderness in the strongholds.' And he fled from Saul. Once he had a chance to kill him, and forbore—Saul too was the anointed. They exchanged useless words of reconciliation at a distance: but no mention of Michal. More than once Jonathan came out in secret to visit his beloved friend and renew the bond: not a word about Michal.

So the years pass, and suddenly, when we finish the story of Abigail, and we read how David married her, and took a second wife,

Ahinoam the Jezreelitess, we come across these casual words: 'Now Saul had given Michal his daughter, David's wife, to Palti the son of Laish, who was of Gallim'.

[202] The reader may perhaps remember Palti, or Paltiel, as the weird little man for whom I have such an aversion—Palti the weeper—and may even begin to share my feelings. From what we have seen of Michal, and from what we shall yet see, we know that she was not forced into the marriage. She entered into it contemptuously, and if a sword lay between husband and wife in the night, it was she who put it there.

Then again a long silence. Again the outlaw life, and a meeting with Saul, and a tearful exchange of words of mutual forgiveness, and again nothing about Michal. There were wild adventures. Abigail and Ahinoam were captured by the Amalekites, and David rescued them. That was more like it, he must have thought, the man saving the woman. Then Saul and Jonathan fell on Gilboa, in battle with the Philistines, and David became king, and the secret anointing was vindicated long after the death of Samuel.

And finally David, reigning in Hebron, sent for Michal the princess, addressing these words to Ishbosheth, Saul's son: 'Deliver me my wife Michal, whom I betrothed to me for a hundred foreskins of the Philistines'.

That was his recollection of her! He was careful to quote the strict terms of the bargain, claiming no credit for the bonus of the extra hundred he had thrown in. He had risked his life to win her, and he had a right to her. I am confused about his motives in sending for her, and I imagine he was, too. It will be suggested that it was a political move; he reclaimed the daughter of Saul in order to strengthen his claim to the throne. To me it [203] seems unlikely that he saw himself beholden to her for any such favor.

She came to Bahurim, we remember, accompanied by the weeping Paltiel, who was sent back by Abner; and she joined David in Hebron. Everything was changed now. David was king of Judah, a man in the middle thirties, with at least two other wives—he married several women in Hebron, and had children by them, before and after sending for Michal. He was no longer the protégé of a romantic princess. The relations were reversed. The house of Saul was all but destroyed, and it was Michal who needed protection. That was not how she had planned it. She came back to David to be one among many.

Seven years David reigned in Hebron, warring on the Philistines and the Amalekites, and preparing the unification of the kingdom. And then he made the decision that has given the world a place-name of unparalleled symbolic sanctity. He moved to Jerusalem; and to signalize his glory and his triumph he had the Ark of the Covenant brought to the new capital, thereafter known, even until this day, as the city of David...

What his mood was like, what visions and exaltations [204] his soul experienced in that time of fulfillment, when he was making his transition from the temporal to the eternal, we can glimpse only in our own highest moments...

[205] Breathless, God-intoxicated, oblivious of everything but the vision, he sang that day, danced and sang, ascending the hill.

And Michal? Where was she? What part had she in the rejoicing, what understanding for the supreme moment in David's life, which was henceforth divided into two parts, that which led up to this glory and that which led from it? Of her who had kept idols in her room we read: 'As the Ark of the Lord came into the city of David, Michal the daughter of Saul looked out at the window, and saw king David leaping and dancing before the Ark; and she despised him in her heart...'

It was not the idolatrous strain in her that was revolted. It was the dethroned romantic realizing that she had never been the savior of this man or the source of his strength. When she saw him whirling half-naked before the ark, her possessive soul felt itself disowned. It was more than she could bear. We read: 'Then David returned to bless his household. And Michal the daughter of Saul came out to meet David, and said: "How did the king of Israel get him honour today, who uncovered himself in the eyes of the handmaids of his servants, as one of the vain fellows shamelessly uncovereth himself!"'

[206] There are women who have a marvelous gift for the wounding word, the word that penetrates to the core of a man's honor and kills his love on the spot; or, when love has faded, all prospect of friendship, and even of mutual tolerance. It is a gift that is not necessarily related to intelligence; it resembles rather the unexpected offensive equipment of certain lower species.

As between Michal and David it was he who was in the wrong up to then; now she put herself in the wrong forever, and provided David with the plausible defense: 'I knew all along what kind of woman she was'. In David's worship of God, his 'shameless' self-abasement, his self-surrender, lay his meaning, his excuse for living, and his hope of self-redemption; and if Michal had only known it, her hope of reaching his heart. Instead she struck unerringly at his self-justification.

What a man retorts under such circumstances is forgiven in advance, because the savagery of the thrust has reduced him to reflex action. But there is little to forgive in David's hot reply, or in what followed. We read:

'And David said unto Michal: "Before the Lord, who chose me above thy father, and above all his house, to appoint me prince over the people of the Lord, over Israel, before the Lord will I make merry. And I will be yet more vile than thus, and will be base in mine own sight; and with the handmaids whom thou hast spoken of, with them will I get me honour." And Michal the daughter of Saul had no child unto the day of her death.'

Adin Steinsaltz

THE PRINCESS AND THE SHEPHERD
(from *Biblical Images: Men and Women of the Book*)*

[145] One of the most fascinating women in the Bible is Michal, the
daughter of Saul. She is perhaps one of the most romantic of all the
biblical heroines both because of the strange situation in which she
found herself and because of her tragic fate.

At the same time, the biblical text shows us a Michal who was
almost totally passive, who spoke and acted very little for herself. Our
glimpses of her are fragmentary, as though we were peeping at her
through cracks in the shutters, through the rents and tears in the
fabric of family life, into the inner palace and her private life there.

The few words Michal utters are important in providing an understanding of her character. The power of the biblical account lies in a
few short, sharp lines, sketches of the people and events in question.
On the whole, we are told almost [146] nothing of the thoughts of the
heroes; there are no complex and complicated dialogues, no character
'build-up'. From this point of view, biblical narrative is in marked
contrast to Greek drama. The latter, in almost all its forms, rests
largely on monologues in which the heroes explain their experiences
and feelings. When the monologue does not suffice, the chorus fills in
the gaps in the story and carries the narrative forward. Thus, the author has the opportunity to express his own educational, moral, and
philosophical ideas. In the Bible, we find almost none of these devices.
Yet the narrative is often strikingly clear and provides us with true-
to-life multidimensional figures. Thus, we discover Michal in three
different situations, each one of which shows us a different aspect.
The combination of the three pictures, the three situations, enables us
to reconstruct not only the events that characterize each one, but also

* *Biblical Images: Men and Women of the Book* (New York: Basic Books,
1984), pp. 141-51. Used by permission.

to understand the personalities involved.

Michal is first introduced with the words: 'And Michal Saul's daughter loved David' (1 Sam. 18.20), hinting at a story of first love. We next meet her when, after David's escape from Saul, she is given to another man, Palti ben Laish (1 Sam. 25.44); and in the third story, we witness a short conversation, a very unpleasant scene, between David and Michal (2 Sam. 6.20-23), in which she comments on the way he dances. Taken in isolation, none of these brief passages presents a full picture; but together, they give us a general portrait of relationships, a portrait that illuminates and reveals aspects of David's character as much as it does those of Michal.

One point that is perhaps crucial to Michal's personality, and for understanding the relationship between her and David, is actually linked to the relationship between the tribes of Judah and Benjamin. Saul and Michal were truly representative of the image and essence of their whole tribe, with all its [147] power and advantages and its concomitant weaknesses. The most marked facet of Michal's character is that she was an aristocrat, a princess. She was the daughter of the nobility, not only because her father was king, but because her whole family was noble. It was a nobility that had beauty and elegance, along with weaknesses. Such aristocratic figures may often include something anemic, a certain inability to adapt to awkward situations. We often find in them passivity instead of action, silence where there should be speech, and thoughtless chatter where there should be silence.

In contrast to these reserved people—some of whom, like Jonathan, were heroic and beautiful in body and soul—someone like David appeared. He was simpler, more earthy, undoubtedly of handsome appearance, and a hero of war. Very understandably, an attachment was formed, a first love, involving the closeted young girl from the aristocratic family. Michal fell in love with the village hero; and his simplicity—or crudeness—was not disturbing to her but doubtless had a certain charm of its own. The same characteristics have had a singular magic for many other young maidens, in similar circumstances, throughout history. Out of this attraction was born a great love: Michal, the daughter of Saul, loved David. A special relationship was created between them, and even Michal, never overtalkative, showed it, so that Saul, for all his introversion, sensed what was going on. From this first contact, Michal and David were bound by a tie of love

that remained constant, despite all the problems that followed. It remained steadfast in the face of the pressures later created by Saul and
was unshaken by the triangle of relations between Saul, David, and
Jonathan.

Michal did not often act of her own accord; yet until her last
moments with David, she remained loyal, and even more [148] than
loyal, to him. In fact, she was even prepared to betray her father for
David's sake, as when she tricked Saul by smuggling David out of the
house to enable him to escape Saul's ire. The situation is reminiscent—and not only from the point of view of 'plot'—of the relationship between Rachel and Laban, perhaps not surprisingly, since
Michal, of the tribe of Benjamin, was a direct descendant of Rachel.
The story of David's escape (1 Sam. 19.13) contains a key word identical to one in the story of Laban's pursuit of Jacob and the theft of his
household images (Gen. 31.34). These two instances are the only references in the Bible to household or family idols. In both cases, they
are treated as a means of cheating the father. In both cases, the inner
motive is similar: the bond with the man, with the new hero, is so
deep that it apparently erases all other ties. This special bond between
David and Michal remains to the end.

In the next passage, the weakness of the aristocracy is disclosed.
While in the first situation, we find a mutual attraction, the combination and pairing of beauty and heroism, of the old nobility and the
'man of the people', in the second, we find Michal's surrender and
passivity when given to another man. She was given away to Palti ben
Laish, a man who was possibly a friend of the family, of the house of
Saul. She moved with him across the Jordan, where she remained with
him for several years. The Talmud tells us several things about Palti
ben Laish, who was apparently closer to Saul's house than was David,
and about his attitude to Michal. However, if we look at Michal herself, we are given a glimpse of her essential being, by what she did not
do. When Palti was forced to renounce Michal, it is said that he went
'along with her weeping behind her' (2 Sam. 3.16). But Michal did
not cry. In a way, it seems as if she had lost her active personality in
this great crisis, acting [149] no longer as a human being but as an
object, a chattel. She was taken and returned by Palti ben Laish—in
silence.

We can imagine Michal's emotional crisis in different ways, but a
crisis it surely was. Her heart was broken. She had been handed over

to another man whom she did not love, and the impression is somehow created that she was no longer capable of caring for anyone, not
even for David. The parting from him (which she believed to be final)
and her being handed over to Palti ben Laish broke her spirit until she
reached a point of total detachment. This emotional detachment was
partly an expression of her aristocratic nature. The nobility was superior; they did not make scenes or have stormy fights, nor did they
destroy social structures. Michal did not rebel; she did not try to
escape from the entanglement by some extreme means, such as suicide, as did her father Saul at the end of his days. She could protest
her lot, but instead she broke, and what remained was the outer shell
of a personality from which the heart was missing. From this point
onward, Michal responded to everything that happened with total passivity, the passivity of one who is past caring. She continued to function, to fulfil her role in accordance with her status, and she did this
right to the end of her life. But inwardly something had snapped; her
personality was no longer what it was, and she was concerned only
with the externals of behavior.

The Michal of the first meeting with David was not the same woman
who was returned to him several years later. She had undergone not
so much a personality change as a kind of death. The heart, the emotion, the excitement had gone out of the woman, and what remained
was the shell: an aristocrat, and nothing more.

All this is sharply expressed in the final episode of the Michal–
David relationship, which reveals a clash between [150] two cultures
as well as between two totally different individuals. It was a clash
between David, so very earthy, passionate, and enthusiastic, and
Michal, reserved, introverted, and deeply concerned with propriety.
Michal's rebuke to David is a key to her whole personality. She
neither saw nor related to the spiritual significance of bringing the
Ark of the Covenant to Jerusalem. She knew that it was an important
celebration, and what bothered her on this great occasion was the fact
that David had exposed himself when dancing in front of the maidservants. How could he do such a thing! The sages have already
pointed out the marvelous sense of modesty in Saul's family: the way
in which he went deep, deep into the cave when he wished to 'cover
his feet'. That same horror of nakedness, which is characteristic of all
Semitic cultures, was marked in Saul, in his personal relations as in
his public behavior. He had a fear of exposing himself. Hence the cov-

ering up, the layers upon layers of garments and clothing.

In contrast to this modesty and circumspection, so characteristic of the aristocracy and nobility everywhere, at all periods of history, we find David. David did not stop to consider how he was dancing, how he was behaving, how he appeared to others. For Michal, the fact of exposure was less important than the humiliation—as she saw it—of cheapening himself before the masses, of descending to their level. She was injured by the fact that David did not treat his throne with respect, that he had no sense of the majesty of kingship, of being divinely chosen to lead. She was the daughter of the nobility contrasted with the man she actually regarded as simple, as a boor, as one who may have taken up the reigns of government but not the grandeur of the kingship.

David, for his part, was no less sharp in his response to [151] Michal, and his sharpness is illuminating. He juxtaposed these contrasting elements, comparing his election as king not necessarily with Michal but with what she represented: the house of Saul, her father. David claimed that the choice of the Almighty had fallen rather on someone like him: a man who expressed real sensitivity, the true emotions of the heart, the excitement, the flexibility to stand firm against difficulties and not break. At the same time, he was the man who could rejoice, who could express his joy and reveal himself.

The sages' saying that the kingship of the house of Saul did not continue because he had no fault, finds an echo in the relations between David and Michal. Outwardly, she was flawless, cold, and noble, the ideal woman viewed from afar. David, in contrast, was passionate, fiery in everything he did, in his virtues and in his sins; he had his flaws and his failings, and he also had the strength to rise above them.

In this context of two opposing life views, the two personalities are revealed, each in its own light. The contrast between them recalls not only the confusion of Michal's life, arising partly from her reserve and inhibition, but also from the tragic clash, the entanglement between this aristocratic woman and the simple man with whom she fell in love.

Michal's heart was broken because David could never be wholly hers: he could never fit her notions of the perfect, and she could not accept him as he was. She could be happy neither with him nor without him.

N.J.D. White

MICHAL
(in *Encyclopaedia Biblica*)*

[363] MICHAL (מִיכָל contracted from מִיכָאֵל 'who is like unto God?').
—The younger of Saul's two daughters (1 Sam. 14.49, Μελχόλ).
Saul, who was wavering between desire to destroy David and reluctance to promote him to be the king's son-in-law, suddenly gave
Merab his eldest daughter to Adriel (1 Sam. 18.19). It now transpired
that Michal had fallen in love with David. For a woman to take the
initiative in such matters is without parallel in the Bible, but it suited
Saul's designs, and David, on his part, lost no time in providing double (not LXX) the dowry demanded. It should be noted that the LXX
(B), followed by Josephus (*Ant.* 6.10.2), simplifies the story by omitting the incident about Merab (1 Sam. 18.17-19, 26b); and Josephus
here, and again in *Ant.* 7.1.4, misses the point of Saul's savage mockery of 'the uncircumcised Philistines' by representing the conditions
imposed on David as six hundred heads of Philistines. David was soon
to owe his life to the wife whom Saul had designed to 'be a snare to
him'. When the emissaries of Saul 'watched the house to kill him' (1
Sam. 19.11-17, Ps. 59 title), Michal baffled them by letting David
down by the window, and delayed pursuit by a clever ruse. Placing
the household god in the bed, she covered the supposed sick man's
head with a mosquito net (RVm), and finally disarmed Saul's jealous
anger by a plausible lie. In this passage the rare word in v. 13
'pillow' כְּבִיד (on which see Driver's note) was read כָּבֵד (constr. of
כָּבֵד) 'liver' by the LXX. Josephus (*Ant.* 6.11.4) seems not to have
understood the LXX translation of 'teraphim', τὰ κενοτάφια, for he
says that Michal placed in the bed a goat's liver, which, as it palpitated

* *Encyclopaedia Biblica* (London: A. & C. Black, 1902), III, p. 363.

and shook the bedclothes, might suggest that David was gasping for breath.

The last scene in which Michal figures (2 Sam. 6.16-23) presents a startling contrast to the time when, for love of David, she had flung aside conventi⸱nalities and braved her father's fury. That love was now all changed into coldness and dislike. When from a window in the palace on Mt Zion Michal looked down on David leaping and dancing before the ark, it was not merely her woman's impatience of the absurd that made her 'despise him in her heart', or that prompted the sarcasm in which that contempt found utterance later on. To appreciate her daring mockery, and the cold anger of David's rejoinder, we must read them in the light of the years that had passed. It is probable that Michal had been happy with Palti, or Paltiel, to whom she had been married on David's banishment (1 Sam. 25.44). From that home she had been torn (2 Sam. 3.15) merely that David might be enabled to claim a sort of hereditary right to the throne, and have by him a living memorial of his early prowess. Now she was but one of many wives, equalled with mere 'handmaids', probably neglected. What wonder if the bitter reflexion that she had indirectly facilitated the humiliation of her own family was coupled with a suspicion that David had from the first regarded her merely as a means of self-aggrandisement? It is difficult not to feel some sympathy with Michal; though the historian characteristically sees in her childlessness a punishment for that ill-omened outburst of spleen on the most glorious day of David's life. The Chronicler omits, as usual, the painful incident, except 2 Sam. 6.16.

It remains to add that in 2 Sam. 21.8 'Michal' is an ancient but obvious mistake for 'Merab' (which is read by Luc. and Pesh.). Josephus (*Ant.* 7.4.3) says that Michal returned to her former husband (Palti), whom he does not name, and bore five children. The AV explanation 'brought up' for 'bare' is that of the Targum and Jerome (*Qu. Heb.*); and the Targ. on Ruth 3.8 mentions 'the pious Paltiel, who placed a sword between himself and Michal...because he had refused to go in unto her'. Similarly Jerome (*Qu. Heb.* on 1 Sam. 25.44) explains that Paltiel wept for joy because the Lord had kept him from knowing her. He also (*Qu. Heb.* on 2 Sam. 3.5; 6.23) mentions a Jewish tradition that Michal is the same as Eglah, who is emphatically styled 'David's wife' because she was his first wife, and that she died when giving birth to a child.

Alexander Whyte

MICHAL, SAUL'S DAUGHTER
(from *Bible Characters: Gideon to Absalom*)*

[171] Never, surely, were man and wife more unequally yoked
together than was David, the man after God's own heart, with Michal,
Saul's daughter. What was David's meat was Michal's poison. What
was sweeter than honey to David was gall and wormwood to Michal.
The things that had become dearer and dearer to David's heart every
day, those were the very things that drove Michal absolutely mad;
furiously and ungovernably mad that day on which the ark of God
was brought up to the city of David.

It was the greatest day of David's life. And, sad to say, it was the
very greatness of the day to David that made it such a day of death to
Michal, Saul's daughter. Michal, Saul's daughter, died that day of a
strange disease—a deep distaste at the things that were her husband's
greatest delight. A deep distaste that had grown to be a deep dislike at
David, till that deep distaste and settled dislike burst out that day into a
downright hatred and deliberate insult. You must understand all that
[172] the ark of God was to David, and the home-bringing of the ark,
before you can fully understand the whole catastrophe of that day. It
would take me till midnight to tell you all that was in David's heart as
he sacrificed oxen and fatlings at six paces, and leaped and danced
before the ark of God all the way up to the city of David. And, even
then, you would need to be a kind of David yourself before you would
look with right reverence and love at David that day. For David was
beside himself that day. David never did anything by halves, and least
of all his worship of God. It was like that day long afterwards in that
same city when we read that His disciples remembered that it was
written, The zeal of Thine house hath eaten Me up. With all his might,

* *Bible Characters: Gideon to Absalom* (London: Oliphants, c. 1898), pp. 171-
81. Reprinted by permission of William Collins Sons & Co. Ltd, Publishers.

then—and you know something of what all David's might in such matters was—with all his might David leaped and danced before the Lord till Michal despised him in her heart.

Those who are deaf always despise those who dance. The deaf do not hear the music. And, on the other hand, those who do hear the music, they cannot understand those who can sit still. David could not understand how Michal could sit still that day. But Michal's ear had never been opened to the music of the ark. She had not been brought up to it, and it was not her custom to go up to the house of the Lord to sing and play like David. Had Michal been married in the Lord; had Michal reverenced her husband; had she cared to please her husband; had she played on the psaltery and harp sometimes, if only for his sake—what a happy [173] wife Michal would have been, and David, what a happy husband! Had her heart been right with her husband's heart when he blessed his household every night; had she been wont with all her heart to unite with her husband when he blessed them every night and sang psalms with them; had she sung with him and said, We will not go up into our bed till we have found out a place for the Lord, an habitation for the mighty God of Jacob: how well it would have been. Lo! sang David alone with the handmaids of his servants, Lo! we heard of it at Ephratah; we found it in the fields of the wood. Arise, O Lord, into Thy rest; Thou and the ark of Thy strength. Had David not been so unequally yoked, Michal would have put on David's shoulder that day an ephod that she had worked for that day with her own hands; and as she put it on him she would have sung and said, I will clothe her priests with salvation, and her saints shall shout aloud for joy. And then all that day in Jerusalem it would have been as it was at the Red Sea when Miriam the prophetess took a timbrel in her hand, and all the women went after her with timbrels and with dances. But it was not so to be. For Michal sat at home that great day in Israel, and forsook her own mercy. Michal was not in the spirit of that day. And thus it was that she despised David in her heart when the very gates of brass and iron were lifting up their heads at David's psalm to let the King of Glory come in.

Not to speak of the past, had Michal done that day what any woman with any sense of decency left [174] in her would have done—had she put on her royal garments and set out with David to the house of Obed-Edom, how differently for her and for David that day would have ended! For, once on the ground; once surrounded with the

assembled people, the magnificent sccne would have carried Michal
away. The fast-dying ashes of her first love for David would have
been blown up into all their former flame as she shared in the splendid
salutation that David received from the assembled land. No ambitious
woman, and least of all Saul's royal-hearted daughter, could have seen
assembled Israel that day without being swept into sympathy with the
scene. But Michal lost her last opportunity that morning. Michal did
not overcome herself that morning. Her proud and unsympathetic
temper got the better of her that morning, till David had to set out on
the royal duties of that day alone. And as the day went on, Michal was
left alone with a heart the most miserable in all Israel that day. And
Michal's heart became harder and darker and fiercer as the day went
on. Harder and darker and fiercer at David, and at all the ordinances
and delights of that day. And then, when all Jerusalem rang with the
ark just at her door, Michal stole to her shut window and saw nothing
but David dancing before the Lord. At the despicable sight she spat at
him, and sank back in her seat with all hell in her heart. You have had
Michal's heart in yourselves, in your measure, on some Sabbath-day
when you remained at home for some wrong reason, and when your
husband [175] came home with his face shining. And on other days,
when you should have been at his side, but some distaste, some dislike,
some pique, some catishness kept you at home to eat your heart all the
time. And then the very high spirits of the party when they came
home made your day end sufficiently like Michal's day. What a pity
that David did not better prevail with Michal to accompany him to the
fields of the wood that day!

The wife see that she reverence her husband, says the apostle. Yes;
but even Paul himself would have allowed that it was impossible for
Michal to reverence David all at once that day. Paul would have
needed to have got Michal's ear early that morning when she tarried
at home in the palace. Nay, he would have needed to have got her
heart while she was yet Saul's daughter in Saul's palace. It is to tell a
waterfall to flow uphill to tell Michal at this time of day to reverence
David. Reverence does not come even at divine command. Reverence
does not spring up in a day. Reverence is the result of long teaching
and long training. Reverence has its roots in the heart and in the character; and the heart and the character only come and bring forth reverence as life goes on. That may be all true, but the apostle does not
say that. He does not say that any of the wives to whom he wrote were

too late now to reverence their husbands. He speaks it to all wives, and he expects that all wives who hear it shall lay it to heart, and shall do it. And yet their husbands, their very best husbands, are in so many things so difficult, so impossible, to [176] reverence. They fall so far short of their young wife's dreams and visions. They are so full of faults, and follies, and tempers, and habits to which no wife can possibly be blind. Most husbands are at so little trouble, after they have been for some time husbands, to make it easy, or indeed possible, for their wives to continue to love, and respect, and reverence them. All our wives have dreary, lonely, sorely disappointed days at home— partly our fault and partly theirs, but mostly ours—that we know nothing about. Now, what are they to do between Paul on the one hand demanding in the name of God that they shall love and reverence us, and us on the other hand with all our might making both love and reverence impossible? Well, with God all things are possible. Let our wives, then, take us, with all our faults and infirmities, and let them think that with all our faults and infirmities we are still their husbands.

And let them take this to heart also, that though we fall ever so far below ourselves, that is all the more reason why they should rise all the more above themselves. It does not divorce a wife from her affection and respect for her husband that he causes her much pain and shame: many a blush in public, and many a tear in private. His sins against good taste, his clownish or churlish habits, his tempers, his prejudices, his ignorance, his rude, insolent, overbearing ways, not to speak of still grosser vices—all that will not absolve a wife from a wife's solicitude and goodwill to her husband. All that will not discharge her from her command over herself. [177] She must often see and feel all that like a wolf under her gown as she sits at the top of the table and her husband sits at the foot. But she must all the more learn to say her own grace to herself before she sits down to her temptation, till she is able to return thanks as she rises to go upstairs. All the time they are talking and eating and drinking at the other end of the table, she must set a watch on her ears and on her eyes and on the blood in her cheeks. She must be as full of guile as her husband is of meat and drink and himself. The keenest and cruelest eye must not find her out. Its deceived owner must be sent home saying, What a fool of a wife that brute, that bore, that goose has! I declare the blind thing is still in love with him! The wife see that she is hypocrite enough to throw dust

into the eyes of her oldest, closest and most familiar friend. Dante
describes Michal as a woman who stood scornful and afflicted at her
royal window. But let not even Dante's terrible eyes see either your
scorn of your husband or your affliction on account of his exposure of
himself. Throw dust even into Dante's blazing eyes. We are poor
creatures, the best of us husbands; and, at our best, we are still full of
appetites and egotisms and all the other dregs of our indwelling sin.
But if Almighty God bears with us, and does not despise us and spurn
us and refuse us His love, neither will you. And you will be well paid
for it all, and well acknowledged. For when we praise God at last and
say, To Him who loved us! we will not forget you. The wife see, then,
[178] that she prays for and puts up with her husband. The wife see
that she makes his self-improvement easy for her husband. And if,
after all is done, there is an irreducible residuum of distaste, and
almost dislike left, well, all the more let her see to it that she work out
his and her own salvation under that secret, life-long, household cross.
To your thorn, as to the apostle's, Christ will come and will say, My
grace is sufficient for it. My strength is made perfect even in such
weakness as yours.

Being the woman she was, and having the husband she had, Michal
could not but feel both scorn and affliction that day. But, when all is
said for her, and all allowance made, she should not have spoken to
David as it is recorded she did speak. She could not command her
proud heart when she saw David dancing, but by the time he came
home she should have had her tongue tamed and under a bridle. David
was, no doubt, a great provocation and a constant cross to Michal.
They were never made for one another. It was impossible they could
ever be happy as man and wife, short of a miracle. David was all
emotion, especially in divine things; whereas Michal was as proud and
cold as if she had been a daughter of Lucifer, as indeed she was.
David that day was like one of our own ministers coming home from
the communion table. It takes a night and a day and more than that till
the agitation and the emotion of a communion day subsides and settles
in a minister's heart. And if he were met with a blow in the face about
his sermon or his prayer or his table service as he opened his own
[179] door, that was exactly the reception that poor David met with at
Michal's hands that day. The wife see, at any rate, that she holds her
tongue. I do not now speak of communion time. There is no fear of
any minister's wife speaking on that day as Michal spoke. But there

are other times with ministers and with all men. Times when husband
and wife do not see eye to eye. Times when their two hearts do not
beat as one heart. Times of distaste, and disapproval, and difference of
opinion, and positive dislike; when Michal, who is written for our
learning, must be called to every wife's mind. Michal with her heart
full of war, and her mouth full of wicked words, and her whole after-
life full of remorse and misery for that evil day in her house in
Jerusalem—Michal is a divine looking-glass for all angry and outspoken wives.

'It was before the Lord', was David's noble answer to Michal's
taunting and insulting words. That was the whole explanation of
David's emotion and the sufficient justification of it. David's overflow-
ing joy that day had its deep and full spring in that far-off but never-
to-be-forgotten day when Samuel came to Bethlehem with his horn of
oil. To understand David and to sing David's psalms, you must have
come through David's experiences. You must have had David's birth
and upbringing; David's election and anointing and call; David's sins
and David's salvation; David's falls and David's restorations; David's
offices and David's services in the church of God. No wonder, then,
that so many of David's psalms are as much beyond your depth [180]
to-day as his dancing was beyond Michal's depth that day. Michal
thought of her royal father Saul that day, and despised David. David
thought of his poor father Jesse that day, and danced before the Lord.
And, as he says, he would have danced all the same, and still more,
had earth and hell both been all let loose to scoff and scout at him.
'Both less and more than king', is Dante's whole remark on David's
dance. As we shall be on that day when we look down at the hole of
the pit from whence we were digged, and cast our crowns at His feet
who took us from the dung-hill and set us beside David.

And then, the truly noble, the truly humble, and the terribly lonely
man that he was, David took up the taunt of his godless and heartless
wife, and wore it as a badge of honour before the Lord that day. Yes,
he said, it will be as you say. I will seek and I will find among the
poorest and the most despised of God's people that which my own
married wife denies me at home. And who can tell how many husbands here are in David's desolate case? Who can tell how many have
to go out of their own homes to find the finest sympathy, and the
fullest utterance, and the completest rest for their hearts? The wife see
that her husband has not to go abroad to find his best friend, his most

sympathetic and fellow-feeling friend, and, above all, in his religion. A minister once told me that he preached best and prayed best when his wife was at home. What a gulf there was between David and Michal; between Jesus and His brethren, [181] not to say His mother; and between my desolate friend and his wife! My brethren, the Holy Ghost knew what He was doing, and for whom He was doing it, when He moved the sacred writer to put that day in David's life into our Bible. And this,—'Husbands, love your wives, even as Christ loved the church, and gave Himself for it'. And this,—'And the wife see that she reverence her husband'.

INDEXES

INDEX OF REFERENCES

OLD TESTAMENT

NEW TESTAMENT

RABBINIC AND OTHER JEWISH TEXTS

INDEX OF AUTHORS

JOURNAL FOR THE STUDY OF THE OLD TESTAMENT

Supplement Series